Ethnic Conflict
and Reconciliation
in Sri Lanka

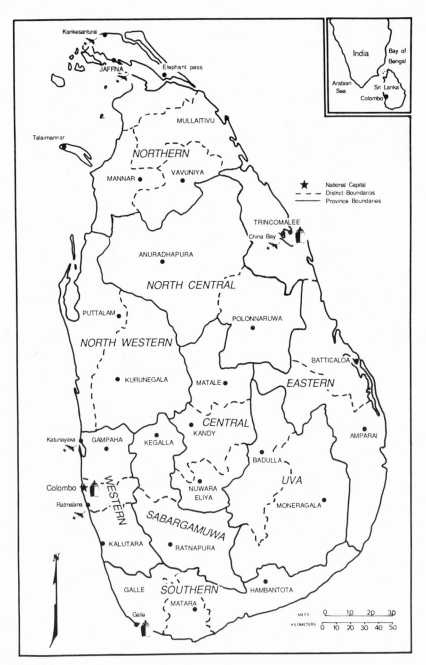

Sri Lanka

Ethnic Conflict and Reconciliation in Sri Lanka

CHELVADURAI MANOGARAN

 UNIVERSITY OF HAWAII PRESS • HONOLULU

Library of Congress Cataloging-in-Publication-Data

Manogaran, Chelvadurai, 1935–
    Ethnic conflict and reconciliation in Sri Lanka.

    Bibliography: p.
    Includes index.
    1. Sri Lanka—Politics and government. 2. Sri Lanka
—Ethnic relations. 3. Tamils—Sri Lanka—Politics
and government. I. Title.
DS489.8.M36 1987   954.9'303   87–16247
ISBN 0–8248–1116–X

The prosperity of a nation does not descend from the sky. Nor does it emerge from its own accord from the earth. It depends upon the conduct of the people that constitute the nation. We must recognize that the country does not mean just the lifeless soil around us. The country consists of a conglomeration of people and it is what they make of it. To rectify the world and put it on proper path, we have to first rectify ourselves and our conduct. . . . At the present time, when we see all over the country confusion, fear and anxiety, each one in every home must contribute his share of cool, calm love to suppress the anger and fury. No governmental authority can suppress it as effectively and as quickly as you can by love and brotherliness.

SATHYA SAI BABA

Contents

Tables

Figures

Preface

THERE has been no comprehensive study by geographers of the ethnic conflict in Sri Lanka which has been partially caused by the inability of a community to preserve and develop a well-defined geographical region considered to be its traditional homeland. My aim has been to analyze among other factors the geographical determinants of the conflict, especially those dealing with the allocation of water on a spatial basis for agricultural development and land settlement.

I have undertaken this ambitious task seriously and the book is the culmination of a decade of intensive study and exclusive research on this topic. I have undertaken numerous trips to Sri Lanka from 1977 to 1983.

The book deals primarily with contemporary issues, but I had to discuss developments prior to independence in order to make readily understandable the origins of the ethnic conflict.

Although the author is a Tamil and shares the concerns of his community, he nevertheless has attempted to look at all sides of the issue and make as disinterested a judgment as possible. So far as is humanly possible, I have tried to approach the topic from the viewpoint of a professional scholar. The reader has to judge for himself/herself how well the author has succeeded in achieving that goal.

I am deeply indebted to my colleague John D. Buenker, an authority on ethnic history of the United States, who read all of the manuscript, offered valuable criticism, and gave encouraging support. In this regard, I greatly appreciate the contributions made by the readers, whose critical reviews forced me to tighten the manuscript and strengthen its substance. My sincere thanks also go to B. J. Nielsen of the University of Wisconsin-Parkside library for her skill and patience in obtaining most of the reference materials used in this book via the inter-library loan system. Donald Litner and Catherine Owen of the Media Services of the university and my brother Ainkaran assisted me with the compilation, drafting, and photographing of illustrations. Two of my former students, Patrick Luchack, a Fulbright Scholar who completed one year of graduate study in Sri Lanka in 1986, and Lydia Morrow, who is employed in the cataloging section of the university library, assisted me in the library research and computer analysis of data.

One of the pleasures of writing this book has been the opportunity to work with the members of the University of Hawaii Press. I am particularly indebted to Damaris A. Kirchhofer for her careful editing and numerous improvements in the manuscript.

Finally, more than these words can convey, I owe a great deal to my family—Devi, Shakila, and Anita—who had to suffer through my moods and anxieties.

thirteenth century to establish an independent kingdom in northern Sri Lanka. Historical records indicate that the Malabar Coast on the western side of the subcontinent was the source of major Tamil migration to the island until about the thirteenth century, when it shifted to the present-day Indian state of Tamil Nadu. Although Sri Lankan Tamils speak the same language and follow a set of cultural traditions similar to those of the Tamils of South India, the impact of the early Malabar migration, their long period of residence in Sri Lanka, and their interaction with the Sinhalese people helped them to become distinct from the Tamils of Tamil Nadu. Sri Lankan Tamils developed a unique community identity when they established the Jaffna kingdom, independent of the Sinhalese Kandyan kingdom of the hill country and Kotte kingdom of the southwest, and of Tamil kingdoms in South India. When the Portuguese and the Dutch occupied Sri Lanka in the sixteenth and seventeenth centuries, respectively, they left intact the administrative structure of the three kingdoms and recognized northern Sri Lanka as the traditional homeland of the Tamils. A vast stretch of mosquito-infested Dry Zone kept the Sinhalese and Tamils apart until the eighteenth century, when the whole country was brought under one administration by the British.

The establishment of a unitary form of government and the development of an extensive system of roads and railroads linking all parts of the island enabled members of the Sinhalese and Tamil communities to come into contact with each other. The British government abolished the three separate systems of administration that had existed for the Sinhalese Maritime provinces, the Tamil Maritime provinces, and the Kandyan provinces during the Dutch period. The country was divided on a territorial basis into five provinces, namely, the Northern, Eastern, Southern, Western, and Central provinces, and each province was placed under the authority of a British government agent who was appointed by the governor of Ceylon. The Tamil Maritime provinces, which have been traditionally inhabited almost entirely by Tamil-speaking people, became the Northern and Eastern provinces of Sri Lanka. The number of provinces was later increased to nine by the addition of the Northern-Western, North-Central, Uva, and Sabaragamuwa provinces, and each province was subdivided into administrative districts and administered by Assistant Government Agents (see Figure 1). Administrative functions were subsequently decentralized at the district level, rather than at the provincial level, and each of the twenty-two administrative districts was placed under the charge of a government agent. The Tamil-speaking people maintained a clear majority in all the districts of the Northern and Eastern provinces, but the ethnic composition of some of these districts, especially Amparai, Trincomalee, and Vavuniya began to change dramatically after the 1930s as large numbers of Sinhalese were settled in these districts under government-sponsored colonization schemes.

The linguistic and religious differences between the two communities proved strong enough that Sinhalese and Tamils continue to be self-conscious about their identification with their respective communities. Although four different ethno-religious-linguistic communities reside in Sri Lanka, more than 92 percent of the inhabitants identify themselves with one of two distinct groups, Sinhalese and Tamils (see Tables 1 and 2). In 1981, the estimated population of the island was 14.85 million, of which the Sinhalese and Tamil communities account for 74 percent and 18.2 percent, respectively. Two-thirds of the inhabitants, predominantly Sinhalese, live in the Wet Zone, while 72.6 percent of the Sri Lankan Tamils, 9.4 percent of the Indian Tamils, and 35 percent of the Muslims, all of whom speak Tamil, live in the Northern and Eastern provinces, where agricultural development is hampered by a lack of water.

Agriculture is the mainstay of the economy of the island. Rice is the staple food of the inhabitants, and paddy lands occupy approximately 13 percent of the island's total land area, with almost two-thirds of the area under irrigation. In addition, tea, rubber, coconut, sugar cane, and minor food crops occupied approximately 17.5 percent of the total land area of the island in 1981. The cultivation of export crops—including paddy, subsidiary food crops, as well as forestry and fishing—contributed approximately 28 percent of the Gross National Product in 1983 (see Table 3).

Given the meager resources of the water-deficient environment of northern Sri Lanka, the Tamils were compelled to seek alternative means of livelihood. By acquiring knowledge of the English language they were able to secure a disproportionate share of public employment in the British-run administration, even in Sinhalese-dominated areas, as well as in the legal, medical, and engineering professions during colonial times. Tamils who were employed in the colonial administration had an average income higher than the rest of the population, including the majority of Tamils living in the Northern and Eastern provinces. Nevertheless, the Sinhalese community

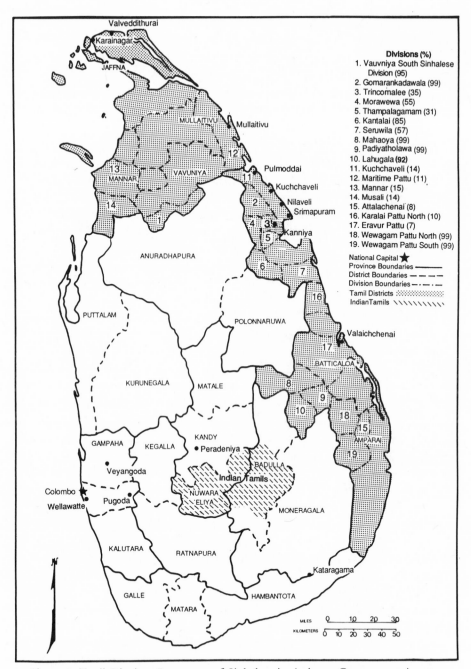

Figure 1. Tamil Districts: Percentage of Sinhalese in Assistant Government Agent (AGA) Divisions (Census 1981)

Table 1. Ethnic Communities in 1981

Ethnic Communities	Sri Lanka		Northern and Eastern Provinces[a]		Ethnic Communities Represented in Northern and Eastern Provinces
	Number	%	Number	%	%
Total	14,850,000	100.0	2,087,943	100.0	
Sinhalese	10,989,000	74.0	276,578	13.2	2.51
Sri Lankan Tamils	1,871,000	12.6	1,358,188	65.0	72.59
Indian Tamils	817,000	5.5	76,754	3.7	9.39
Muslims (Moors)	1,054,000	7.1	368,277	17.7	34.94
Others[b]	119,000	0.8	8,146	0.4	6.80

Source: Department of Census and Statistics, *Census of Population and Housing, Sri Lanka, 1981: Preliminary Release No. 1.*

[a]These two provinces were approximately 26 percent of the total area of the island in 1978.
[b]Includes Burghers (Eurasians) and Malays.

Table 2. Population by Religion in Sri Lanka, 1981

Religion	Numbers	Percentage Distribution
All Religions	14,850,000	100.0
Buddhists	10,291,000	69.3
Hindus	2,302,000	15.5
Muslims (Moors)	1,128,000	7.6
Christians	1,114,000	7.5
Others	15,000	0.1

Source: Department of Census and Statistics, *Census of Population and Housing, Sri Lanka, 1981: Preliminary Release No. 1.*

viewed all Tamils, irrespective of whether they resided in Tamil- or Sinhalese-dominated areas, as having an income higher than that of the Sinhalese population. Therefore, Sinhalese politicians demanded a larger share of the economic resources of the country for their community in order that the consequences of inequalities between the two communities might be redressed.

The Sinhalese also became resentful of the Tamils of Indian origin whom the British settled in the predominantly Sinhalese areas of the hill country in the 1830s to work on the tea plantations. The Indians were considered by the Sinhalese to be foreigners who had no abiding interest in the island and who were prepared to work for low wages on

Table 3. Sector Composition of Gross National Product and Employment, 1983.
(GNP at 1982 Constant Factor Cost Prices)

Sector	Composition GNP (millions of Rupees)	Percent of GNP	Employment (thousands)	Percent of Total
Agriculture, Forestry, and Fishing	26,294	28.0	2,172.7	45.8
Mining and Quarrying	2,413	2.6	63.7	1.3
Manufacturing[a]	13,710	14.6	568.2	12.0
Construction	8,039	8.5	229.1	4.8
Electricity, Gas, and Sanitary Services	1,161	1.2	18.0	0.4
Transportation, Storage, and Communications	8,920	9.5	197.4	4.2
Wholesale and Retail	16,910	18.0	490.8	10.4
Services	8,672	9.2	648.1	13.7
Others[b]	10,864	11.5	349.6	7.4
Gross National Product	94,047	103.1		
Net Factor Income from Abroad	−2,936	−3.1		
Total	94,047	100.0	4,737.7	100.0

Source: Department of Census and Statistics, *Statistical Pocket Book of the Democratic Socialist Republic of Sri Lanka,* and Central Bank of Ceylon, *Review of the Economy.*

[a]Includes tree crop processing.
[b]Includes banking, insurance, real estate, ownership of dwellings, public administration, and defense.

the plantations that were established on lands cultivated—or with the potential to be cultivated—by the Kandyan peasantry. As Tamils of Sri Lankan origin and Tamils of Indian origin moved into Sinhalese areas to seek employment, it was not difficult for politicians to revive the ancient fear of a Tamil threat to the survival of the Sinhala race, its language, and culture. Thus the early decades of the twentieth century saw the resurgence of Sinhalese nationalism to which Buddhist activists gave a religious bent by warning that the people should strive to prevent the Tamils and Muslims from dominating the economy of the island. Nevertheless, there was no open confrontation between Sinhalese and Tamil politicians until the 1920s.

Ethnic rivalry became an issue in the 1920s when the British government began giving serious consideration to greater Ceylonese participation in the political process. Sinhalese politicians insisted that communal representation, which had hitherto been the vehicle through which Ceylonese participated in the colonial government, be replaced by some form of territorial representation that would be reflective of the size of the Sinhalese community relative to that of the Tamils. Tamil demands to retain communal representation were rejected.

During the early years of British rule in Sri Lanka, the governor, who was appointed by the Crown, exercised all executive and legislative power with the aid of an advisory council. The governor's autocratic powers were reduced with the establishment of the first Legislative Council in 1833, which included both official and unofficial members. Three of the six unofficial members of the Legislative Council were nominated by the governor from the English-educated Ceylonese elite. The nomination was on a communal basis, since one Tamil, one Burgher (Eurasian), and one low-country Sinhalese were selected to represent their respective groups in the Council. The executive powers were vested in the governor and the Executive Council, and the Legislative Council continued to be mainly an advisory body. In 1912, an "educated Ceylonese," who could speak, read, and write in English, was elected by educated Ceylonese to the Legislative Council, but all the other Ceylonese on the Council were nominated by the governor on a communal basis. With the official majority in the Legislative Council, the unofficial members had very little power to enact laws. In 1924, more than half the members of the Legislative Council were elected and for the first time the unofficial members formed a majority in the Council. Even those nominated on a communal basis were elected by communal electorates. The governor, however, continued to exercise his powers through the Executive Council without having to consult with the members of the Legislative Council.

The Donoughmore Constitution of 1931 introduced drastic changes in the system of representation and in the exercise of real power by the people of Sri Lanka. All adults over the age of twenty-one were granted franchise and the members in the newly constituted State Council were territorially elected. The State Council was also vested with both legislative and executive powers. The minorities, especially the Tamils, objected to the abolition of communal electorates on ground that territorial representation would create a Sinhalese-dominated State Council that would ultimately discriminate against them. When a new legislature was convened, after the elections of 1936, Tamil representatives for the first time were excluded from the cabinet and a pan-Sinhalese ministry was formed. Tamil politicians became apprehensive that their community would be discriminated against by a Sinhalese-dominated government and demanded that the Soulbury Commission, charged with drawing up a constitution for an independent Sri Lanka, safeguard minority interests. G. G. Ponnambalam, a Tamil representative to the State Council of the Jaffna constituency in the Tamil north, demanded that half the seats in the parliament of independent Sri Lanka should be assigned to minorities. Thus, the formation of the pan-Sinhalese ministry and a pro-Sinhalese council, the Sinhala Maha Sabha, followed by the "50-50" demand of G. G. Ponnambalam, paved the way for the emergence of contemporary ethnic conflict.

The constitution of independent Sri Lanka provided for the establishment of a British-style parliamentary system of government in 1948. The parliament consisted of the Queen, and the House of Representatives, and the Senate. The Queen was represented by the governor-general, who was appointed by the Queen on the advice of the prime minister. The governor-general had very little power to govern the country. The link to the Crown was maintained because it did not infringe on Sri Lanka's independent status and provided an opportunity for the country to become a member of the worldwide commonwealth of nations. In 1972, Sri Lanka became a free, sovereign, and independent republic within the Commonwealth.

The Senate had thirty members, of whom fifteen were elected by the House of Representatives, in accordance with the system of proportional representation by means of single transferable vote, and fifteen were appointed by the governor-general on the advice of the prime minister. Senators served for a period of six years, one-third retiring every two years. The president and the deputy president of the Senate were elected by its members. The Senate was abolished in 1972 by a constituent assembly of the people of Sri Lanka, convened to adopt and enact a new constitution.

The House of Representatives had 101 members, 95 popularly elected and 6 appointed by the governor-general to insure that minorities were represented. The duration of the House of Representatives is five years unless parliament is dissolved earlier. All citizens of Sri Lanka over the age of eighteen were entitled to elect the members to the House of Representatives from 89 electoral districts. Five electorates had more than one seat. The electorates were delimited according to one seat for every 1,000 square miles and one seat for every 75,000 inhabitants. The area provision was incorporated to ensure that minorities in the less-populated Eastern Province were adequately represented. As the population increased, the total number of electoral districts was increased to 145 in the 1960s. There was a corresponding increase in the members of the House of Representatives from 101 to 157. Of the 157 members, 151 were elected and 6 were appointed. The 1972 constitution called for a unicameral republican structure and established the National State Assembly to replace the two houses. The National Assembly of the elected representatives of the people was vested with the legislative, executive, and judiciary power of the Republic. The duration of the National Assembly was set at six years, unless it is dissolved earlier. The National Assembly, which was elected in 1977, has not been dissolved even though it completed its six-year term in 1983. One hundred and sixty-eight members were elected to the National Assembly at the general election held in 1977.

From 1948 until 1977, the prime minister and his cabinet, chosen from the party which had the majority in the House of Representatives, constituted the executive branch of the government. The prime minister as the head of the cabinet, was in charge of the Ministry of Defense and External Affairs, while the other ministers were in charge of departments assigned to them by the prime minister. While the prime minister, the leader of the largest party to be represented in the House of Representatives, was appointed by the governor-general, other ministers were appointed by the governor-general on the advice of the prime minister. The position of governor-general was abolished by the constituent assembly in 1972, but the prime minister was given the authority to nominate the president, who became the head of the state, head of the executive, and commander-in-chief of the armed forces. He was, however, responsible to the National Assembly in the exercise of the powers that were delegated to him under the constitution. In actual practice, the president had very little powers and the cabinet of ministers with the prime minister as its head were in complete charge of the government of the Republic of Sri Lanka until 1977.

A major change was introduced in the British-style parliamentary form of government in 1978, when the constitution of the Democratic Socialist Republic of Sri Lanka made provisions for the president to be directly elected by the people for a fixed term of six years. The president serves as head of the state, the government, as well as a member and head of the Cabinet of Ministers. The prime minister does not exercise the same degree of executive power he or she exercised under the British-style parliamentary system. Nevertheless, as the leader of the majority party in the National Assembly, the prime minister has sufficient influence over the elected representatives in parliament. Since the prime minister and the president are from the same party, no major conflicts have appeared over issues between the National Assembly and the president. In the future, however, if the prime minister and the president were to be elected from different political parties, the National Assembly could pass or reject laws contrary to the president's wishes. The life of the present parliament, which was elected in 1977, has been extended until 1989 by means of a referendum conducted in 1982.

When Sri Lanka became independent in 1948, Sinhalese politicians used their majority in the newly elected parliament to improve their community's economic and political positions. The Tamils of Indian origin became the first target of discrimination when the parliament enacted legislation excluding them from Ceylon citizenship in 1948. Some Sinhalese leaders realized that a better life for their community could not be achieved by merely acquiring political power—the sensitive issue of ethnic identity had to be exploited to accomplish this. S. W. R. D. Bandaranaike was one of the eminent politicians who championed the cause of the Sinhalese masses by demanding the overhauling of the administrative, educational, and political structures, legacies of the colonial system that had bestowed "undue" privileges on Tamils. No sooner had he become the prime minister in 1956 than the Sinhalese-dominated parliament passed legislation making Sinhala the official language of the country in place of English. Tamil politicians adopted various strategies to show their disapproval of this legislation. C. Suntharalingam, a prominent Tamil politician who served in the post-independence cabinet, threatened that the Tamils would solicit the support of Tamils in South India in order to establish an independent state. The call for the establishment of a separate Tamil state was considered very serious by Sinhalese politicians, especially because the Dravida Munnetra Kazhagam Movement in India was clamoring for the establishment of an independent Dravida state in South India. Some Sinhalese politicians warned of the possibility of the creation of a pan-Dravidian Tamil state that would ultimately undermine the future of the Sinhala race, its culture, and Buddhism. It is obvious that political leaders in both communities used the issue of ethnicity to outbid their political opponents.

The Tamil electorate, however, continued to support the Federal

Party whose objective was not to establish a separate state but to form a semi-autonomous Tamil linguistic state within a federal union of Sri Lanka, although some radicals in the party clamored for an independent state. Nevertheless, the Buddhist clergy, some opposition parties, and a few powerful Sinhalese extremists began to view all Tamil demands as seeking to establish a separate state. These groups have generally succeeded in blocking the passage of any legislative measures designed to grant political, language, territorial, and economic concessions to the Tamils since 1956. Tamil opposition to discriminatory laws and regulations under the direction of the Federal Party took the form of nonviolent disobedience campaigns designed to persuade the government to grant concessions. In many instances, however, thugs or the police broke up these peaceful demonstrations. Some of the demonstrations led to anti-Tamil riots, such as those in 1956 and 1958, which swept the island. The leader of the Federal party, S. J. V. Chelvanayakam, attempted to work with various Sinhala governments to resolve the ethnic problem. The Bandaranaike-Chelvanayakam Pact of 1957 and the Senanayake-Chelvanayakam pact of 1965 were negotiated in good faith but were not implemented because of strong opposition from a section of the Buddhist clergy and a few extremists. In both cases the Tamils were willing to accept constitutional provisions for the decentralization of limited governmental functions to Tamil provinces and to abandon their original demands for making Tamil an official language and for establishing a Tamil linguistic state within Sri Lanka.

Not only was the Federal Party unsuccessful in securing Tamil rights from successive governments, it was also unable to dissuade the government from discriminating against the Tamils with regard to recruitment for government jobs and admissions to universities and from settling Sinhalese peasants in Tamil areas. Despite appeals from the Federal Party, laws were passed and regulations issued to facilitate the gradual exclusion of Tamils from public service, to restrict the number of Tamil students gaining admission to universities on the basis of merit, to accelerate the planned colonization of Tamil areas, and to encourage the development of Sinhalese districts relative to Tamil districts. The government also pursued an aggressive policy of settling Sinhalese families in Tamil districts by inaugurating major irrigation projects and repairing existing ones, while the economy of the predominantly Tamil areas was allowed to deteriorate.

In the early 1970s, a major change occurred in the strategy

employed by Tamils to fight for their rights because of two factors. First, the 1972 constitution of Sri Lanka did not recognize Tamil as the language of a national minority, while Sinhala was reaffirmed as the only official language of Sri Lanka. Also, there were no provisions granting devolution of powers to Tamil provinces, but Buddhism was given special status as the religion of the state. Second, Tamil youths, frustrated with the inability of their leaders to secure the legitimate rights of the Tamils, demanded that all Tamil parties unite to become an effective force against Sinhalese domination. As a result, all the major Tamil parties were dissolved and the Tamil United Liberation Front (TULF) was formed under the leadership of Chelvanayakam in 1972. Many Tamil youths, however, disapproving of the peaceful methods adopted by their elders, demanded more vigorous action. Deeply concerned about their future and that of their community, some of them decided to follow the dictates of their own leaders to carry arms in order to establish an independent state in which they could hope to enjoy the privileges denied to them by Sinhala governments. Indeed, as the degree of discrimination against Tamils intensified, Tamil demands for the establishment of a semi-autonomous state changed in 1976 to a call for the creation of an independent and sovereign state to be named Eelam. Tamil militants formed underground movements, the most prominent of which was the Liberation Tigers of Tamil Eelam, and employed violent methods to express their disapproval of government policies against their people.

Tamil representatives continued to use their influence in parliament to persuade the government to grant political, economic, and language concessions to the Tamils, but with little success. However, the ultimate objective of all TULF members was to establish the state of Eelam, and that elicited an expression of moral support from the Dravida Munnetra Kazhagam of Tamil Nadu. This Indian connection revived Sinhalese fears of South Indian domination of Sri Lanka and, in 1977, when the TULF won the elections in the Tamil-dominated districts on a mandate to establish Eelam, reports linking Tamil militants to the killing of a Sinhalese policeman started a major riot in which many Tamils were killed and made homeless. The riot alienated Tamil militants, and they showed their disapproval by attacking security forces. Soon the ethnic violence, which had hitherto been limited to the burning and looting of Tamil homes and properties in Sinhalese areas, took on a multifaceted character. Tamil militants also attacked government establishments and government informants in

Tamil-dominated areas. The security forces retaliated by attacking innocent civilians. The government, in turn, introduced emergency regulations, the Prevention of Terrorism Act, and other repressive measures to halt terrorism, but youths continue to harass security forces.

Since 1977, many civilians have been killed and made homeless by Sinhalese mobs, government security forces, and by the militant wing of the Tamil separatist movement. The intensity and the severity of anti-Tamil riots, as determined by the loss of lives and damage to property, have been increasing with each incident. The 1983 riot is considered the worst, since it was allegedly instigated and organized by employees of a government ministry. After 1983, Tamil militants expanded their attacks to include Sinhalese civilians in the Northern and Eastern provinces. Many Tamils were killed and rendered homeless as government forces attempted to flush out militants indiscriminately from these provinces. This circle of violence has taken such a heavy toll of innocent lives and inflicted such suffering and humiliation on the Tamil community that time must pass before the memories of the bloodshed and bitterness can be forgotten. Even if a political settlement to the ethnic problem were to be negotiated in a spirit of mutual accommodation, the prospects for national reconciliation seem remote. The governing United National Party appears to want a solution to the ethnic problem, but its reluctance to grant substantial powers to Tamil provinces and its carrot and stick approach in dealing with ethnic conflict have delayed any peaceful resolution to the conflict.

The purpose of this book is to document accurately and fairly the historical perspective of Sinhalese/Tamil relationships in Sri Lanka. It will be shown that the roots of the ethnic conflict can be traced to early historical times. The long-standing grievances of the Sinhalese people concerning their language rights, the status of Buddhism, employment and education opportunities, and political control of the state by the Sinhala majority have been resolved. Likewise, it will be demonstrated that the Tamils are no longer a privileged community, although many Sinhalese continue to insist that their rights, rather than those of Tamils, should be protected. The aggressive policy of discrimination in areas such as language, freedom of expression, university education, employment in the public and private sectors, colonization of Tamil districts, and the agricultural and industrial development of Tamil districts has made the Tamils an oppressed minority in Sri Lanka. The Tamils are underrepresented in the army, navy, air force, and police, and the government has stationed its Sinhala-dominated security forces in Tamil districts to harass the local population. Yet, Sinhalese extremists are unwilling to recognize that Tamils have been alienated through discrimination and that their attitude toward the Tamils has greatly affected the ability of the Sinhalese and Tamils of the moderate persuasion to negotiate a political settlement of the ethnic problem. Indeed, the Sinhala-Tamil ethnic conflict could have been resolved in the past had the moderate Sinhalese and Tamils persuaded the small minority of extremists in both communities to accept proposals that guaranteed some of the legitimate rights of the Tamils involving the use of the Tamil language, regional autonomy for Tamil areas, colonization of Tamil areas, and the development of Tamil areas where there are severe problems of unemployment and food scarcity.

Another purpose is to show that the ethnic composition of some of the Tamil districts has been drastically altered by state-sponsored colonization schemes and that Tamils are increasingly apprehensive that Sinhalese settlers will ultimately deprive them of their political power and even deny employment opportunities to those who are educated in the Tamil medium. It will be apparent that Tamil demands for regional autonomy are based on the desire to preserve and develop Tamil districts for the benefit of the Tamil community, especially when Sinhalese-dominated areas are no longer safe for Tamil residents and where employment opportunities are largely restricted to those educated in the Sinhala medium.

Chapters 1 and 2 provide a historical perspective on the ethnic problem. Ethnic differences between the two major communities are analyzed and the sequence of political events that followed the granting of independence to Sri Lanka and the introduction of Sinhala as the only official language are discussed with special emphasis on Sinhala nationalism, ethnic movements, and the formation of the Tamil Federal Party. Negotiated pacts between Sinhalese and Tamil leaders to settle the ethnic problem are critically analyzed to show how Sinhalese leaders were swayed by sections of the Buddhist clergy and a few extremists of their own community to abrogate some of these agreements. The history of Tamil opposition to Sinhala governments is traced from: (1) the origin of the Federal Party to the rise of the Tamil United Liberation Front; (2) the change in demands from a semi-autonomous state to a separate, sovereign Tamil state called Eelam; and (3) the change from nonviolent to violent tactics by Tamil youths to resist Sinhala domination. Several government regulations and acts, including the Prevention of Terrorism Act, are discussed in conjunction with the rise of the Tamil Liberation Tiger movement, the confrontation between the security forces and the Tamil militants, and the killing of civilians in Tamil districts. The causes and consequences of the 1983 communal riots and the inability of the government to solve the ethnic problem by implementing the District Development Councils legislation of 1980 are also analyzed. The failure of the 1984 All-Party Conference because of the inability of the government to implement the proposals that were negotiated between Indian and Sri Lankan officials and the events that led to the collapse of the Thimphu peace talks are also discussed. Finally, events leading to the formation of a united front among the leading Tamil militant groups, the willingness of Tamil militants to negotiate with the government on the question of regional autonomy as a suitable alternative to Eelam, and the determination of the government to find a military solution to the ethnic conflict are analyzed.

Chapter 3 examines the concept of a Tamil homeland and evaluates the environmental factors that contributed to the persistence of Tamil settlements in northern Sri Lanka while environmental disasters such as floods and droughts forced Sinhalese populations to move from the Dry Zone to the Wet Zone in the thirteenth century. This discussion substantially dispels the notion that Tamil invasions were entirely responsible for the decline of the Sinhalese civilization in the Dry Zone, the destruction of irrigation works, and the flight of Sinhalese to the Wet Zone. A brief history of government-sponsored colonization schemes in the Dry Zone is included.

The chapter also examines the climatic potential for cultivating crops on a regional basis, both in the Wet and Dry Zones. The lack of suitable agricultural and industrial resources in the Tamil regions, it is argued, compelled the local inhabitants to seek employment elsewhere, including Malaysia. It was not the lack of land but the paucity of water resources that limited agricultural development in Tamil districts, especially in the Northern Province. It is also indicated that while governments are genuinely concerned about solving rural agrarian problems associated with landlessness and lack of water in Sinhalese districts, very little capital has been invested toward augmenting the supply of water in rivers and tanks of the Tamil-dominated

Northern Province. Regional distribution of water resources is analyzed by presenting quantitative information on water discharged by
rivers through Tamil and Sinhalese districts.

This analysis is necessary to stress the fact that while Tamil areas
lack adequate water supply to raise one crop a year, many Sinhalese
districts have a sufficient supply of water to raise two crops of rice,
one with the help of supplementary irrigation during the wet season
and the other with the aid of irrigation during the dry season. Moreover, government investments on projects to augment the supply of
water to farms have increased crop yields in Sinhalese districts. This
chapter also analyzes the temporal and areal changes in rice production in order to evaluate the degree of self-sufficiency in rice of
selected Sinhalese and Tamil districts in the Dry Zone. The results of
this analysis will show that Tamil districts are less self-sufficient in rice
than Sinhalese districts and that this disparity in rice production
between Sinhalese and Tamil districts is due mainly to government
neglect of Tamil areas.

Chapter 4 delves into the sensitive issue of how governments have
discriminated against Tamils with regard to their making a living in
Sri Lanka. It is intended to show that the government has not only
neglected the economic development of Tamil districts but has also
issued orders and regulations that limit the number of Tamils seeking
employment in the public and private sectors of the economy and
securing admission to universities. The notion that the Tamil population is generally more literate and educated than the Sinhalese population because of better educational facilities is dispelled by presenting appropriate data. It will be also shown that at no time has the
number of Tamils in the public service exceeded that of the Sinhalese.
It is true that in the past the Tamil community was overrepresented in
the public service and professions relative to the proportional size of
its population, but with the passage of the Sinhala-only legislation
and the introduction of other regulations the number of Tamils in
different government departments has dropped drastically. The number of Tamils employed in public-sector corporations has remained
static, or even declined, because most of the state-sponsored industries established since the 1950s have been concentrated in Sinhalese
areas. The serious problems associated with landlessness, high unemployment, and high population densities in Tamil districts as well as
the lack of government support for agricultural and industrial development are also discussed. Finally, the chapter analyzes the numerical

changes in the ethnic composition of Tamil districts as a result of government-sponsored colonization schemes.

Chapter 5 analyzes various options to devolve specific legislative, executive, and administrative powers to regional governments in order to solve the ethnic problem. It discusses the reasons why attempts made by Sinhalese and Tamil leaders to negotiate agreements to decentralize administrative functions to provinces and districts in the past were unsuccessful. The structure, composition, and functions of the District Development Councils and their failure to solve the ethnic problem are explored. The District Development Councils were established by the government more than five years after it implemented an Integrated Rural (District) Development Program (IRDP) under which several Sinhalese districts received funds from the government and from foreign sources for rural development. Both the District Development Councils and the Integrated Rural (District) Development Program, which were designed to encourage balanced regional development, are discussed.

The Epilogue traces the chronology of events that have taken place between December 1985 and June 1987, in order to evaluate the prospects for national reconciliation in Sri Lanka. The desirability of reorganizing the prevailing governmental structure to discourage future conflict between the communities and between ethnic-based regional political parties is analyzed. Indeed, the main aim of any political settlement of the long-standing conflict should be to foster national unity and integration.

Sinhalese-Tamil Ethnic Differences and the Beginnings of Conflict

THE Sinhalese majority and the Tamil minority of contemporary Sri Lanka assert their respective identities on the basis of language, religion, ancestral territory, and cultural attributes, although the "Tamil identity does not have a specific religious or Hindu dimension."[1] It is not known whether the members of the ethnic communities were conscious of their separate identities when they came into contact with each other during the early days of settlement of the island. Semilegendary narratives, historical accounts, and religious teachings in the *Pali Chronicles,* the *Dipavamsa,* and the *Mahavamsa,* composed by *bhikkhus* (Buddhist clergy) between the fourth and the sixth centuries A.D., suggest that the Sinhalese were the first civilized people to settle on the island before the Veddhas and the Dravidians appeared on the scene.[2]

Veddhas are the descendants of the aboriginal tribes of ancient Sri Lanka. They are dwindling in numbers as many of them have been absorbed by the Sinhalese. The remaining Veddhas continue to rely on hunting for their food and live under extreme primitive conditions in the jungles of Bintenne in Eastern Sri Lanka.

Origin of Sinhalese and Tamil Settlements

According to the most popular legend in the *Mahavamsa,* the first contingent of Aryan settlers, led by Vijaya, landed on the island the very day Gautama Buddha attained *nibbana* (died) in India about 500 B.C. The *bhikkhus* who compiled the *Mahavamsa* attached religious significance to Vijaya's arrival on the island as an indication that the Sinhalese people, as the descendants of Vijaya, are destined by divine will to protect and foster Buddhism in Sri Lanka.[3] Prominent Sinhalese historians emphasize that the myth of this religious-ethnic destiny was contrived by the Buddhist clergy in order to propagate the theme that the Sinhalese are the protectors of Buddhism.[4] Gananath Obeyesekere states that the "myths are also an expression of the self-perceived historical role of the Sinhalese as a nation" and that this Sinhalese-Buddhist identity was used effectively in ancient times to fight the Tamil-speaking "Saivite unbelievers" from South India.[5]

Despite the myths and legends contained in the *Mahavamsa,* there is consensus among Sinhalese historians that there is an element of truth in the Aryanization of Sri Lanka. Accordingly, the origin of the Sinhalese people is traced to the year 543 B.C. when a group of seven hundred men led by Vijaya, a crown prince who was banished by his father from the city of Sinhapura in Bengal, northeast India, landed on the western shores of Sri Lanka. Vijaya acquired control of the island by marrying Kuveni, the queen of the nonhuman Yaksha people, but after a few years he banished her with his son and daughter into the forest. This story of the banishment of his family was deliberately contrived to imply that Vijaya and his men did not propagate the Sinhalese race with nonhuman Yaksha women. Instead, Vijaya married the daughter of the Pandyan king of Madura, South India, and his men married Pandyan women of high caste. Historians C. W. Nicholas and S. Paranavitana contend that Pandyan people were not Dravidian Tamils, but Aryan Pandus of epic fame who occupied central and South India during this period.[6] Other studies indicate that the three kingdoms of Pandya, Chola, and Chera of the Tamil-speaking Dravidians existed in South India prior to the fourth century B.C. and that "Aryan contacts with South India before the fourth century B.C." were few or nonexistent.[7] Even if the Pandyans were Dravidians, however, this link was severed with Vijaya's death when his brother's son, Pandu Vasudeva of Bengal, who succeeded him as the king of Sri Lanka, is supposed to have landed on the eastern shores of the island with another contingent of Aryan followers.

The Aryan settlers, as indicated by the legend of the banishment of Vijaya's Yaksha wife and children to the forest, maintained their separate identity and propagated the Sinhalese race. The *Mahavamsa* also indicates that the Veddhas were not the aboriginal people of Sri Lanka but were propagated by Vijaya's Yaksha son and daughter in the isolated parts of the island. Apparently, the Veddha connection to Vijaya is emphasized to insure that the Sinhalese are considered the original inhabitants of the island and that no ethnic links are established between the aboriginal tribes of Sri Lanka and those of South India of the pre-Dravidian period. N. D. Wijesekera, however, indicates that the physical characteristics of the Veddhas can be traced to the successive fusion of Mediterranean, Australoid, and Negrito racial groups in South India.[8] Moreover, the physical characteristics of the Balangoda man, who roamed the island in prehistoric times, closely resemble those of the pre-Dravidian tribes in South India. Apparently, the present-day Veddhas are not the direct descendants of Balangoda man but are "the mixed descendants of Balangoda man, Sinhalese, and the Tamils."[9] The Veddhas, in turn, contributed, at least in part, "to the making of the Sinhalese population."[10]

Some scholars have postulated that the Yakshas and Nagas, who are referred to in the *Mahavamsa* as nonhumans, are the aboriginal tribes of India and Sri Lanka. These scholars refer to historical traditions and the semilegendary accounts in Indian epics like the *Mahabharata* and *Ramayana*, which were written in the sixth century B.C., as well as to Ptolemy's description of the aboriginal people of Sri Lanka to suggest that the Yakshas and Nagas were Tamil-speaking people who worshipped the cobra (Naga) and demon (Yaksha), respectively, in the protohistorical period dating back to 1000 B.C.[11] Even the *Mahavamsa,* like the *Ramayana,* mentions prosperous kingdoms, townships, and rural settlements that existed on the island when the Sinhalese arrived.[12] G. P. Malalesekere's authoritative interpretation of the account of the Yaksha kingdom in the *Mahavamsa* corroborates well with the accounts of the *Ramayana,* in which Sri Lanka is mentioned as having "possessed a certain degree of civilization" and it is noted that the "Yakshas had their own cities, social institutions, a fairly developed language, and indubitable signs of accumulated wealth."[13]

Although there is a strong possibility that the Yakshas and Nagas were the original Tamil-speaking inhabitants of Sri Lanka, the *Mahavamsa* does not make any references to the origin and development of Tamil settlements in Sri Lanka. Nevertheless, some historians are of the opinion that the Tamils began settling on the island as peaceful immigrants and invaders from very early times.[14] Although the dates of the establishment of the Sinhalese and Tamil settlements are shrouded in obscurity, some historians believe that the island has been inhabited by both communities for more than two thousand years.[15] While there is also general consensus among historians that Sinhalese settlements preceded Tamil settlements on the island by a

few centuries, some scholars claim that the "Tamil-speaking Dravidians . . . were very likely on the island at the time of the Sinhalese
arrival."[16] This claim is based on the hypothesis that the origin of the
Dravidian group of languages can be traced to the formerly widespread Megalithic culture that existed in peninsular India and Sri
Lanka prior to 700 B.C.[17] To substantiate this, South Indian historians
claim that the Yakshas and Nagas were the ancestors of Tamil-speaking Dravidians who belonged to an earlier colony of settlers that
migrated from South India to Sri Lanka.[18] They presume that this
colony of settlers established the Yaksha kingdom described in the
Mahavamsa. Linguistic, archaeological, cultural, and racial evidence
also suggest that some Dravidian-speaking people were present in the
northwestern part of India and other Dravidian-speaking people were
scattered throughout India, "including sections of the South," when
the Aryans moved into India.[19] If this were true, some of the Dravidian groups could have crossed the narrow stretch of water into Sri
Lanka by way of a land bridge that is supposed to have connected the
two countries in the distant past. In spite of this evidence, we can
only speculate that the ancestors of the present-day Tamils were
already in Sri Lanka when the Sinhalese began colonizing the island.

Historical evidence indicates that South Indian Tamils became
directly involved in Sri Lankan affairs by the third century B.C.,
although they may not have formed a substantial portion of the permanent population until the seventh century.[20] Certainly, a mul-
tiethnic society seems to have existed on the island from ancient
times, and there were racial and religious harmony, cultural contacts,
and physical mixing between the two groups. There is also evidence
to show that Tamil rulers became patrons of Buddhism and Hindu
deities were worshipped by Buddhists.[21] This racial harmony was,
however, shattered by the fifth century A.D., when the rulers of three
powerful South Indian Tamil kingdoms succeeded in undermining
the influence of Buddhism on Hindu society in South India and
threatened the political stability of the island's Sinhalese kingdom.[22]
Unlike in India, Buddhism was preserved and fostered in Sri Lanka
by the state and the Buddhist order of monks termed the Sangha.

The Sangha, the Myth of Sinhalese Origin, and Dravidian Invasions

Buddhist traditions indicate that Buddha and later Asoka, the North
Indian king who was instrumental in the spread of Buddhism outside
India, found the island to be an ideal place to establish a Buddhist

society. Therefore, large numbers of *bhikkhus*, including Mahinda, a close relative of Asoka, were dispatched to Sri Lanka to convert the king and his subjects during the reign of Devanampiya Tissa (307–267 B.C.). Sinhalese people were drawn to the new faith because legends and myths in the *Pali Chronicles* suggested that Buddha himself had asked Sakka, the king of gods and the protector of Buddha's doctrine, to furnish protection to Vijaya, the founder of the Sinhalese race, in order to establish the Sinhalese-Buddhist nation of Sri Lanka. The religious significance attached to the Vijaya legend and the myths of Buddha's visit to Sri Lanka on three separate occasions have always been an important factor in Sinhalese national consciousness. Therefore, when Sinhala rulers and the Buddhist clergy became apprehensive of the growing threat from Hindu rulers in South India, they mustered support from the Sinhala people to defend the kingdom by appealing to their religious and racial sentiments. Indeed, one of the most successful strategies adopted by the Buddhist clergy to stir nationalistic sentiment was to expound the theme that the Sinhalese are destined by divine will to defend the Sasana (Buddhism) against the Tamils, who are opposed to Buddhism. Semilegendary and historical accounts in the *Pali Chronicles* emphasize that Sinhalese people should protect both the spiritual and ethnic integrity of Sri Lanka.

The Buddhist clergy was genuinely concerned about the plight of Buddhism in the event that Sri Lanka came under the permanent rule of Dravidian Hindu kingdoms. Political domination by Dravidians would have meant an end to the power they traditionally wielded over Sinhalese rulers. Sinhalese rulers were eager to maintain close relationship with the Sangha and to support Buddhism in order to receive the overwhelming support of the people, and the prosperity of the Sangha and its ability to foster Buddhism varied with the political stability of the Sinhalese state. Moreover, Sinhalese villagers relied on the clergy to instruct the children, to conduct religious ceremonies, and to guide the people in the conduct of their lives according to Buddha's teachings.[23] Thus the Buddhist clergy had a profound impact on the people as well as the rulers, and Buddhism, as the state religion, had become a powerful instrument in shaping the outlook of the people by the sixth century. The ruler and his subjects were intimately connected through Buddhism, and this connection between religion, culture, language, and national identity has continued to exert a powerful influence on the Sinhalese.[24]

The Buddhist clergy has also influenced Sinhalese national consciousness by deliberately exaggerating historical events dealing with Sinhalese-Tamil conflict. The Buddhist clergy incorporated legends and myths in historical accounts to inculcate the notion that the very existence of Sri Lanka as a sovereign state is under constant threat of "racial and cultural assimilation from Dravidian South India."[25] To the Sinhalese, myths were real; they expressed their historical role as defenders of the country and the Sasana and, on occasion, became "rallying points for Sinhalese nationalism."[26] One example of an appeal to the Sinhala people's nationalist sentiment was the glorification in the *Mahavamsa* of Prince Dutugemunu as the greatest Sinhalese hero of all times for his second-century defeat of Elara, the Chola general from South India who ruled Anuradhapura for forty-four years, and for thereby rescuing Buddhism. It is surprising to note, however, that Elara is portrayed in the *Pali Chronicles* as a benevolent king who extended patronage to Buddhism. There were also other Tamil rulers who assumed the traditional role of protecting and fostering the state religion while "Sinhalese kings sometimes pillaged temples and robbed monasteries of their wealth."[27] The *Pali Chronicles* even suggest that Elara had the support of a large number of Sinhalese, including a few generals, in his encounter with Dutugemunu. Evidently, ethnicity was not an important factor at the time of the Dutugemunu-Elara conflict.[28] Yet, racial and religious motives are attributed to the Dutugemunu-Elara conflict, and some Sinhalese scholars even regard the defeat of Elara by Dutugemunu as the beginning of Sinhala nationalism.[29] Over the years the myth that Dutugemunu saved the Sinhalese race and the Sasana "developed into one of the most powerful instruments of Sinhalese nationalism in modern times."[30]

Contrary to the accounts in the *Mahavamsa* that project a racial motivation onto the Dutugemunu-Elara conflict, some modern historians believe that racial conflict did not occur until the fifth and sixth centuries A.D. when Sri Lanka came under constant attack from powerful South Indian Dravidian states that were militantly Hindu—the Pandyans, Pallavas, and Cholas.[31] By this time the Tamil settlers in Sri Lanka are supposed to have become conscious of their ethnic identity and to have extended their support to the South Indian invaders. Thus, although Dutugemunu may have been viewed as the savior of the Sinhalese race, his victory over Elara did not put an end to Tamil-Sinhalese conflict nor did it deter Sinhalese rulers from having contact with South Indian rulers. Indeed, Sinhalese rulers sought the assistance of Indian rulers to settle dynastic disputes, got involved in conflicts between the Cholas and Pandyans, and concluded matrimonial alliances with South Indian families. Despite the South Indian invasions, Anuradhapura remained the capital of Sri Lanka from the time of Dutugemunu's triumph over Elara until the eleventh century, except for a brief period in the fifth century A.D. when the capital was moved to Sigiriya.

The Collapse of the Sinhalese Kingdom and the Establishment of the Jaffna Kingdom

Anuradhapura was sacked in 1017 by the Cholas to punish the Sinhalese ruler for assisting the Pandyans against them in South India. Sri Lanka remained a province of the Chola empire for seventy-five years, during which time the capital was moved from Anuradhapura to Polonnaruwa. Vijayabahu defeated the Cholas in 1070. The reign of the Cholas came to an end with the accession of Parakramabahu I (1153–1186), but Tamil invasions continued to plague the Sinhalese kingdom in the twelfth century. When the Sinhalese kingdom collapsed in the thirteenth century, the Sinhalese began drifting southwest to the Wet Zone. This drift was occasioned by a combination of factors, including invasions from India, internal dissension, natural disasters, decline in the fertility of the soil, silting of tanks and canals, lack of administrative control to organize labor to maintain irrigation facilities, and a malaria epidemic of major consequences (see chapter 3).[32] The Sinhalese chronicle *Rajavaliya,* which was written in the seventeenth century, places the blame for the ultimate disintegration of the Polonnaruwa kingdom on Magha of Kalinga, who invaded the island in 1215.[33] References in the *Rajavaliya* to the plundering of Buddhist shrines by Tamils, the forced conversion of Buddhists to Hinduism, and the burning of the Rajarata, the "king's country," by an invading army from South India have had great impact on Sinhalese national consciousness.

Despite periodic invasions from South India, including the Chola campaigns of the eleventh century, the Sinhalese kingdom, with its tank civilization, its rich Buddhist treasures, and its monumental architecture, persisted until the thirteenth century. Indeed, it maintained its independence for centuries except for brief periods. Nevertheless, the collapse of the golden age of Sinhalese civilization, Vijayabahu's victory over the Cholas, and other minor incursions by Tamil armies into Sri Lanka are highlighted in the Pali and Sinhalese chronicles to portray the Tamils as aggressors who have continuously attempted to destroy Buddhism and subjugate the Sinhalese. This theme has been used effectively by some sections of the Buddhist clergy and by Sinhalese extremist nationalists to argue against language and political concessions for Tamils in present-day Sri Lanka.

With the collapse of the Sinhalese kingdom in the Dry Zone, the island was subdivided into three distinct kingdoms. The northern part of the island, from the Vanni, the area between Jaffna and Anuradhapura, to the Jaffna Peninsula came to be occupied by Tamil settlers and ruled by the king of Jaffna. The coastal area of the southwest came under the Kingdom of Kotte, and the central hill country became the Kandyan kingdom. There is no consensus as to the date of the establishment of the Jaffna kingdom, but some Tamil scholars believe it was founded soon after the invasion of the island by Magha of Kalinga. Even Sinhalese historians C. W. Nicholas and S. Paranavitana have suggested that the Tamils secured control of the Northern Province in the thirteenth century. Whether the Tamils established the Kingdom of Jaffna in the thirteenth century or earlier cannot be confirmed because of the absence of archaeological data. Nevertheless, prominent Sinhalese and Tamil historians agree that the kingdom was certainly in existence by 1325. Gananath Obeyesekere believes that the Tamils of the present-day Batticaloa and Trincomalee districts owed allegiance to the king of Kandy rather than to the king of Jaffna, while others believe that by 1325 the Tamil rulers were strong enough to hold suzerainty over a large area in northern Sri Lanka as far as the coast of Puttalam.[34]

In the sixteenth century, the Portuguese were successful in establishing suzerainty over the lowlands of Sri Lanka, which formed part of the Kingdoms of Jaffna and Kotte, but they failed to consolidate their hold on the Kandyan kingdom, even though they sacked it more than once. The kingdom's mountains, forests, and rivers furnished the Kandyans with adequate protection from their enemies. Kandyan rulers conspired with the Dutch to expel the Portuguese from the island in the seventeenth century. The Kandyan kingdom maintained its independence from the Dutch, but its kings were unable to restrict Dutch rule over a limited area along the coast. Although no formal war was declared between the Dutch and the kings of Kandy, the Dutch expedition of 1762 into the Kandyan kingdom was completely routed.

The Kandyan kingdom, however, became weakened by the eighteenth century when the Dutch virtually monopolized trade by forcing Kandyans to sell their products below the market value, as well as preventing them from trading with the people of the lowlands. The kingdom was also weakened by dynastic disputes and, in 1747, when the male line to the Kandyan throne died out, it passed to a descendant of the female line belonging to a Dravidian dynasty of Madura in South India. The Sinhalese nobility and the Dravidian court were unable to maintain peaceful relations; Sinhalese chieftains even intrigued with the British to overthrow the kingdom. The king eventually lost the support of his people. When the British invaded Kandyan territory in 1815, Sri Vikrama Rajasinha did not even have the support of many of his soldiers to defend the kingdom.

The history of Sri Lankan Tamils becomes more complete and continuous from the thirteenth century A.D. with the large-scale settlement of Tamils in northern Sri Lanka following the Chola invasions. Once the Jaffna kingdom was established, Sri Lankan Tamils developed a social organization, customs, traditions, and speech of their own that are distinct from those of South Indian Tamils. Laws and customs pertaining to inheritance and property rights evolved from a combination of laws and customs that were prevalent in the present-day states of Kerala and Tamil Nadu from which they had emigrated to the island in ancient times.

Some historians view the call for the establishment of a separate state by the Sri Lankan Tamils as a recent historical phenomenon, contending that the kings of Jaffna were never content to be merely rulers of a part of the island.[35] There is little doubt, however, that the establishment of the Tamil kingdom gave the Sri Lankan Tamils an opportunity to develop a sense of collective identity based on Tamil language, Tamil culture, and Tamil territory, which are the prerequisites of nationality.[36] Indeed, to the Tamils, the northern and eastern parts of Sri Lanka are their "single most treasured possessions," a traditional homeland "which thus served to underline their attribute of nationality and distinctiveness from, and, non-assimilability by, the Sinhalese."[37] They have also shown no desire to amalgamate politically or culturally with the Tamils of South India. They "have maintained their own separate and distinct linguistic and cultural continuum in the island for so many centuries that in reality the Tamil literary and cultural heritage of South India operates only as a source of historical inspiration, particularly in the present text."[38]

British Administration, Indian Tamils, and the Buddhist
Revitalization Movement

The Tamil kingdom lost its independence to Western colonial powers, first to the Portuguese in 1619, then to the Dutch and the British. In 1833 the British established a centralized form of government, developed roads and railroads connecting the Tamil and Sinhalese areas, and created opportunities for English-educated Tamils to seek employment in the South, all of which brought the two communities into direct contact with each other in the nineteenth century. From the 1830s, a large number of South Indian Tamil laborers were also settled on the British-owned coffee and, later, tea and rubber plantations located primarily in the highlands in the central part of the country. The British government employed foreign workers in their plantations because the Sinhalese peasants were reluctant to trade the casual schedule of rice cultivation for the low-paid and strictly regulated work on the plantations.

Although Indian Tamils and Sri Lankan Tamils are of the same racial stock, speak the same language, and are Hindus, they are separated from each other by centuries of history as well as geography. The Sri Lankan Tamils live predominantly in the Northern and Eastern provinces while the Indian Tamils are largely concentrated in the Central, Sabragamuwa, and Uva provinces. The differences between them were strong enough to restrain the two groups from forming a united front against the Sinhalese in the past. Indeed, it seems clear, as one observer noted, that if "race were all that mattered, the Ceylon and Indian Tamils would make a common cause against the Sinhalese."[39] The Sinhalese attitude toward the Indian Tamils, who numbered approximately 1.2 million in the 1940s, has been one of hostility, but unjustifiably so, since the large acreage of land devoted to plantations was alienated not to the Indian Tamils but to British plantation owners. Nevertheless, the plantations deprived the Kandyans of the land they urgently needed to support their increasing population and forced them to live among foreign-born people of different ethnicity who had no abiding interest in the island. The Indian Tamil community is still characterized "as an unassimilated and unassimilable element in the Ceylonese nation."[40]

While Sinhalese peasants of the rural villages came into direct contact with the poorly paid Indian Tamils, there was little opportunity for interaction between the former and the majority of Sri Lankan peasants of the Northern and Eastern provinces. Sri Lankan Tamils did not purchase land to cultivate crops or to settle in large numbers in the rural areas of the South. Therefore, the majority of the Sri Lankan Tamils and Sinhalese have been geographically separated from each other since the eleventh century. It was thus natural for the Sinhalese of the rural areas to project their negative attitudes about the Indian Tamils onto the Sri Lankan Tamils, since they spoke the same language. Even the leaders of the Buddhist Revivalist Movement of the nineteenth century made little effort to distinguish the Tamils of Indian origin from the Tamils of Sri Lankan origin and lumped them into the category of Indians. Leaders of the Buddhist and Sinhalese Revivalist movements never made any conscious effort to describe Sri Lankan Tamils as people with longevity of residence who are an integral part of the Sri Lankan community. Indeed, these leaders spent many years reinforcing the negative attitudes of the rural Sinhalese about the Sri Lankan Tamils. Nevertheless, some Sinhalese and Tamils, especially of the middle-class elite, developed positive attitudes toward each other as they made contact at places of employment, educational institutions, and public places in the mid-nineteenth century. However, as the nation moved into the twentieth century their interests collided, especially with regard to communal versus territorial representation in the Legislative Council, established in 1833.

A handful of Sri Lankans who belonged to the rising middle class of the English-educated elite were nominated to the Legislative Council to represent their respective communities. At this stage of political evolution in Sri Lanka, national issues were placed in the forefront and sectarianism was discouraged. In fact, national consciousness was limited to a section of the westernized elite, but everyone extended full-fledged cooperation to the British authorities in governing the country. The first threat to colonial rule came in the mid-nineteenth century when the Buddhist Revivalist Movement campaigned for the restoration of Buddhism to the former high status it held during the golden age of Sinhalese civilization. The movement concentrated its attack on foreign rule and Western influence, since Buddhism was neglected and Christianity was fostered during the colonial period. Communal issues were not the primary focus of the Buddhist Revivalist Movement at this time. By the late nineteenth and early part of the twentieth centuries, however, there were indications of the emergence of Sinhalese revivalist sentiments among those who were in the forefront of the Buddhist Revivalist Movement.[41] By the turn of the century, most Sinhalese revivalists regarded Moors (Muslims) and Indian traders as "non-nationals," whom they claimed dominated the country's trade and money lending. Sri Lankan Tamils were also included in the category of "non-nationals," since the term non-national was in many instances equated with "non-Sinhalese" by them.

Sri Lankan Tamils did not feel threatened by the Buddhist and Sinhalese revivalist movements although it was clear that "there were men who saw possibilities of exploiting (Buddhist) religious sentiment for political purposes."[42] In fact, the Sri Lankan Tamils "were in the forefront of the movement to create a Ceylon national-consciousness and to use this consciousness to wrest concessions from a reluctant [colonial] administration."[43] Tamil members of the Legislative Council, such as Sir Ponnampalam Ramanathan, were more concerned about the social and political welfare of Sinhalese than were their Sinhalese counterparts in the Council and were able to obtain much-needed concessions on issues pertaining to the Wesak holiday, the Buddhist Temporalities Bill, and taxes from the British government.[44]

Representation in the Legislative Council was based on the principle of communal representation, wherein the governor nominated members of the Sri Lankan elite to represent the Burgher (Eurasian), Sinhalese (Kandyan and Low Country), Tamil, Indian, Moor (Muslim), and Malay communities. The constitutional reform of 1910 maintained the principle of communal representation, but it permitted the English-educated, westernized elites, for the first time, to elect a Sri Lankan to the Legislative Council. A Sri Lankan Tamil, Sir Ponnampalam Ramanathan, was elected, in preference to a Sinhalese of the Karava caste, to the Council in 1912. It has been suggested that Ramanathan's election was largely the result of the support he received from leaders of the Sinhalese Goyigama elite, who, as the leaders of established order, were against the rising power of the Sinhalese Karava elite.

As members of the fisherman caste, the Karavas hold a lower position in the Sinhalese caste hierarchy than the Goyigamas, who belong to the cultivator caste. Despite their lower position, however, the Karavas emerged as a wealthy caste because they had better access to English education and more opportunities to become involved with plantation agriculture and modern commercial enterprise.[45]

Communal Versus Territorial Representation and the Beginnings of Ethnic Conflict

Even as late as 1912, there was no visible evidence of conflict between the Sinhalese and Tamil elites in the Council, although Ramanathan may not have been elected were it not for the caste rivalry among the Sinhalese. It was fortunate that Ramanathan was elected because he, in the wake of the Sinhalese and Muslim riots of 1915, played an effective role in condemning the way the government mishandled the riots as well as in convincing the government that Buddhist leaders had not incited them. There is no doubt that Sir Ponnampalam Ramanathan's success in persuading the government to lift martial law and to release Sinhalese leaders played a significant role in strengthening the political unity between the Sinhalese and Tamils and contributing to the establishment of the Ceylon National Congress (CNC) in 1919. Although communal bitterness had been aroused as early as 1910 when Ramanathan was elected to the Educated Ceylonese seat in the Legislative Council, his role in championing the Sinhalese cause during the 1915 disturbances helped to ease tensions. However, communal fears were revived as plans for constitutional reforms involving the allocation of seats in the Council were discussed.

Since 1833, unofficial membership in the Legislative Council had been allocated among the various ethnic communities so that no single community, irrespective of whether it was the majority community, could impose its will on the other communities. Even before the CNC was organized, Sinhalese politicians had objected to this method of communal representation and demanded that the number of Sinhalese representatives in the Council should be greater than that of the other communities. Ramanathan's brother, Sir Ponnampalam Arunachalem, was the leader of the constitutional reform movement and one of the founding members of the CNC. Constitutional reform was introduced in 1920 in response to agitation from the CNC, which sought provisions to enlarge the number of unofficial members nominated on a territorial basis to the Legislative Council. Hitherto, the number of Sinhalese and Tamils unofficial members of the Council had been nearly equal, but after 1921 there were more Sinhalese than Tamils because of the greater emphasis placed on territorial representation. The thirty-seven members of the reformed Council were to include twenty-three unofficial members, who for the first time were to hold a majority, but only twelve members were to be elected.

Although there were more Sinhalese unofficial members in the Legislative Council of 1921, they did not hold a clear majority in the Council since an education and property qualification for franchise limited the number of members who could be elected both on a territorial and communal basis. The Sinhalese members of the CNC wanted control of the Council by limiting its membership to only those elected on a territorial basis and objected to this arrangement, to the surprise of the minorities. They demanded that the franchise should be widened so that more Sinhalese could be elected. At this stage, the minorities, led by the Tamils, "were anxious for self-government, but did not wish to exchange British domination for Sinhalese domination."[46] Tamil members of the CNC, especially Sir Ponnampalam Ramanathan, had supported the CNC's original demand for territorial representation because the education and property qualification, in addition to communal representation, would insure adequate representation of Tamils in the Council. Nevertheless, the Tamils were willing to make concessions to insure that the Sinhalese had a majority in the Council, provided the Sinhalese leaders in the CNC actively supported the proposal for the reservation of a special seat for the Tamils residing in the Western Province. To their disappointment, support for this plan was not forthcoming from the CNC Sinhalese leadership.

Most of the Tamil elite were not prepared to accept the weakened position of Tamils in the Legislative Council under the system of territorial representation, and Sir Ponnampalam Arunachalem resigned from the CNC. The Tamil leadership became increasingly aware that many Sinhalese political activists, including constitutional reformists and Buddhist revivalists, "possessed a streak of Sinhalese national consciousness" and were inclined to sacrifice Tamil interests.[47] This became clear when the Sinhalese Buddhist activist Anagarika Dharmapala began a campaign for the revival of Sinhala national consciousness at the turn of the century. In the Buddhist Revivalist Movement of this period, "the older forms of identity were given a new lease on life, resulting in communalism, casteism, a distortion of history, a revival of myths of origin and hero-myths, along with visions of a past 'golden age.' "[48] Dharmapala's teachings, which stressed that Sri Lanka belonged exclusively to the Sinhalese Buddhist with no place for exploiters such as the Tamils, had a profound impact on the schoolteachers, Buddhist clergy, native physicians, and various categories of government officials at the local and national level who "were educated in Sinhalese schools, but were cut off from the sources of political and economic power."[49] When Sri Lanka became independent in 1948, these Sinhalese-educated rural people and the Buddhist clergy, which became a powerful force in S. W. R. D. Bandaranaike's Sri Lanka Freedom party, demanded preferential treatment for their community. Even those in the CNC, who had been committed to fostering Ceylonese national consciousness as against Sinhalese national consciousness, were swayed by the Sinhalese Revivalist Movement. Many members of the CNC and the Council came to realize that economic benefits would accrue to the Sinhalese if the Indians were repatriated to India and Sri Lankan Tamils were no longer permitted to use English for recruitment to the public service. Clearly, Dharmapala's pronouncements that "non-Sinhalese had no place in Sri Lanka" contributed to the emergence of "Sinhalese nationalist-sectarianism . . . from within the bastion of Ceylon nationalism."[50]

The CNC, which became a Sinhalese-dominated organization when the Tamils resigned from it, established the Sinhala Mahajana Sabha (Great Council of the Sinhalese), with its local rural sabhas, to mobilize popular support for the liberation of the country from foreign rule. From the very start its proceedings were in Sinhala, and "this emphasis on Sinhalese had the inevitable effect of strengthening ethnicity as a cohesive force within the Sabhas, and from this it was but a short step to emphasizing ethnicity as a point of distinction or separation from rival groups."[51] The Sinhala Mahajana Sabha was also anti-Christian in its outlook and "in this sense . . . , very much in the tradition of the religious nationalism of men like Anagarika Dharmapala, and precursors of the Sinhala Maha Sabha of the 1930s and 1940s, and the Mahajana Eksath Peramuna (MEP) of the mid- and late 1950s."[52]

Anagarika Dharmapala's Buddhist Revivalist Movement, the establishment of the Sinhala Mahajana Sabha in 1919, and the CNC's demand to do away with communal electorates aroused the suspicions of Tamil leaders and compelled them to adopt new strategies in order to safeguard Tamil interests. They became aware that they could no longer rely on Sinhalese caste rivalry to secure their objectives. In their view, the Goyigama elite was determined to minimize the power of the Tamils by demanding the abolition of communal representation.[53] Tamil political leaders realized, for the first time since 1833, that they represented a minority community and that they should demand adequate constitutional safeguards from the colonial rulers to defend Tamil rights in the face of the rising tide of Sinhalese nationalism. They failed, however, to convince the members of the Donoughmore Commission to continue with the system of communal representation for safeguarding minority interests. The Donoughmore Commission was appointed in 1927 to study the constitution of 1924 and make recommendation on ways to facilitate the participation of a large percentage of the population in the election of Ceylonese to the Legislative Council, as well as to devise a constitution that would give substantial power to the Ceylonese representatives in the Council to govern the country. To their dismay, when territorial representation was combined with universal suffrage, the relative ratio of Sinhalese to Tamil representation was 5:1; a dramatic increase from the former ratio of 2:1 in the previous Legislative Council.[54]

The Donoughmore Constitution of 1931, granted the franchise to all adults over twenty-one, so as to broaden the basis of political power. Indeed, Sri Lanka became the first country in Asia to have universal suffrage. The constitution abolished communal electorates and members of the newly formed State Council were elected through a territorial system. Under this system the country was divided into electorates based on area and population and this ensured the Sinhalese a substantial majority in the State Council. The State Council was vested with both legislative and executive powers, since its fifty elected and eight nominated members were divided into seven Executive Committees. The chairmen of the committees and three British officers of state formed the Board of Ministers. The internal administration of the country came under the direction of the Ceylonese ministers, while the powers reserved to the governor were handled by the British officers of state. For the first time in the history of constitutional development in Sri Lanka, Ceylonese were provided with the real opportunity to gain experience in the problems of government.

Tamil leaders were not pleased with the provisions of the Donoughmore Constitution but refrained from contesting the 1931 elections because the Tamil Youth Congress, which was inspired by the Indian freedom movement, as exemplified by the Indian National

Congress, called for a boycott of the elections. The Tamil Youth Congress had passed a resolution in 1929 demanding complete independence for Sri Lanka. The Youth Congress welcomed the provisions in the Donoughmore Constitution that abolished communal representation, seeing it as a way for the establishment of an independent, united Sri Lanka by ending communal-oriented politics. Those Sinhalese who clamored for complete independence for the country praised the stand taken by the Tamil Youth Congress, although prominent Sinhalese leaders did not support it and there were threats made against the people of Jaffna. These threats merely helped to reinforce Tamil suspicions that the majority community was determined to suppress minority rights. In spite of these suspicions, the Tamil leaders remained willing to work together with the Sinhalese to establish an independent united Sri Lanka.

The "Pan-Sinhalese" Ministry, Sinhala Maha Sabha, and Ponnambalam's "50-50"

Following the general elections of 1936, Sinhalese leaders were able to secure for themselves the chairmanships of the seven Executive Committees in the State Council that formed the Board of Ministers. Tamil members of the State Council became suspicious of this "pan-Sinhalese ministry" and accused the ministers, who were in charge of the administration of government departments, of neglecting the needs of Tamil constituencies. Tamils also accused the Board of Ministers of preferring to negotiate privately with the British government on matters dealing with constitutional reforms. Although the establishment of a Sinhalese ministry was communally motivated, Sinhalese leaders convinced the British governor, Sir Andrew Caldecott, otherwise. They emphasized that the formation of the pan-Sinhalese Board of Ministers was essential "solely for the purpose of securing unanimity to press the imperial power to make concessions toward self-government."[55] Moreover, there were no indications that the inclusion of Tamils in the ministry would have created a serious problem or hindered the country's progress toward self-government. Indeed, Tamil leaders did not even consider that "the Tamil interest was threatened to such a point to be impelled to collaborate with the British and to thwart the country's progress toward self-rule."[56] Nevertheless, Tamil leaders were completely excluded from sharing in the political power in 1936. The Tamil Congress leader G. G. Ponnam-balam, who was elected to the State Council from Jaffna, was deliber-ately excluded from the Board of Ministers.

Obviously, many Sinhalese constitutional reformists who dominat-ed the Ceylon National Congress and the State Council had been influenced by the upsurge of Sinhalese nationalism at the turn of the century. Although the Sinhalese leaders of the State Council did not agree with all the objectives of the Sinhala Revivalist Movement, "economic nationalism had a place in their program."[57] This explains why they objected to the granting of basic rights to Indian Tamils. Like the Sinhalese Revivalists, the Ceylon nationalists in the Council regarded the Indian Tamils as "non-nationals," even though some of them had long resided or were even born in Sri Lanka. The CNC advocated restricting the immigration of Indian Tamils from 1930. Although the CNC could not have prevented colonial rulers from granting voting rights to most of the Indian immigrants under the Donoughmore Constitution, Sinhalese Council members under the direction of the CNC were determined to deny some of the basic rights of the Indian Tamils. As a first step toward discriminating against them, the State Council deprived them of the benefits of the Land Development Ordinance of 1935 and the Village Development Ordinance of 1937.[58] From 1939, Indian Tamils were gradually pro-hibited from seeking daily paid employment in government depart-ments. The members of the CNC and the State Council defended these discriminatory measures as being politically and economically rather than racially motivated. They indicated that the presence of a large number of Indian Tamils on the island, particularly in certain electorates, deprived the indigenous population of its political rights and employment opportunities. It was obvious that the future for the Indian Tamils in Sri Lanka was bleak when then minister of agricul-ture D. S. Senanayake proclaimed in 1940 that "unless we stem the tide of this growing domination of Indians in Ceylon in the economic and social life, our extinction as a Ceylonese nation is inevitable."[59]

With the Indians being gradually stripped of their rights in the country, Sri Lankan Tamil leaders became increasingly skeptical about their own community's future. They protested the treatment of Indian Tamils to the Board of Ministers and accused the ministers of discriminating against the native Tamil community in the areas of agriculture, education, disbursement of public funds, and public ser-vice appointments.[60] Evidently, some of the new members of the

Goyigama elite, the "Goyigama arrivistes," were not satisfied merely with the process of Ceylonization but were anxious to proceed with the more drastic process of Sinhalese nationalism.[61] In 1937 one of the prominent Goyigama arrivistes, S. W. R. D. Bandaranaike, founded a communal organization known as the Sinhala Maha Sabha (The Great Council of the Sinhalese) with the support of others in the CNC to actively agitate for the revival of Sinhala traditions, Sinhala culture, Sinhala language, and Buddhism. The formation of the Sinhala Maha Sabha in turn compelled G. G. Ponnambalam to form the All-Ceylon Tamil Congress in 1944 to champion the cause of the Tamils against Sinhala-Buddhist domination.

As Sri Lanka moved toward independence, Sinhalese and Tamil leaders continued to disagree with each other regarding Tamil representation in the parliament, which came into existence in 1947. The Tamil Congress complained to the Commission on Constitutional Reform, headed by Lord Soulbury, which was drafting the new constitution, that the Board of Ministers of the State Council had deliberately discriminated against the Tamils in the past and that provisions should be made in the constitution to protect the legitimate rights of the Tamil community in a free Sri Lanka. The fears of Sinhala domination were so intense that G. G. Ponnambalam even advocated that one-half of the seats in the new legislature be reserved for minorities, so that the "Sinhalese majority would not hold more than 50 percent of the seats in the legislature and this balance would be reflective in the executive and would be a series of checking clauses against discriminating legislation."[62] He believed that given the discriminatory measures adopted by the Board of Ministers of the State Council under the watchful eye of the colonial rulers, the Tamils had to secure substantial assurances in the constitution to prevent discrimination by the majority, even if their demands were extreme. This "50-50" scheme was rejected by the Soulbury Commission as being contrary to democratic principles, especially since the Sinhalese accounted for nearly 70 percent of the population. The Commission assured the Tamils that, with the inclusion of constitutional safeguards against discrimination, the creation of multimember constituencies (electorates from which more than one member can be elected to parliament) for Tamil areas that provided for additional minority representation in the legislature, and the formation of electorates based on the area as well as the population of provinces, the rights of Tamils would be protected. It was these assurances from the

Commission that persuaded the Sri Lankan Tamil councillors to approve the draft of the new constitution. However, even if the modified proposal of the Board of Ministers conceding 43 percent of the seats in the new legislature to the minorities had been accepted, the Sinhalese-dominated parliament of independent Sri Lanka would have been able to abolish this provision and replace it with territorial representation.

It is often claimed that G. G. Ponnambalam's "50-50" scheme "greatly agitated Sinhalese Buddhist resentment," and it is "cited by many Sinhalese as the beginnings of contemporary communal problems in Sri Lanka."[63] However, G. G. Ponnambalam was not responsible for initiating contemporary ethnic conflict; he was willing to cooperate with the Sinhalese leaders after 1947 and even supported measures later adopted to deny citizenship and voting rights to the Indian Tamils. It is more appropriate to trace the beginning of contemporary ethnic conflict to S. W. R. D. Bandaranaike, who as the leader of the communally structured Sinhala Maha Sabha appealed to anti-Tamil sentiments in all sections of Sinhalese society. The language issue, which mobilized the same forces that were in the forefront of the Buddhist and Sinhala revivalist movements at the turn of the century, led to the cleavage between the Sinhalese and Tamils and contributed to a series of anti-Tamil riots that started in 1956. There is no doubt that both Bandaranaike and Ponnambalam taught other ambitious politicians how easy it was to secure political power by appealing to people's anti-Tamil/anti-Sinhalese emotions. Indeed, some sections of the Buddhist clergy, as well as leaders of opposition parties in parliament, have on many occasions appealed to the Sinhala people's anti-Tamil emotions to force Sinhalese leaders to abandon their plans to grant language and political concessions to the Tamils.

Denial of Citizenship and Voting Rights to Indian Tamils

The 1948 constitution of independent Ceylon did provide guarantees against discrimination for ethnic minorities in the Ceylon Orders in Council, 1946 and 1947, Article 29, Section 2 (b) and (c).[64] These provisions and the assurances given by Prime Minister D. S. Senanayake that Tamil rights would be protected convinced G. G. Ponnambalam and a majority of his Tamil Congress to cross the floor and join the governing United National Party (UNP) in 1948. Only Tamil leader S. J. V. Chelvanayakam and a few of his followers, who later organized the Tamil Federal Party (FP), remained in the Opposition. Under the new constitution, five elected members of the Tamil community joined the United National Party to form the first national government. To ensure communal or ethnic balance, a Tamil was appointed by the governor-general to a nominated seat in the Senate, and relations between the two ethnic communities seemed to be cordial at the outset.[65] The interests of almost all communities were taken into consideration in the formation of the government with a major exception: those of the Indian community, consisting of plantation workers, were ignored. Contrary to the assurances made by the prime minister that no harm would come to the minorities, the government passed legislation under the Citizenship Act No. 18 of 1948 making Indian Tamils effectively stateless. The following year, the Indian and Pakistani Residents (Citizenship) Act No. 3 of 1949 was enacted by Parliament to define the conditions under which Indian Tamils could claim citizenship by registration. These two acts and the Parliamentary Elections (Amendment) Act No. 48 of 1949, which were designed to deny citizenship and voting rights to Tamils of Indian origin, had the approval of some of the Tamil members of parliament, including G. G. Ponnambalam, who may have felt a greater sense of shared historical experience and future aspirations for Sri Lanka with the Sinhalese than with Indian Tamils. Some of these Tamil parliamentarians who continued to cooperate with the Sinhalese government were even re-elected to parliament in the 1952 general elections.

From the early days of Sri Lanka's independence it was apparent that Sinhalese-dominated governments were determined to deny the legitimate rights of Tamils of both Indian and Sri Lankan origin. The legislation denying citizenship and voting rights to most Indian Tamils was passed by a Sinhalese-dominated parliament to satisfy the Kandyan Sinhalese, who were resentful of the Indian Tamils living and working in the predominantly Sinhalese areas where agricultural land and employment opportunities for the indigenous population were limited. Kandyan Sinhalese resented the presence in their electorates of Indian voters who they considered foreigners and who allegedly had no long-term interests in Sri Lanka. Moreover, the Kandyans and many Sinhalese politicians belonging to right-wing parties became concerned that the Sri Lankan Tamils and Indian Tamils might unite in order to dominate the Sinhalese. Their suspicions were particularly aroused when members of the Tamil Congress as well as the Tamil representatives in the Opposition, led by S. J. V. Chelvanayakam, vehemently opposed the passage of this legislation. In fact, it was these acts that led S. J. V. Chelvanayakam to leave the Tamil Congress and form the Tamil Federal Party in December 1949. The Federal Party not only opposed the legislation to disenfranchise Tamils of Indian origin but objected to the state-aided colonization of Tamil areas by Sinhalese peasants sponsored by the government of the United National Party.

The situation was further aggravated by the influx of illicit Indian immigrants from south Indian coast and the emergence of a militant local Dravida Munnetra Kazhagam (DMK) organization in the plantation areas.[66] Indian Tamils had also alienated the ruling United National Party by organizing themselves into trade unions and supporting left-wing-oriented parties in their efforts to secure better wages and working conditions. They often voted for Marxist candidates in the general elections, to the dismay of candidates from the UNP, and even expressed militancy during the period 1930–1940. Indeed, the UNP was eager to eliminate "a bloc of Marxist representatives" from the parliament in order to win additional seats for itself from the Kandyan areas, where the indigenous population was willing to support overwhelmingly right-wing parties more concerned about the plight of the Kandyan peasantry than about the Indian Tamils.[67]

The denial of voting rights to Tamils of Indian origin adversely affected the capacity of the Sri Lankan Tamils to defend their legitimate rights as citizens. When 90,000 Indian Tamils lost their voting rights, the parliamentary strength of the Sinhalese was increased from 67 percent in 1947 to 73 percent in 1952. It was further increased to 78 percent in 1959 through delimitation of electorates. At present, Sinhalese representation in the legislative bodies is as high as 80 percent, and this has given the Sinhalese leaders "the ability to alter the constitution, and to hold the minorities at their mercy in respect to fundamental rights."[68] Indeed, the legislative acts of 1948 and 1949 denying voting and citizenship rights to Indian Tamils were the first of the many legislative acts passed by the Sinhalese-dominated parliament designed to chip away first at the privileges and then at the basic rights of the Tamils. Being outnumbered, Tamil representatives were unable to prevent the passage of discriminatory legislation aimed at the Tamil community.

CHAPTER 2

Problems of National Integration

SRI LANKAN Tamils were still hopeful, despite the position taken by the United National Party (UNP) on the Indian Tamil issue, that their rights would be guaranteed under the Soulbury Constitution. Their fears of being discriminated against were further allayed by Prime Minister D. S. Senanayake's position that the concept of a secular state would be upheld and that "he sought the reconciliation of the legitimate interests of the majority and minorities within the context of an all island polity."[1] Unfortunately, the Sri Lankan nationalism propagated by D. S. Senanayake did not enjoy popular support and was opposed by the Sinhalese-Buddhist majority, and especially by the Sinhalese intelligentsia, perturbed by the continuing emphasis placed on English as the official language of administration. Even before independence, some Sinhalese politicians, including J. R. Jayewardene, had demanded preferential treatment for their community in the exercise of political power and in the sharing of economic resources on the grounds that the Tamils, by virtue of their proficiency in the English language, held a disproportionately higher percentage of employment in the public service.[2]

S. W. R. D. Bandaranaike, a prominent member of the Goyigama-dominated UNP, read the pulse of the Sinhalese electorate accurately and adopted strategies appropriate to capitalize on this political situation. He had already organized the Sinhala Maha Sabha in response to Sinhala-Buddhist nationalism and aspired to transform it into a political force. His first move in the quest for political power was to cross over to the Opposition and form the communally oriented Sri Lanka Freedom Party (SLFP). As a leader of the SLFP, he was able to use the theme of Sinhala-Buddhist nationalism to secure, in due course, support from a large number of Sinhalese from both the Goyigama and non-Goyigama castes.[3] Bandaranaike was confident that his future lay in the support he would receive from the Sinhala-educated physicians, teachers, and *bhikkhu*s who had espoused Sinhalese-Buddhist nationalism since the days of Anagarika Dharmapala. In order to appeal to this sentiment, he had rejected British rule and, above all, had demanded that both Sinhala and Tamil be elevated to the status of official languages of the country. Nevertheless, Bandaranaike was unable to make an impact on the rural electorate and lost the election of 1952 held after the death of D. S. Senanayake. He had not as yet taken up the "Sinhala only" theme. The UNP's landslide electoral victory, under the leadership of Dudley Senanayake, "took place in an atmosphere of emotionalism following the death of D. S. Senanayake, and in fact the massive victory won by his son was in many ways a ringing endorsement given by the electorate to the father's lifework."[4] However, Dudley Senanayake was forced to resign as prime minister in October 1953 when several demonstrators who had taken part in a Marxist-sponsored strike against the increase in the price of rationed rice were killed when the police opened fire.

Although increasingly apprehensive of the emergence of Sinhalese nationalism, the Tamil community was still willing to extend its support to the UNP in its efforts to create a united Sri Lanka in which Sinhalese and Tamils could live in harmony. It was with this in mind that they elected G. G. Ponnambalam to represent them in the parliament and in the United National Party government, which was committed to Sri Lankan nationalism. Unfortunately, Sir John Kotelawala, who succeeded Dudley Senanayake, excluded Ponnambalam from his reshuffled cabinet. While it is true that Ponnambalam was considered by some Tamils to be a traitor to their cause because of his willingness to join the Sinhalese-dominated government and vote for the legislation that denied citizenship and voting rights to Indian Tamils, he was still highly regarded. Thus, many Tamils who had hitherto given full support to the UNP were disturbed by Kotelawala's decision not to reappoint Ponnambalam to the cabinet, especially at a time when the Sinhalese intelligentsia and the Buddhist clergy were demanding that the Sinhala language, Sinhala culture, and Buddhism of the majority people be given special recognition.

Evidently, as Sinhalese politicians and *bhikkhu*s began to view their language, religion, and traditions exclusively as Sri Lankan, more Tamils were inclined to vote for the Federal Party, which stood for the preservation of the Tamil language, Tamil culture, and the traditional Tamil homeland.[5] In fact, many Tamils were beginning to question the ability of the UNP to defend their rights in the face of rising Sinhalese nationalism. Moreover, some Sinhalese nationalists were already demanding that Sinhala should be made the sole official language of Sri Lanka. In order to allay their fears and to secure their support for the UNP, Kotelawala assured the Sri Lankan Tamils, during a visit to Jaffna in late 1954, that appropriate legislation would be adopted to make both Sinhala and Tamil the official languages of the country. Many Sinhalese were outraged by this and regarded the prime minister's initiative as inappropriate, since the government had never striven to satisfy the aspirations of the Sinhalese people. Bandaranaike capitalized on this situation by declaring that the SLFP would make Sinhala the sole official language of the nation and at the same time provide for the "reasonable use" of the Tamil language if his party was elected to power. This was the same Bandaranaike who had pressured the Sinhalese-dominated CNC in 1944 to agree to Sinhala and Tamil as the official languages of the country in place of English.

S. W. R. D. Bandaranaike and other members of the SLFP recognized the power of language as an aspect of group identity and used that fact effectively to achieve their political ambitions. Bandaranaike began to champion the cause of the *bhikkhu,* the native physician, the rural schoolteacher, and the large numbers of low-paid minor employees who had hitherto lacked opportunities to acquire the English education necessary to secure lucrative employment.[6]

The language-employment problem was closely intertwined with Sinhala nationalism because the Sinhalese sought "their identity in the Sinhalese language, in Buddhism, and the traditions of the *Mahavamsa*—an identity sharpened and popularized by the Buddhist revival" that began in the nineteenth century.[7] Sinhalese extremist nationalists warned of the danger that would befall the Buddhist religion and Sinhalese tradition if Sinhala were allowed to fall into decay under the powerful influences of English and Tamil. The "Sinhala only" theme was used effectively to garner the backing of the Sinhala-educated rural people who aspired to share in the political and economic power of the country but were excluded because of the emphasis placed on English education. Indeed, politicians convinced the Sinhalese electorate that the Tamils had usurped more than their fair share of the jobs and the only way to trim the

advantage they held was to make Sinhala the official language. The
SLFP was also supported by the Buddhist clergy and other parties that
were committed to the "Sinhala only" cause. The Eksath Bhikkhu
Peramuna, consisting of concerned *bhikkhus*, accorded overwhelming support to the SLFP because it promised to restore the monk's traditional role of unlimited influence in the government and education.[8] In November 1955, four distinct groups consisting of the SLFP,
VLSSP (Viplavakari [Revolutionary] Lanka Sama Samaja Party), the
Basha Peramuna (Language Front), and independents formed the
Mahajana Eksath Peramuna (MEP) to oppose the UNP and vowed to
make Sinhala the sole official language. Indeed, the MEP was basically a SLFP-Marxist coalition. The UNP, perturbed by the support
the MEP was receiving for this stand, changed its original position in
February 1955, declaring that Sinhala should be the official language
of the country. With this declaration, the UNP lost the little support
it previously had from the Tamil people.

The "Sinhala Only" Legislation, Sinhalese Nationalism, and Tamil Nationalism

It was not surprising that the MEP, led by S. W. R. D. Bandaranaike,
won a landslide victory in the election of 1956. Likewise, the Federal
Party, led by S. J. V. Chelvanayakam, was given a clear mandate
from the Tamil people to seek, through peaceful and parliamentary
methods, the establishment of a Tamil linguistic state within a federal
union of Sri Lanka. The electoral victory of the MEP in Sinhalese-
dominated electorates and the FP in Tamil-dominated electorates
marks the beginning of the period when Sinhalese and Tamil nationalism replaced the concepts "of multi-racial polity, a Sri Lankan
nationalism, and a secular state."[9] From then on, politicians in both
communities were increasingly tempted to manipulate the ethnic
issue, even at the risk of endangering political stability, national
unity, and integration in Sri Lanka, as long as it contributed to the
political advantage of their party or faction.

The 1956 general elections and the formation of the government
by the MEP became an important turning point in the relationship
between the two ethnic communities in Sri Lanka. Henceforth,
Tamils who were elected from the FP to represent the interests of the
Tamils in parliament were completely excluded from holding minis-
terial or other positions of power in the government. This made it

impossible for them to influence the decisions of the cabinet or for the Sinhala government to interact on a regular basis with the elected representatives of the majority of the Tamils. On the other hand, successive Sinhala governments were obliged to listen to the wishes and aspirations of the rural Sinhalese, the influential *bhikkhus* of the Eksath Bhikkhu Peramuna, and the Sinhalese nationalists who had elected them to power. Henceforth, Sinhala governments were forced to pay heed to the demands of powerful groups that were opposed to the granting of concessions to the Tamils. One observer, commenting on the outcome of the MEP victory in 1956, aptly stated that "the rural masses and the Sinhalese Buddhists intelligentsia now came to grips with the realities of political power. Bandaranaike, who had reflected as well as articulated their needs and aspirations, found it difficult to hold the more militant sections in check."[10] In particular, the Eksath Bhikkhu Peramuna, which campaigned for the MEP and received a pledge from Bandaranaike that its ten demands would be met, including the implementation of the controversial Buddhist Commission Report and the institution of Sinhala as the official language of Sri Lanka, became a very potent political force. Since the MEP had used the anti-Tamil sentiment to defeat the United National Party in the Sinhalese electorates, it was unable to grant any concessions to Tamils because opposition parties, especially the UNP, accused the MEP of yielding to Tamil demands. It became apparent that Sinhala governments were unable to accede to the demands of the Tamils because such a move would be exploited by opposition parties to gain power. Therefore, since 1956 ambitious politicians have not hesitated to inflame popular passions by appealing to communal sentiments, "making virtually impossible a reconciliation of conflicting Sinhalese and Tamil claims through reasoned accommodation and compromise and creating an atmosphere of disorder and hostility that was readily exploited by fanatics, adventurers, and goondas."[11]

The "Sinhala only" legislation, enacted into law by the MEP government as the Official Language Act No. 33 of 1956, marked the end of the political control exercised by the westernized, English-speaking elite, including the Tamils, in all spheres of life in Sri Lanka and symbolized the end of foreign domination of Sri Lanka.

The "Sinhala only" Act made the Sinhala language the only official language of Sri Lanka in 1956. However, provisions were made in the Act to permit the use of the English language in government departments until December 31, 1960, provided that the ministers in charge of such departments were convinced that it was impracticable to commence the use of Sinhala for any official purposes. The Act also specified that ministries should be prepared to commence the use of the Sinhala language before the expiry date, and if this change could be affected by administrative order, regulations might be made to effect such a change. No provisions were made in the Act for the use of the Tamil language for official purposes in the Tamil districts.

"Sinhala only" legislation provided, for the first time, an opportunity for 74 percent of the population who did not have proficiency in the English language to conduct official transactions in their native language. At the same time, however, Tamils, many of whom were proficient in the English language and not Sinhala, were prohibited from using the English language. Its use was prohibited partly because it was a foreign language and partly because it gave undue advantage to Tamils in education and employment. Tamils objected to the attitude that they had intentionally and deviously robbed the Sinhalese of their jobs and therefore should be punished. Tamils insisted that they had no alternative, given the paucity of environmental resources for successful agriculture in their traditional areas, but to secure lucrative nonfarming jobs by mastering the English language.

Under colonial rule, more than 90 percent of the island's population was not literate in English and had to seek aid from persons proficient in English to decipher information pertaining to income taxes or inheritance. Once Sinhala was declared the official language, the majority of the Sinhalese people were spared the problem of having to rely on translators to complete forms dealing with legal and personal matters. On the other hand, the Tamils had to continue, as they had during the colonial period, to rely on translators to transact business with the government and to complete legal documents as well to learn an alien language in order to secure public service appointments. While colonialism had ended for the Sinhalese, it continued for the Tamils. The Tamils were also deeply concerned that the official language policy would destroy their language and distinctive culture, which they have zealously cultivated from the time of their arrival from South India in ancient times.[12] The Tamil masses and their political leaders did not question the aspirations of the Sinhalese people who desired to "retrieve their cultural heritage, which they felt was endangered by the incursions of the West, and to assert their position and prerogatives as the majority of the island's population."[13] Tamils, however, were unwilling to be governed in the Sinhalese language in the very areas they considered to be their traditional homeland.

The Official Language Act No. 33 of 1956, despite the promises made by Bandaranaike in the MEP manifesto, did not contain any special provisions that granted concessions to the national minority, the Tamils, with regard to the use of the Tamil language for education, for administration in the Tamil areas, and for correspondence with government departments. Tamil leaders realized for the first time that the Sinhalese leaders were prepared to deny Tamils any of their legitimate demands if it were politically advantageous to do so. First, the UNP let the Tamils down by changing its language policy from one of amending the constitution to guarantee parity of status for both languages in 1953 to one that advocated Sinhala only in 1955. Then in 1956, the MEP gave in to demands to delete from the Official Language bill the provisions for the "reasonable use of Tamil" because of pressure from Sinhala nationalists, the Eksath Bhikkhu Peramuna, and from prominent Sinhalese leaders like Mettananda, the influential leader of the Karava Buddhist lobby of the MEP, as well as the UNP.[14] The Buddhist clergy and a large number of Sinhalese Buddhists were not willing to accede to Tamil demands because they believed that the Sinhala national myth of reconquering the island, whether from the Tamils or Europeans, had been accomplished, after 2,500 years of frustration, by the passage of the "Sinhala only" legislation and that the elevated status of Sinhala and Buddhism should be maintained.[15]

The passage of the Sinhala only legislation had additional significance because it coincided with the 2,500th year of Buddhism, the year that Buddhist traditions predicted would mark the beginning of an unprecedented spiritual awakening that would spread Buddhism throughout the world. Therefore, the Sinhalese masses strongly believed that this new era in the history of the Sinhalese race had been inaugurated with the blessings of Buddha, and that it was their duty, as the "chosen race" with a "divine mission," to establish, preserve, and develop a Sinhala society based on the "sacred values" of the ancient past.[16] The Sinhalese masses were also persistently warned by the Buddhist clergy that Tamils should not be granted rights and privileges of the kind they sought in a Sinhala-Buddhist state because the Dravidian-Tamils have the reputation of destroying Sinhalese kingdoms, wrecking the Sinhala-Buddhist culture, usurping the political rights of the Sinhalese, and depriving the Sinhalese of opportunities to secure employment and prestigious positions in the public sector.[17]

To the Sri Lankan Tamils, the manner in which the language issue was formulated and expounded by Sinhalese politicians, both within and outside parliament, threatened their very existence as a recognizable national minority. They wanted their language to be safeguarded, their distinct culture to be preserved, the right to conduct the administration of their traditional homeland in the Tamil language to be assured, and the right to develop their traditional homeland according to their needs to be guaranteed. To show their disapproval of the passage of the discriminatory "Sinhala only" law, the Federal Party staged a peaceful demonstration in the vicinity of parliament, but the demonstrators were beaten up by Sinhalese mobs. This violence was accompanied by an anti-Tamil riot, resulting in the killing of more than one hundred Tamils at the government-sponsored Gal Oya colonization scheme in Amparai District. The anti-Tamil riots did not deter the federalists from continuing their demonstrations. In August 1956, they called a convention in Trincomalee, located in Eastern Province, to demand, among many concessions, the creation of a federal form of government that would give them regional autonomy, enact legislation giving parity of status to both Sinhala and Tamil as official languages of Sri Lanka, grant citizenship rights to Indian Tamils, and end the planned Sinhalese colonization of Tamil areas.

Thus from the very beginning the federalists insisted that cooperation from the Tamils to develop a strong national economy would not be forthcoming unless the latter's rights were guaranteed. Such a situation, they argued, could not be secured unless Tamils were granted a federal system of government which would allow them to use their language for administrative purposes, preserve their culture, provide employment opportunities for Tamils, and develop the Tamil areas according to the economic needs of the inhabitants, without interference from the Sinhala government.[18] They wanted economic rather than political independence for their people at this stage of their struggle for Tamil rights. Moreover, the claim by Sinhalese extreme nationalists that Tamils would seek foreign assistance to subjugate the Sinhalese, once regional autonomy was granted under a federal setup, had no validity because defense, foreign affairs, and other essential services related to national security would be under the control of the central government. The Federal Party threatened to stage a mass civil disobedience campaign if the government failed to implement the resolutions passed at the Trincomalee convention within one year. Prime Minister Bandaranaike was convinced that the Tamils were determined to defend their legitimate rights and, in order to avert a major ethnic conflict, he agreed to negotiate a political settlement to the conflict in July 1957.

The Bandaranaike-Chelvanayakam Pact

The only agreement negotiated in good faith by the leaders of the Sri Lanka Freedom Party, which, as the majority party in the MEP coalition government, represented the majority of the Sinhalese people in the parliament, and the leaders of the Federal Party, who represented the majority of the Tamil people in the parliament, was the Bandaranaike-Chelvanayakam Pact of 1957 (see Appendix I).[19] Had this agreement been implemented at this early stage of communal confrontation, much of the contemporary violence and bloodshed could have been avoided. The pact recognized Tamil as the language of a national minority and made provisions for its use as the language of administration in the predominantly Tamil areas of the Northern and Eastern provinces, without altering the position of Sinhala as the only official language of Sri Lanka. It would have minimized the threat of Sinhalese colonization of Tamil areas and permitted Tamils to develop their traditional homeland as they deemed necessary. Moreover, it would have provided for the devolution of administrative powers to regional councils in the Tamil areas.

Bandaranaike, realizing that the opposition from the Buddhist clergy and Sinhalese extremist forces, as well as the UNP, was growing, delayed the implementation of the agreement and issued an order requiring all motor vehicles to display the Sinhalese character "Sri" on license plates throughout the island in order to assure the Sinhalese extremists that the Bandaranaike-Chelvanayakam pact would not nullify the Sinhala Only Act. On the other hand, the FP became dubious about the prime minister's declared intention and launched "a protest campaign against the sending of nationalized public transport buses with Sinhalese-lettered number plates to Ceylon Tamil areas."[20] In addition, the FP persuaded principals of Jaffna schools to rescind their proposal to conduct Sinhala classes for the benefit of Tamil students. As expected, one action intensified the other. Sinhalese mobs retaliated against the obliteration of Sinhalese license plates in Jaffna by defacing Tamil homes and businesses, as well as by harassing Tamil people. The reprisals by Sinhalese mobs and the peaceful, nonviolent demonstration by two hundred *bhik-khus* of the Eksath Bhikkhu Paramuna in front of the prime minister's residence, compelled Bandaranaike to abrogate the pact in April 1958. The Bandaranaike-Chelvanayakam Pact was one of the many promises to the Tamils that Sinhalese politicians failed to honor during more than a quarter of a century.

The Federal Party, disappointed by Bandaranaike's refusal to implement the pact, called a convention in May 1958 to plan a mass disobedience campaign in Vavuniya District. This gathering was opposed by some Sinhalese extremist nationalists, and what began as the stoning of buses and trains that were transporting Tamil delegates via Polonnaruwa ended in the massacre of Tamils in many areas, especially in Colombo. The atrocities committed by Sinhalese mobs against Sri Lankan Tamils, who were using peaceful means to express their disappointment with the Sinhala government, ranged from rape to outright killing. Some of the killings and the burning of Tamil property were instigated by casual workers and squatters who lived in government-sponsored colonization schemes located in the vicinity of Tamil districts.[21] A few Tamil residents in the Eastern and Northern provinces retaliated, but the violence was predominantly orchestrated by Sinhalese extremists. No area of the island was secure for the Tamils except their traditional homeland, which became a safe haven for the 12,000 refugees who were evacuated from Colombo. The 1958 anti-Tamil riots marked the beginning of a series of ethnic confrontations involving violence and bloodshed that would continue in the years to come. With each successive riot, Sri Lankan Tamils became more convinced that their very survival was contingent on the ability to secure their traditional homeland for themselves.

The government used its emergency powers to quell the communal riots of 1958 and to detain prominent members of the Federal Party as well as to enact the Tamil Language (Special Provisions) Act No. 28 of 1958, which incorporated provisions for the use of Tamil as the medium of instruction in schools and universities. Tamil students were even permitted to take entrance examination to public service in Tamil, although entrants were required to pass a Sinhala proficiency examination within a specified time. These provisions seemed to be important concessions to the Tamils, if government regulations had authorized that Tamil parents could educate their children in the Sinhala language.[22] The act also allowed for the transaction of business with the government in the Tamil language and for the use of the Tamil language for "prescribed administrative purposes" in the Northern and Eastern provinces "without prejudice to the use of Sinhala Only."[23]

To the members of the Federal Party who were under house detention when the Tamil Language Act was passed and to others in the Tamil community, the "special provisions" reduced Tamil-speaking people to second-class citizens because their language was not recognized as a "national language" along with Sinhala. The FP emphasized that the "special provisions" did not satisfy the minimum provisions of the Bandaranaike-Chelvanayakam Pact with regard to the devolution of political power to regional councils and procedures for selecting colonists for state-sponsored colonization schemes. The independent member of parliament from Vavuniya, C. Suntharalingam, criticized the Tamil Language Act and even questioned the ability of the Federal Party to wrest substantial concessions for the Tamils. He also proclaimed that the future of the Tamils rested in the establishment of a separate state rather than on federalism.[24] He was the first Tamil politician to use the name "Eelam" to refer to the independent Tamil state of Sri Lanka, which the Tamil United Liberation Front and militant Tamils proclaimed in the 1970s. As it happened the Tamil Language Act of 1958 was not implemented because of Bandaranaike's assassination by a Buddhist *bhikkhu* in 1959.

The Federal Party did not give up hopes of securing language rights and political concessions similar to those provided in the Bandaranaike-Chelvanayakam Pact. It waited for an opportunity to strike a political alliance with any party that promised to deliver substantial concessions to the Tamils. This political alliance was essential since the FP "might at some moment hold the balance between rival Sinhalese parties in the often closely divided Parliament. They would then be in a position to bargain for the attainment of Tamil aims."[25] The opportunity came when neither the UNP nor the SLFP had a clear majority to form a government after the March 1960 general elections. At the outset, the FP tried to strike an alliance with the UNP. The UNP had been called to form a government as the party with the largest number of supporters in parliament, though not with a clear majority. The UNP rejected the alliance because the proposals submitted by the FP for its support were close to the provisions of the Bandaranaike-Chelvanayakam Pact. When the UNP rejected the federalist demands, the Sri Lanka Freedom Party, under the leadership of Srimavo Bandaranaike, the former prime minister's widow, solicited the support of the FP to form an alternative government, with an understanding between the two parties that the Bandaranaike-Chelvanayakam Pact would be enacted into law. Instead of calling upon the SLFP and FP to form the government, however, the governor-general dissolved parliament and called for a new election. The Federal Party's hopes evaporated when the SLFP won a landslide victory and formed a government without FP support. The SLFP was instead obligated to the Sinhalese masses who returned it to power and thus reneged on its agreement with the FP.

The SLFP government implemented its original language policy making Sinhala the only official language and ignored the provisions of the Tamil Language (Special Provisions) Act of 1958. The government even failed to recognize Tamil as a regional language and declared that Sinhala should be the language of administration even of Tamil areas. Legislation was also introduced making Sinhala the only language of the courts. This sudden emphasis on "Sinhala only" was partly intended to counter criticisms by the UNP and Sinhalese Buddhist militants to the effect that Mrs. Bandaranaike was preparing to sacrifice Sinhalese interests through a secret understanding with the Tamils. The Federal Party responded by embarking on a major civil disobedience (satyagraha) campaign that brought the activities of the government to a halt in the Tamil areas. It also defied the government by establishing a separate postal system to serve the Tamil areas. The government, in turn, responded by arresting Tamil leaders, banning the Federal Party, restoring its administrative control over the Tamil areas under a state of emergency, and dispatching army units to Jaffna. Some members of the army assaulted peaceful demonstrators and innocent bystanders in Jaffna.

The state of emergency, which was imposed on April 17, 1961, was lifted after 743 days. During the state of emergency the government's attention was directed toward improving the economic conditions of the nation and "Sinhalasization" of Sri Lanka. Many Tamil public service employees, who were unable to become proficient in the Sinhala language, were denied annual salary increments or forced to retire during this period. The language issue is the one through which the Tamils have suffered the most overt discrimination. The Federal Party was prepared to renew its civil disobedience campaign in August 1964 but called it off when Mrs. Bandaranaike's government decided to take steps to implement the provisions of the Tamil Language (Special Provisions) Act of 1958. The government also intended to introduce legislation for establishing district councils that would facilitate administrative decentralization and transaction of business in the language prevailing in the area. Unfortunately, these proposals were not enacted into law because Mrs. Bandaranaike's coalition government collapsed in December 1964.

The coalition government of Mrs. Bandaranaike was defeated in the general elections of 1965, but the victorious UNP was ten seats short of an absolute majority. It sought alliance with the FP, which had by now watered down its demands to include the implementation of the Tamil Language Act of 1958 and some of the more important provisions of the Bandaranaike-Chelvanayakam Pact. A "National Government" comprising the UNP, the FP, and the Tamil Congress was formed and a non-elected Tamil member of the FP was appointed to the cabinet for the first time since 1956. It was apparent from the outset that the UNP was anxious to negotiate a political settlement to the Tamil problem in return for the support it had received from the FP to defeat the SLFP-Marxist coalition. The government also took precautionary measures to implement the Tamil Language (Special Provisions) Regulations of 1966 without giving any room for the opposition to criticize the UNP. In particular, it emphasized that all regulations would be drafted to conform to Bandaranaike's Tamil Language Act of 1958 and the SLFP-Marxist coalition proposals of 1965 (see Appendix III). These regulations, which were approved by the parliament in January 1966, are still in force. They provide for the use of the Tamil language in the Northern and Eastern provinces for the "transaction of all government and public business and for the maintenance of public records." Official government communications are both in Tamil and Sinhala, and Tamil can be used in correspondence between Tamil-speaking persons living anywhere in the country and government officials, and for correspondence between local government bodies of Northern and Eastern provinces and the central government.

These provisions were acceptable to the Federal Party and the Tamil masses as long as they represented only the first step toward redressing the legitimate grievances of the Tamils. On the other hand, the coalition parties in the opposition and the Eksath Bhikkhu Peramuna accused the UNP of granting "parity of status" to the Tamil language and thus permitting the Tamils to exploit the wealth of the country. They claimed that the removal of restrictions imposed on Tamils seeking public service jobs paved the way for the eventual takeover of the country by Tamils. The regulations were actually similar to ones proposed by Mrs. Bandaranaike's coalition government the previous year. Nevertheless, the opposition parties sponsored strikes and demonstrations on the day the Tamil Language (Special Provisions) Regulations were tabled in the parliament, and these contributed to anti-Tamil disturbances in Colombo (see Appendix III). The "Buddhist bhikkhus were among those who denounced the regulations, and a bhikkhu was accidentally killed by police firing against demonstrators."[26] Despite these anti-Tamil demonstrations, the Tamils remained calm and even assisted the government in implementing the Tamil Language Act and the "Sinhala only" legislation. It is necessary to emphasize, however, that the belated recognition of Tamil as a regional language was "as much a result of the consciousness of its practical difficulty of enforcing it in the Tamil areas as an attempt at political appeasement."[27] Soon after the enactment of the language regulations into law, public servants in Tamil areas sought Sinhala training and accepted Sinhala as the official language. More than seven hundred Sinhalese teachers assumed duties in Tamil schools on invitation from the Tamils of the Northern and Eastern provinces. The number of motor vehicles with Sinhala license plates proliferated in the Northern and Eastern provinces, and signs in government departments and public places were posted in both Tamil and Sinhala.

By agreeing to the provisions of the Tamil Language (Special Provisions) Act, the Tamils had virtually accepted Sinhala as the only official language but the opposition parties continued to accuse the UNP of having surrendered Sinhalese interests to the Federal Party. It was thus not surprising that the District Councils bill, which was drafted by the "National Government," failed to gain support from parliament, even though a similar one had been proposed by Mrs. Bandaranaike's government before the 1965 elections.

The District Councils Draft Bill of 1968 was designed to establish district councils in each of the twenty-four administrative districts. These councils were to be vested with powers and responsibilities in respect of subjects to be mutually agreed upon between Mr. Senanayake and Mr. Chelvanayakam. These powers and functions included the "formulation and recommendation to the Government" regarding "development loans schemes important to the district and to raise with the approval of the Minister of Finance for works or public services to be undertaken by the district." Although these powers were limited in scope and were to function under the control and direction of the central government, the hitherto neglected economic development of Tamil districts could have been accomplished to some extent, provided, however, that the central government allocated adequate funds for development projects.

The members of the council were not to be specifically elected by the people of the districts. The council was to be composed of the government agent, "elected Members of Parliament of each electoral district which lies within such administrative district, Appointed Members of the House of Representatives, Mayors of Municipalities and Chairmen of Local Bodies within the administrative districts." Indeed, the district councils were merely designed to extend some of the central government functions that were hitherto performed by Kachcheries, and therefore the Bill did not contain any provisions that would have made the district councils responsible for the people at the district level.

Unfortunately, the District Council Bill did not furnish authority to the councils to "select settlers for the colonization schemes in the area under their administration," and have "powers over land development and colonization," as was agreed in the "Senanayake-Chelvanayakam Pact." Therefore, even if this Bill had been enacted into law, the most pressing concern of the Tamils regarding the conversion of Tamil-dominated areas into Sinhalese-dominated areas via government-sponsored colonization schemes would not have been alleviated. The Federal Party withdrew from the National Government in 1968 and the District Councils proposal was not pursued any further by Prime Minister Dudley Senanayake.

To the Tamils, the implementation of Tamil Language Regulations did not produce any substantial benefits. They had hoped that the National Government would enact legislation granting regional autonomy to Tamil areas similar to that proposed in the Bandaranaike-Chelvanayakam Pact. For the Tamil masses the ethnic issue had become more political than economic in nature. They were outraged with the government-sponsored colonization schemes designed to settle people from Sinhalese districts on lands they considered to be their traditional homeland. Nevertheless, opposition parties succeeded in mobilizing public sentiment against the National Government on many issues, including the language regulations, the district councils proposal, and the measures it adopted to deal with strikes and demonstrations staged by the opposition parties, including ruling the country for more than a thousand days under a state of emergency. The Federal Party had hoped that it could re-negotiate with the UNP on the issue of regional autonomy for the Northern and Eastern provinces, if the latter were returned to power in the 1970 general election. Unfortunately for the Tamils, Mrs. Bandaranaike, whose SLFP had joined with two Marxist parties to form the United Front (UF), was victorious and formed the new government.

The 1972 Constitution

The United Front government was in no great hurry to introduce legislation to establish district councils, which Mrs. Bandaranaike had proposed in 1964, since the coalition government did not owe any political favors to the Federal Party. Mrs. Bandaranaike, however, was obliged to satisfy the communal aspirations of her pro-Sinhala supporters, who were made to believe that the Sinhala Only Act had been compromised by the previous government in order to meet Tamil demands. In order to allay their fears, a new constitution was adopted in 1972 reaffirming the position of Sinhala as the only official language and conferring special status on Buddhism. An important clause in the constitution declared that "it shall be the duty of the state to protect and foster Buddhism."[28] This provision aroused the Tamils' suspicions that government funds would be used to try to convert Tamils by establishing Buddhist schools, as had been done in the past, and instructing Tamil children in Buddhism and in Sinhala. The new constitution also eliminated a clause that read: "parliament has no right to enact legislation which would confer an undue advantage to a race, religion, or community." This clause had provided the basis for the only legal recourse the Tamils had against the government. Henceforth, laws passed by the National State Assembly could restrict the fundamental rights and freedoms incorporated in the new constitution. Therefore, the Tamils, whose leaders had pioneered the constitutional reform movement and had made significant contributions to the political evolution and economic development of the country, were relegated to the status of second-class citizens by the constitution. Tamil members of parliament had no alternative, but to boycott the constituent assembly that was drafting the constitution.

From 1972, Tamil leaders adopted new strategies to clamor for the establishment of a federal state, a solution they had refrained from advocating as long as the UNP assured them of their language rights and a degree of regional autonomy for the Tamil provinces. The official language controversy in the 1950s drove a deep wedge between the communities, but no major Tamil parties proposed a total separation prior to the 1970s. The beginnings of concerted action by Tamil leaders to resist Sinhalese domination can be traced to the formation of the Tamil United Front (TUF) in 1972. The Tamil Congress and Federal Party united and, for the first time since 1949, the Ceylon Workers Congress, which represents the Tamils of Indian origin, agreed to coordinate its political activities with Tamils of Sri Lankan origin. The formation of the TUF was precipitated by many factors, including the adoption of the 1972 constitution. Tamil leaders were convinced that it was the lack of unity among the Tamils that had encouraged Sinhalese parties to ignore their demands in the past and for the SLFP and the UNP to manipulate the ethnic issue for their own political gains. They could no longer overlook the fact that Sinhala governments had, on several occasions, reneged on their promises to enact appropriate laws to redress Tamil grievances, and they realized they had to change their strategy in order to secure political and linguistic rights for their community. Tamil leaders believed that without regional autonomy the Tamils could not improve economic conditions in their traditional homeland, which have deteriorated to the point that there is widespread unemployment, underemployment, and general despair among the people.

The Rise of Separatist Movement and the Tamil United Liberation Front

Initially, the major objective of the TUF was to secure regional autonomy for Tamil areas, but over the course of time its members were compelled by circumstances to demand the creation of an independent Tamil state, to be called Eelam. One of the most potent factors in propelling the TUF toward separatism was "the rapidly increasing impatience and militancy among the youths of the North, including those associated with the TUF Youth Organization," who questioned the effectiveness of the conventional tactics employed by the older generation of leaders to secure the legitimate rights of the Tamils.[29] These young people accused their leaders of being inconsistent in their demands for regional autonomy for Tamil areas, having expected them to cling to their original demands for the devolution of legislative and executive powers to the Tamil areas under a federal form of government. Instead, the leaders had shown themselves willing to negotiate pacts that would have devolved only administrative functions to Tamil areas, at first through the regional councils proposal and then through the district councils proposal. They were further outraged at the way agreements negotiated between Tamil and Sinhalese leaders to deal with pressing problems relating to colonization of Tamil districts, educational and employment opportunities, the use of the Tamil language for regional administration, and funds for the development of irrigation, agriculture, industries, and the Kankesanthurai harbor in north Sri Lanka had been repudiated by Sinhalese leaders under pressure from *bhikkhu*s and a few Sinhalese extremists. They felt that the civil disobedience campaigns of the FP and the TUF merely encouraged Sinhala governments to ignore Tamil demands and to renege on their promises.

They were appalled by the level of unemployment among educated Tamil youths and with how the Sinhala only policy, with its more indirect forms of discrimination, had made it more difficult for them to find suitable employment. It is true that the acute problem of unemployment at this time was not limited to the Tamils. It was estimated that as much as 24 percent of the labor force and approximately 47.7 percent of those who had earned a diploma in the General Certificate of Education or its equivalent, the Senior School Certificate, were unemployed in 1973.[30] As in many other developing nations, the rate of economic growth has not kept pace with the growth of population, and both communities have been suffering, but Tamil youths have been more adversely affected. Tamil youths not only lacked employment opportunities but were also discriminated against with regard to university admissions. As one observer noted, "in the years 1970–1975 the mode of access to higher education was altered in such a way as to benefit the Sinhalese—largely at the expense of Ceylon Tamils."[31] The government had instituted standardization of examination scores between language media, with the result that persons taking the examination in the Tamil language were required to achieve a higher score than those taking the examination in Sinhala in order to gain admission to a university (see chapter 4). In addition, admission to universities was based on the percentage of total population resident in a district under the district quota system. Under this system, the Jaffna District, where most Tamil students are concentrated, was only entitled to 5.54 percent of the total allocated seats. The Tamil students were those "most adversely" affected by both the standardization of scores and the district quota system, since the "total share of Tamil admissions fell to 20.9 percent (from 25.9 percent in 1973 and 35.3 percent in 1970)"; by 1983, this figure had plunged to 19.3 percent.[32] The seriousness of these discriminatory measures can only be gauged if the 5.5 percent for the seats allocated to Indian Tamils were added to the 12.6 percent of the Sri Lankan Tamil population. Tamil youths had anticipated in the early 1970s that this would happen in the 1980s.

The youths also predicted that the unemployment situation would worsen in the 1980s, since the government did not represent the interests of their community. After 1983, when Tamil parties were proscribed and Tamil members of parliament elected from Tamil districts could no longer serve as members of the opposition, the UNP government appointed three Tamils to serve as members of the cabinet. To the Tamil youths, these three Tamil ministers, who are not the elected representatives of the Northern and Eastern provinces were merely stooges of the government. The government maintained that Tamil interests were represented by the handful of Tamils who held high positions of responsibility in the government. However, these Tamils could have reached their high positions through seniority and/or could have been arbitrarily selected to demonstrate to the international community that the Tamils are not discriminated against. Indeed, if the Tamil ministers and the few Tamil public servants had been as influential as the government claimed, they would have been able to persuade Sinhala governments to redress some of the Tamil grievances and even to have prevented the periodic massacres of Tamils by members of the armed forces. As it was, as a result of preferential treatment, the Sinhalese were able to gain complete control over the exercise of political power and the economic resources of the country.

Tamil youths watched as the constitutional provisions for reasonable use of Tamil language in limited areas became a dead letter; they saw the government's failure to devolve substantial powers to government bodies in Tamil areas and its reluctance to halt the planned resettlement of large numbers of Sinhalese in Tamil districts. With the adoption of the 1972 constitution, they realized that all hopes for the recognition of Tamil as the language of a national minority and the devolution of substantial legislative and executive powers to Tamil areas were nullified. Their frustration with the political strategies adopted by their elders since the early 1950s is thus understandable; the strategies were clearly ineffective in securing concessions "from a series of governments brought to power principally by Sinhalese votes."[33]

The beginnings of the Tamil militant movements can be traced to March 1973 when more than one hundred Tamil youths were arrested for staging a black-flag demonstration during the visit of Mrs. Bandaranaike's cabinet ministers to Jaffna. Militant youths for the first time were able to persuade the Tamils of Jaffna to boycott schools and colleges. In the same year, the government, using emergency powers, arbitrarily arrested more than two hundred Tamil youths suspected of being militants and held them in custody for four months. These arrests provoked youths to retaliate and confront the government. They soon became a political force powerful enough to compel the TUF to reconsider its long-cherished objective to establish a federal system of government. Its Action Committee "resolved upon a separate state of Tamil Eelam as its goal" in May 1973. The youths were able to pressure the TUF to move quickly toward a drastic solution, which in their view could not be achieved as long as there was a Sinhalese majority in parliament in control of the government. The solution to the Tamil problem as they saw it was to persuade TUF leaders to use whatever means at their disposal to create an independent Tamil state. The leaders responded, at a conference, by recasting the TUF as the Tamil United Liberation Front (TULF) and by reiterating its call for the establishment of the secular state of Tamil Eelam on May 14, 1976. The influential Ceylon Workers Congress did not give its support to this separatist movement. It was willing to support the TULF as long as the main objective of the party was to establish a linguistic state within the framework of a federal system of government, but it drew the line when it came to the call for an independent Tamil state.

The members of the TULF, for the most part, hold moderate views on the methods to be adopted to secure a separate state for the Tamils. Although the leadership of the TULF had changed hands from S. J. V. Chelvanayakam, who was committed to the use of Gandhian methods to secure Tamil rights, the policies of his successor, Appapillai Amirthalingam, were a continuation of Chelvanayakam's. However, some of his speeches openly advocating the establishment of a separate Tamil state, with appeals to the Indian government and the people of Tamil Nadu to support the Tamil cause. These appeals, delivered partly in desperation and partly in response to militant demands, enraged Sinhalese leaders. The TULF's desire to establish an independent Tamil state won the moral support of some leaders in Tamil Nadu, which "in turn led to a widespread Ceylon Tamil conviction that without sovereignty, the Ceylon Tamil people are destined to second-class status in the larger Sinhalese polity as well as to a collective life of economic and cultural subservience under hostile repressive Sinhalese governments."[34] Nevertheless, TULF has remained committed to the use of democratic methods to establish such a state.

The youth movements, on the other hand, most of which are underground organizations with links to South India, have embraced violence as the only means to establish an independent Tamil state. The stage was set for direct confrontation between the government and the Tamil militants in January 1974, when Mrs. Bandaranaike's United Front coalition government, which was becoming increasingly sensitive to the rise of youth movements, failed to give unconditional approval for the holding of the fourth world conference on Tamil Language and Tamil Culture in Jaffna from January 3 to January 10, 1974. A public meeting held on the last day of the conference was broken up when "the police on the pretext of an unwarranted public meeting charged into the crowd with tear gas and baton, bringing down the electric pylons and killing nine people in the process."[35] This enraged the Tamil youths, more so because there was no inquiry into the incident and the government offered no apology for it. The militants considered this an intentional act designed by the government to warn them and the TULF of its determination to crush movements that advocated terrorism and separation.

Violence by Government Security Forces and Tamil Militants

The government imposed restrictions on the activities of Tamil militants and, in retaliation, the militants organized a series of robberies and even committed acts of violence against the police, military personnel, and others whom they considered to be traitors to the Tamil

cause. Alfred Durayappah, the mayor of Jaffna and a member of the
SLFP, who was trying to build an organizational base for the party in
the North, became their first victim in 1975. Following his assassination more than one hundred suspected youths were arrested at random, detained, and tortured. These repressive measures drove the
militant movements underground. The TULF, however, contemplated returning to the parliament with a new mandate from the Tamil
people.

In the parliamentary elections of 1977, the United National Party
was returned to power and TULF candidates swept all the fourteen
seats in the Northern Province, captured 70 percent of the total vote
in the province, and received a simple majority in the Eastern Province. This victory gave a clear signal to the government that sizable
numbers of Sri Lankan Tamils were generally behind their leaders in
their demand for the creation of a separate state.[36] Nevertheless,
many Tamils hoped, even at this stage, that the need to establish a
separate state would not arise if the United National Party would take
appropriate measures to remedy Tamil grievances as promised in its
manifesto. Their hopes were shattered one month after the elections
when Sinhalese police in the Jaffna Peninsula ran amok when they
were not allowed to enter a carnival as nonpaying guests. Unruly
mobs repeated the carnage of the anti-Tamil riots of 1958 by burning
and looting homes and businesses, killing more than three hundred
people, and forcing approximately 35,000 Tamils to seek shelter in
refugee camps. Ethnic violence, which had hitherto been limited to
the burning and looting of Tamil homes and properties in Sinhalese
areas, affected the people of the Jaffna Peninsula for the first time.
This police rampage, which was also linked to a false rumor concerning the killing of a Sinhalese policeman by Tamil militants, fueled
anti-Tamil riots in other parts of the island.

It was this rampage by the police that precipitated the formation of
the Tamil Liberation Tigers, an underground movement which,
according to newspaper reports, was planning to smuggle arms pur-
chased abroad into Sri Lanka. During the early stages of the militant
movement in 1976, there was no indication as to how many youth
movements were operating in Sri Lanka. Therefore, the name Tamil
Liberation Tigers was used to describe the movement as a whole. It
was only in April 1978, after a well-known Tamil police inspector,
who was instrumental in arresting Tamil youths for certain acts of violence, was ambushed and killed that one of the militant groups

claimed responsibility for this incident and declared itself the Liberation Tigers of Tamil Eelam (LTTE). Although the LTTE was formed in 1977, it was not known until 1978 that it was this particular group that was carrying out most of the violence against government troops and government informants.

The reasons for the 1977 anti-Tamil riots were outlined in the *Report of the Presidential Commission of Inquiry into the Incidents which Took Place between 13th August and 15th September, 1977*. It attributed the cause to many factors, including the TULF's anti-Sinhalese propaganda advocating separatism, Sinhalese extremists' statements claiming that Tamils intended to wipe out the Sinhalese race, and acts of violence committed by the Liberation Tigers.[37] The immediate cause of the violence, however, was the rumor that Tamil militants had attacked Sinhalese policemen in Jaffna. In retaliation, Sinhalese extremists moved against Tamils living in Sinhalese areas. Tamils were infuriated when they learned that the government had not taken swift action to contain the riot. Public statements made by some Sinhalese politicians following the riots disheartened them further. For their part, Sinhalese were outraged by the rhetorical threats made by some TULF members to the effect that South Indian assistance would be sought to establish an independent Tamil state. In the past, Sinhalese extremists had objected to political concessions on these very grounds—that they would lead to the formation of "an independent Tamil state, which would be bound to seek links with India."[38] Tamils had never contemplated seeking South Indian assistance to secure their legitimate rights in the past, and a majority of Sri Lankan Tamils still desired that the problem be amicably solved between the Sinhalese and Tamils. Those who wanted to seek military assistance to create a separate Tamil state in Sri Lanka felt driven by Sinhalese chauvinists to do so. Thus the public hearing on the 1977 anti-Tamil rioting was used effectively by both Sinhalese and Tamils to blame each other for inciting people to riot, but the violence of 1977 and the events that followed it convinced many Tamils, of both extreme and moderate views, of the need to establish a separate state.[39]

The Tamil Liberation Tigers stepped up their program of violence against the police and army personnel, who represented for them the Sinhala government that was intent on imposing its rule on the Tamil people, as well as against certain Tamils. In turn, the armed forces and the police escalated their violence against innocent citizens in order to stem the tide of the youth movement and to discourage people from supporting the movement. In 1977, before the riots, five Tamil youths were arrested and detained for killing a government informant. These five youths and forty-eight other detainees were murdered by fellow Sinhalese prisoners in a maximum security prison during the riots of July–August 1983. The government proscribed the Liberation Tiger Movement and other similar organizations by introducing Order No. 16 of 1978, which permitted security forces to torture youths whom they detained.

The UNP government became increasingly concerned that the 1977 anti-Tamil riots had alienated the Tamils and that there was an urgent need to appease them. As a first step, the government adopted a new constitution in September 1978 that recognized Tamil as a national language in Sri Lanka and improved on the Tamil language provisions in order to offer better employment opportunities to Tamils in the public sector.[40] The violence continued, however, government regulations proscribing underground movements notwithstanding. On September 7, 1978, a time bomb exploded on the Air Ceylon Avro 748 on a flight from Jaffna to Colombo. This incident, plus the continued violence against security forces and informants, compelled the government to pass a series of harsh acts, some of which have become permanent.

The relationship between the Tamils and Sinhalese was severely strained and there was a danger of the outbreak of another communal disturbance. Two months after the new constitution was adopted in 1978, Tamils had another problem to contend with. In November 1978, when the new university bill was debated, Cyril Mathew, the minister of Industries and Scientific Affairs, alleged that Tamil lecturers in universities had virtually handed inflated scores to Tamil students so that more of them could gain admission to universities, thereby depriving Sinhalese students access to university education. The government, however, was neither willing to inquire into these allegations nor willing to withdraw the regulation dealing with the racial quota system, which gave preferential treatment to Sinhalese seeking admission to universities (see chapter 4). Tamils were also angered when the government introduced legislation to incorporate a portion of the Anuradhapura District into the newly redrawn Vavuniya District. The TULF complained that this legislation would increase the number of Sinhalese living in the Northern Province, and they boycotted parliamentary proceedings. In March of 1979,

TULF leader Appapillai Amirthalingam appealed to the Government of India and to the people of Tamil Nadu to support the cause of Sri Lankan Tamils for establishing a separate state, thus enraging the Sinhalese. The Dravida Munnetra Kazhagam (DMK) of Tamil Nadu had on many occasions reiterated its enthusiastic support for the Sri Lankan Tamils in their bid to establish an independent Tamil state in Sri Lanka. Even Tamil expatriates living abroad, many of whom have relatives in Sri Lanka, supported the establishment of Eelam. At this juncture, the TULF members in parliament were accused by the government of advocating the division of Sri Lanka and of jeopardizing the country's development programs by influencing foreign governments against the Sri Lankan people. At the same time the president vowed to wipe out terrorism in Sri Lanka. Communal tension at this point was so intense that the government was forced to declare a state of emergency in the Jaffna District on July 12, 1979. On July 19, the Prevention of Terrorism Act No. 48 was passed in keeping with the president's promise to do away with such activity. The act permitted suspects to be held incommunicado for up to eighteen months without trial, thus creating classic conditions for torture. Atrocities committed by security and military forces under the protection of the Prevention of Terrorist Act have been well documented by human rights groups.[41] No sooner was the act passed than the government, adopting a "carrot and stick" approach, declared its intention to appoint a commission to find a solution to the ethnic problem.

The Ill-Fated District Development Councils

The United National Party had conceded, during the 1977 election campaign, that some of the Tamil grievances were justified and that appropriate measures should be adopted to address these issues. It emphasized the need for summoning an all-party conference to resolve the ethnic problem within the consensus of public opinion. Past experiences had shown that no government could expect to implement agreements negotiated between Tamil and Sinhalese leaders unless opposition parties and nonsecular groups were consulted. In particular, President J. R. Jayewardene was "persuaded that means could—and indeed must—be found to bring a real measure of decentralization without inevitably risking partition."[42] By July 1979, when the government appointed a Presidential Commission to inquire into Tamil grievances and to recommend appropriate remedial measures, the political situation had deteriorated to its worst level since 1956 and there was a danger of a further outbreak of communal violence. As expected, the SLFP refused to serve on the commission, but the TULF agreed to nominate a member. In order to silence its Tamil critics, TULF made public statements on the same day that its objective was to establish an independent Tamil state but that it was still willing to consider, and even accept, any proposals that would incorporate the regional councils provisions of the Bandaranaike-Chelvanayakam Pact.

The TULF and the government negotiated an agreement that became the District Development Councils Act No. 35 of 1980, although it did not incorporate many of the provisions of the regional councils as set up in the Bandaranaike-Chelvanayakam Pact. The purpose in setting up the District Development Councils was to decentralize certain administrative functions to the twenty-four administrative districts and to encourage economic development in rural areas, especially at the district level. In outlining the reasons why the TULF accepted the proposal, its spokesmen declared that the TULF desired to restore communal harmony, to improve the economy of Tamil districts, and to work within the parliamentary framework to achieve its ultimate objective—Tamil Eelam (see chapter 5). As expected, Tamil militants took a harder line in dealing with the government. They stressed that the District Development Councils (DDCs) were a poor substitute for the concept of Eelam and that Tamils should continue to fight for a separate state. They claimed that "extra-parliamentary action could weary the Sinhalese into yielding to Tamil Eelam."[43]

The elections for the Jaffna District DDC were held in June 1981 under the watchful eye of the armed forces that were stationed in the district. The government even nominated a slate of UNP candidates in Jaffna and took security precautions to supervise the elections. Strict security measures were imposed because the government was aware that "extremists within the separatist movement . . . were ardently opposed to any activity within the existing political framework and viewed participation in the elections as compromising the objective of a separate state."[44] Tamil militants assassinated a prominent UNP candidate a few days before the elections and a week later two policemen were killed and two others were injured at a TULF rally. In retaliation, off-duty Sinhalese policemen and Sinhalese soldiers went on a rampage, looting, killing, and setting fire to the Jaffna public library with its 95,000 volumes of rare books of historical

and cultural significance to the Tamils.[45] Indian Tamils suffered heavily at the hands of roaming mobs of hoodlums who destroyed property and killed innocent victims. Indian Tamils who had been previously settled in Vavuniya District, as refugees from the plantation
areas, were harassed by the army, and their Sri Lankan Tamil benefac-
tors were taken away for questioning.[46] Much of this violence was
instigated by racist statements made by Sinhalese extremists and
UNP backbenchers, during the DDCs election campaign, against
TULF leader Amirthalingam, who was also head of the Opposition.[47]

Despite the violence, the election proceeded according to schedule
and, much to the disappointment of the government, the TULF captured more than 80 percent of the votes and all the seats in the Jaffna
District Development Council. It also won control of five out of the
six DDCs in the other parts of the Northern and Eastern provinces.
The voter turnout in Jaffna was, however, low, and this might well
have been an indication that the people of the district disapproved of
the DDCs Act, or that they were shifting allegiance from the TULF to
militant separatists, or that they were intimidated by the presence of
the military. Disappointed by the failure of the UNP to secure seats in
the North, a UNP member of parliament brought a no-confidence
motion against Amirthalingam on July 24, 1981, for inciting the
Sinhalese to riot with racist statements he made during the DDCs
campaign. However, President Jayewardene, who was anxious to end
this bitter confrontation with the Tamils, negotiated an agreement
with Amirthalingam on November 3, 1981, to implement the DDCs
Act.

Peaceful coexistence between the Sinhalese and Tamils lasted until
the first popular election for president was held in December 1982.
At this time, the dialogue between the Tamils and Sinhalese
appeared to break down, and the government placed the blame on
the Tamils. It cited many factors, including the antigovernment attitude of the TULF toward the presidential system of government, the
continuation of violence by extremists in northern Sri Lanka, and the
nomination by the TULF of a convicted terrorist to a seat in parliament.[48] Tamils, on the other hand, blamed the government for this
breakdown on the grounds that the latter had failed to implement
constitutional provisions regarding the use of Tamil as the language
of administration in the Northern and Eastern provinces, had given
inadequate powers and insufficient funds to the DDCs for developing Tamil districts, and had been reluctant to withdraw the Preven-

tion of Terrorist Act, which gave unlimited powers to the armed forces to deal with suspected terrorists and civilians. They also blamed the government for "the recurrence of acts of indiscipline in the security forces," and for the failure to conduct by-elections in Eastern Province, where former members of parliament had failed in their campaign against the 1982 referendum to extend the life of parliament until 1989.[49] In the meantime, Tamil militants stepped up their attacks on security forces and the latter retaliated by victimizing civilians. The violence escalated as more youths joined the movement. Moreover, the movement had "split into six or more rival and sometimes violently hostile groups, . . . divided by ideology, caste, and personal antagonism."[50] It became increasingly difficult for the government to patrol the streets of Jaffna. Under these circumstances, the government enacted Emergency Regulation 15a of July 3, 1983, which allowed security forces to bury or cremate the bodies of people shot by them without establishing their identities or without inquests.[51]

The government received no cooperation from the civilian population to counteract terrorism in the North, where the population was Tamil-speaking and the army of occupation mainly Sinhalese. In fact, the separatists had no difficulty attacking police stations, army units, government establishments, and government informers as long as they were able to mingle with the population at large after each incident. Under these circumstances, the soldiers, who became frustrated by their ineffectiveness in combatting terrorism and apprehending the militants, moved against the civilian population. Moreover, under the Emergency Regulation and the Prevention of Terrorism Act, the security forces had a free hand to arrest civilians and to commit acts of violence against innocent citizens, as happened one day in mid-July 1983 when soldiers went on a rampage killing fifty-one people in the Jaffna Peninsula.[52] The Tigers, who called themselves the Liberation Tigers of Tamil Eelam, retaliated by ambushing a truckload of thirteen army personnel on July 23.[53]

In the violence that followed, 175 Tamil houses in Jaffna were burned, ten Tamils were killed or wounded by naval personnel in Trincomalee, and fifty-three Tamil inmates of Welikade Prison were murdered by fellow prisoners on July 25 and July 27. Many innocent Tamils living in Sinhalese areas, primarily in Colombo, "were left dead, many injured, thousands displaced, [with] great losses of property, economic and physical dislocation, and a shocked population."

Nearly one-half of the 141,000 Tamils living in Colombo were home-less" and approximately 2,000 were killed, according to unofficial estimates.[54] The riot of 1983 became a communal holocaust because it was well organized, according to Gananath Obeyesekere, by the Jatika Sevaka Sangamaya, a powerful trade union "which has an effective say in the working of government offices and corpora-tions."[55] The Union's anti-Tamil attitude is ascribed to its Sinhala-Buddhist political ideology as expounded by its president, Cyril Mathew. However, government leaders made certain that the blame was not placed on the union, with which some prominent ministers were associated. Instead they attributed the violence to the Sinhalese people in general. Even the president failed to impose a curfew until the damage was done, apparently due to bad advice, and no effort was made by any Sinhalese leaders to show any compassion toward the Tamil community for the untolled suffering it was subject to at the hands of Sinhalese mobs. This outraged the Tamil community and further convinced its leaders that unless the Tamil community was granted substantial political concessions to take care of its affairs in the Northern and Eastern provinces it will continue to be vic-timized in this manner. Following the riots large numbers of youths were rounded up by security forces in the Northern and Eastern prov-inces and thousands of Tamils fled from Sri Lanka to become refugees in South India. It has been estimated that since the 1983 ethnic vio-lence 30,000 Sri Lankan Tamils have moved into government-funded camps in Tamil Nadu and between 10,000 and 40,000 Tamils may have entered Europe.[56] By 1986, more than 100,000 Sri Lankan Tamils had taken refuge in South India.

Of the violence perpetrated by Tamil militants, the government claimed that "between 1976 and a major terrorist incident in July 1983, 73 persons were slain by the Tiger underground movement, and in the five-year period 1978–1983 the Tigers were responsible for more than 265 bombings, robberies, assaults, and other criminal acts," but the government did not maintain any figures on the thou-sands of Tamils who have been slain by Sinhalese mobs and security forces.[57] Since the mid-1950s, thousands of Tamils have been killed, rendered homeless, and had their businesses destroyed by Sinhalese mobs. The government accused the TULF and a few leftist political parties of inciting the 1983 anti-Tamil riots and proscribed them in August 1983.

The All-Party Conference and Mediation from India

President Jayewardene was fully aware of the futility of these violent acts and announced, in late 1983, that he would call an "all-party conference" to discuss Tamil grievances and to seek appropriate solutions. It had taken seven years, the trauma of the 1983 riots, and initiatives on the part of the government of India to persuade the Sri Lankan government and the TULF to attempt a political settlement to the problem by convening an all-party conference in January 1984, as the UNP had promised to do in its manifesto of 1976.

There were many factors that compelled India to assist the Sri Lankan government to resolve its ethnic conflict. First, many thousands of Tamils had fled from Sri Lanka as refugees into South India following the riots of 1983. Second, with the TULF proscribed and its members excluded from parliament, many prominent South Indian Tamils, party leaders, and Sri Lankan Tamil leaders, including former Sri Lankan members of parliament who had to forgo their seats in the legislative body because of their stand on the separatist issue, appealed to the Indian government to persuade the Sri Lankan government to put an end to the violence. Third, India desires to maintain the neutrality of the Indian Ocean, and this can only be accomplished if major powers are not invited to take sides in the ethnic conflict. Fourth, India desires to maintain friendly relations with its neighbors. This need to maintain friendly relations with Sri Lanka, according to some, is motivated by the desire on the part of India to keep the super-powers out of the Indian Ocean and to persuade Sri Lanka to return to the nonaligned fold. Finally, India became aware that the Tamil Nadu Tamils were genuinely concerned about the plight of the Sri Lankan Tamils. In fact, the government may have been aware that the Tamil militants were using South India as a base for their operations against security forces in Sri Lanka, but it was not certain to what extent Indian Tamils were sympathetic to the Sri Lankan Tamil cause. Tamil militants had been using Tamil Nadu as a base for their operations since 1980 with the support of some Tamil Nadu politicians. Only when five militant leaders were arrested by the Tamil Nadu police after a shooting incident in May 1981 was it revealed that they had bases in South India. It was then that the government became aware of the strong moral support that the Sri Lankan Tamil militants had from the Tamil Nadu Tamils, because there was pressure from nearly all the political parties in India not to extradite the five Liberation Tiger leaders captured by the police.[58] With the 1983 anti-Tamil riots the Indian government made serious efforts to bring about a peaceful settlement of the ethnic conflict between the Sinhalese and Tamils.

Preliminary talks took place between Prime Minister Indira Gandhi's special envoy, G. Parthasarathy, and Sri Lankan officials, and it was agreed that the all-party conference would consider the proposals documented in Annexure C, which was prepared by Indian government officials under Parthasarathy's direction with the approval of Sri Lankan government officials (see Appendix IV). These proposals provided for: (1) the creation of regional councils if the people of the region so desired; (2) the election of the chief minister of the council; (3) regional councils with legislative powers to "enact laws and exercise executive powers in relation thereto on certain specified listed subjects"; (4) regional councils to be endowed with power to levy taxes, mobilize resources through loans and other financial resources provided by the central government according to a formula; (5) all settlement schemes to be based on ethnic proportion; and (6) the armed forces to reflect the national ethnic position. In the Northern and Eastern provinces, the police force for internal security would also reflect the ethnic composition of these regions. The proposals specify that the laws dealing with the official language Sinhala and the national language Tamil be accepted and implemented. The conference was attended by government leaders, officials, representatives of eight political parties, including the TULF, and representatives of ethnic and religious groups. The participation of prominent members of the Buddhist organization was considered essential, since it was the Sangha that had persistently resisted the granting of political and language concessions to the Tamils. Unfortunately, the SLFP, whose cooperation is vital for the implementation of any proposals dealing with this issue, withdrew from the conference soon after it was convened in January 1984, claiming that the UNP, its traditional rival for power, was giving away too many concessions to the Tamils.

The provisions in Annexure C would have given some measure of regional autonomy to Tamil provinces and empowered regional councils to have jurisdiction over large areas to enact laws on specific subjects; to maintain internal law and order; to administer justice; to provide for social and economic development; to have control over cultural matters and land policy; and to collect funds to initiate major development projects. Tamil-dominated areas would have been able to preserve their territorial integrity through the Regional Councils. President Jayewardene, however, under pressure from the Buddhist clergy, Sinhala extremists, and opposition parties, did not present the proposals. Instead he submitted for consideration a modified version of the ill-fated District Development Councils concept of 1980 (see Appendix V), which dealt with interdistrict coordination and collaboration without any reference to the regional councils referred to in the Annexure C proposals. The District Development Councils proposal itself did not grant any measure of autonomy to Tamil-dominated districts, and the district councils lacked legislative powers to develop the Northern and Eastern provinces in order to solve their unemployment and food shortage problems. The idea of regional councils and the TULF's proposal that all the districts in the Northern and Eastern provinces that have substantial Tamil populations should be administered as a single unit were rejected by the Buddhist clergy and representatives of Sinhalese parties on the grounds that the large Tamil unit, with its human and physical resources, might pose a challenge to the central government's resources and power. The government's modified proposal, which would permit district councils to form provincial councils, was not acceptable to the Tamil leaders.

In December 1984, the TULF announced that the government's proposals were not acceptable because they did not resolve the concerns of Tamils on matters dealing with: (1) the preservation of the territorial integrity of Tamil areas; (2) the procedure for selecting allottees to colonization schemes in Tamil provinces; and (3) the procedures for financing major projects (see Appendix VI). These concerns of the Tamils were never considered by the conference because the president cancelled it abruptly on the grounds that the demands of TULF were unreasonable. Without the support of the SLFP, and being pressured by the Buddhist clergy not to grant substantial concession to Tamils, the president had no alternative but to cancel the conference. Although there was no indication that the talks were cancelled because the Sinhalese population agitated against the establishment of regional councils, the president was aware that the TULF would never compromise on the issue of regional councils and that it would be unwise to negotiate on modified proposals that would definitely be rejected by the TULF, as well as displease most of the Sinhalese participants in the talks. He therefore used TULF's press announcement that it would not accept the government's modified proposals as a pretext to cancel the conference.

The conference did not accomplish any positive results except to bring the Sri Lankan government, representatives of Sinhalese political parties and the Buddhist clergy, and the TULF to the negotiating table. The Tamils of the Northern and Eastern provinces, who had been most directly affected by the violence and backed the TULF in its demand for the devolution of powers to regional councils, were disheartened by the collapse of the conference. The militants, who were all along pessimistic about the outcome of the talks and warned the Tamil community that the only means to secure Tamil rights was through force, stepped up their violence against government forces. The government, on the other hand, wanted to reassure the Sinhalese community that it did not convene the talks because of its inability to fight the militants and in turn stepped up its efforts to wipe out the militants. The Indian government's efforts to bring about a negotiated settlement to the ethnic issue had failed, but it did not abandon the peace process. Within six months of the failure of the all-party conference it had convinced both the Sri Lankan government and Tamil militants to agree to a cease-fire and begin peace talks in Thimphu, the capital of Bhutan.

The Tamil Militant Movement

The Tamil militant movement consists of more than twenty militant organizations that espouse violent methods to resist the imposition of Sinhala rule over Tamil-dominated areas and to establish a separate independent Tamil state called Eelam.[59] The number of groups operating in the Northern and Eastern provinces is not known, but they are collectively referred to as "Tigers" by the Sinhalese. To the Sinhalese, the Tamil militant movement is synonymous with "Tiger Movement," since the Liberation Tigers of Tamil Eelam (LTTE), led by Veluppillai Prabakaran, was the first militant group to use violent methods to confront the government. The Tiger Movement, which continues to wage war against the Sinhala government, had its beginnings in 1972, but its violent methods were not actively pursued until 1976, when it was renamed the LTTE. Personality clashes between Prabakaran and Uma Maheswaran, the chairman of the executive committee of the LTTE, compelled the latter to break away from the organization and form the People's Liberation Organization of Tamil Eelam (PLOTE) in 1980. In the early 1980s, PLOTE stormed police stations, killed a number of policemen, and robbed banks of large sums of money, but it has claimed no responsibility for incidents involving the killing of Sinhalese civilians and members of security forces in Tamil areas, unlike the LTTE. The LTTE continues to reject any type of negotiations with the government, even though the latter is making use of helicopters and light planes to bomb militant bases in an attempt to find a military solution to the ethnic problem.

In addition to the LTTE and the PLOTE, three other organizations have played an active role in the militant movement. The Tamil Eelam Liberation Organization (TELO), which was originally formed by Thangathurai, one of the Tamil inmates who was killed in the Welikade Prison riots of 1983, has claimed credit for the storming of well-fortified police stations in Chavakachcheri and Murugandy, as well as the bombing of a train transporting soldiers from Colombo to Jaffna. TELO was led by Sri Sabaratnam until he and most of his men were massacred by the LTTE in 1986 because of rivalry between the two groups.

The Eelam People's Revolutionary Front (EPRLF) and the Eelam Revolutionary Organization of Students (EROS), whose origins can be traced to the mid-1970s, have become prominent only in the 1980s. The EPRLF, which is led by K. Padmanabha, has claimed responsibility for the successful rescue of prisoners from the Batticaloa Prison in 1983, the abduction of an American couple in 1984, and the attacks on the army camp in Gurunagar and the naval base in Karainagar. EROS, which expounds radical ideologies, was founded in London in 1975, and its activities are presently directed by V. Bala-kumar in Madras and Rajanayagam in London. It does not advocate random killings and robberies but believes in the effectiveness of sab-otage, such as the bombing of the Oberai Hotel in Colombo and the unsuccessful attempt to destroy the TV antenna at Mount Pedro in the central hill country.

Ideological differences and disputes over tactics with which to con-front the government and its security forces as well as personality clashes, most of which have been confined to the leadership of these organizations, have, to a large extent, reduced the ability of the Tamil militant movement to achieve its objectives. Although the five main groups have approximately 10,000 trained fighters, there is no con-certed action by the organizations against defined targets. Each group tends to operate and get its support from different areas of Sri Lanka. The LTTE appears to be entrenched in the Jaffna Peninsula while the PLOTE seems to receive its support from a larger region, including the Muslim-dominated areas in the Eastern Province. Substantial support for the EROS and the EPRLF comes from the plantation workers in the hill country.

The militant movement is also weakened by the inability of its leaders to agree on a common strategy with which to fight the enemy. The hit-and-run surprise attacks on security forces by the LTTE are considered by the PLOTE to be ineffective. PLOTE apparently believes that guerrilla tactics are not adequate to fight security forces and that a liberation people's army consisting of members of all organizations should be formed to rout the enemy and end the struggle. LTTE believes that guerrilla warfare is an integral part of the people's war and that the people will ultimately adopt guerrilla tactics to liberate the Tamil areas. Hit-and-run tactics, according to the TELO, have to be adopted to demoralize the enemy, but once it has been demoralized, the people's liberation army will be able to inflict heavy losses on the enemy in a pitched battle. Therefore, while the main objective of all the militant organizations is to establish an independent socialist state of Eelam, there appears to be no consensus on how this objective is to be achieved.

The cycle of violence, which was confined to the Tamil-dominated areas until May 14, 1985, spread into Sinhalese areas and resulted in the killing of 146 Sinhalese civilians by Tamil separatists in Anuradhapura, apparently in revenge for a series of incidents involving the killing of Tamil civilians in army reprisal attacks in several districts prior to 1985. Following this and a number of other atrocities committed by the armed forces on civilians in predominantly Tamil areas, the government, the leaders of TULF and militant separatist groups agreed to a "cessation of hostile activity" on June 18, 1985, in order to create "a proper climate" for a political settlement. The Indian government played a major role in arranging for this cease-fire and in persuading the leaders of Tamil militants and TULF to meet with the representatives of the Sri Lankan government in Thimpu to work out a political settlement. Under pressure from the Indian government and Sri Lankan Tamils in Sri Lanka and abroad, the LTTE, EROS, EPRLF, PLOTE, and TELO formed the Eelam National Liberation Front (ENLF) in order to negotiate with the Sri Lankan government officials at the Thimphu talks in 1985. Unfortunately, the government rejected most of the proposals submitted by the ENLF and TULF, including the linkage between the Northern and Eastern provinces, as well as the Annexure C proposals, and failed to present any new proposals that deviated markedly from the president's proposals on District Development Councils which were submitted during the unsuccessful all-party conference of January 1984. The basic disagreement between the Sri Lankan government and the militants remained the critical issue of devolution of power to Tamil areas. Although the Thimphu talks failed, the five militant organizations in the ENLF continued to speak with one voice on Tamil demands in 1986, but operate as separate organizations with regard to military activities. Armed confrontations between Sri Lankan forces and Tamil militants are forcing thousands of Tamil people to flee their homes and take refuge in camps. Incidents involving killings by rival groups continue to plague the militant movement as a whole and personal rivalry between leaders of some groups limits the effectiveness of the movement.

It is clear that the government is not inclined to grant substantial devolution of power to Tamil areas and that the Tamil militants, as well as the TULF, are equally determined to reject any proposals that will perpetuate the present political structure and discriminatory policies of the government. The Tamils reiterate that they possess the same aspirations as the Sinhalese and long to reap the social, economic, and political benefits of the freedom from colonial rule that Sri Lanka has enjoyed since 1948. True freedom, according to the Tamils, can only be achieved if the government can recognize their right of self-determination, the identity of Tamils as a distinct nationality, and the territorial integrity of Tamil areas. To many Tamils, these conditions can only be met when substantial legislative, executive, and fiscal powers are in the hands of a single legislative body that will have jurisdiction over the Northern and Eastern provinces. The government, on the other hand, continues to reject Tamil demands on the grounds that it has granted substantial concessions to the Tamils under its new proposals and that any further devolution of power would lead to Tamil domination. Likewise, what the Sinhalese leaders are offering to the Tamils, according to A. Jeyaratnam Wilson, is a "case of 'too little too late,' and a solution acceptable some ten to fifteen years ago could now be jibbed at by the Sri Lankan Tamils."[60] This is not to imply that the Sri Lankan Tamils, especially the militants, are unwilling to abandon their objective of establishing Eelam through violent struggle. The fact that the militants were willing to negotiate with the government at the Thimphu talks suggest that they are prepared to work within the framework of a united Sri Lanka, provided substantial regional autonomy were granted to Tamil-dominated areas. With the failure of the peace talks, however, the government decided to take military action against the Tamil militants.

The government's decision to find a military solution to the ethnic problem is based on the premise that its security forces have become better equipped and trained in 1986 than previously to destroy militant bases from the air and to capture militants on land by "search and destroy operations." Incidents involving the bombing of suspected militant hideouts in the densely populated Jaffna Peninsula and the "search and destroy missions" elsewhere in the Tamil-dominated areas demonstrate that innocent citizens rather than the militants are often the main victims of these operations. Unless the militants are equipped with surface-to-air missiles, it would be impossible for them to furnish protection to the people, and this might hurt their cause. On the other hand, pressure from the international community, especially India, would compel the government to abandon such military operations involving the bombing of Tamil areas. Whether these military operations will persuade the militants to modify their demands for a separate autonomous state in Sri Lanka, especially since India is opposed to these demands, is not certain. India is deeply committed to a negotiated settlement of the ethnic problems and there were signs during the early months of 1986 that a large number of Tamils, living within and outside Sri Lanka, were willing to accept the TULF's proposals for the establishment of a Tamil linguistic state within a federal union of Sri Lanka. The TULF, however, does not command the support of the Sri Lankan Tamils, and although many Tamil civilians have been killed by government forces in reprisals for militant attacks, the militants continue to command respect from the Tamil population for their aggressive actions against government forces.

Unless the Tamil militants and the Sri Lankan government are directly involved in the peace negotiations, however, there will never be any lasting political settlement to the ethnic problem. Events of the last three decades have shown that, in the words of the executive director of the International Human Rights Law Group, "It is not with guns and tear gas that peace and security will be restored to Sri Lanka. Determination to end communal strife and dedication to the rule of law are what will save Sri Lanka now."[61]

Tamil Districts: Conflict over Traditional Homelands, Colonization, and Agricultural Development

THE Tamil districts are located in a well-defined region of the Dry Zone where Tamils make up the dominant ethnic community (see Figure 1). It is not known when Tamils became the dominant community in these districts or who occupied the Dry Zone prior to the establishment of the Sinhalese and Tamil settlements. Archaeological evidence suggests that a culture, resembling that of the Megalithic culture of South India, existed in the northwestern coastal area of the island during prehistoric times.[1] Whether these prehistorical people were the Nagas, Yakshas, or Dravidians is not known, but Sinhalese historians believe that the first Sinhalese immigrants landed somewhere in the Dry Zone, most probably along the northwestern coast of the island, which is the closest point to the South Indian coast and not far from the archaeological site of Megalithic remains.[2] In the course of time, the settlers moved southeast along the river called Aruvi Aru (Malwattu Oya) and established tank settlements. It is also suggested that a second group of Sinhalese immigrants landed somewhere along the northeast coast and moved inland up the river called Mahaweli Ganga before establishing permanent settlements (see Figure 2).[3] Although no reference is made in the *Pali Chronicles* to the origin of Tamil settlements in the Dry Zone, it is believed "that some Sri Lankan Tamils may have come to Sri Lanka as early as or even before the Sinhalese."[4] There is little doubt that many of the Tamil settlements of the Tamil districts are of ancient origin, since many of them, especially in Mannar, Trincomalee, and Batticaloa districts, are closely associated with Hindu temples that were built in the early Christian era.[5] Most of the Sinhalese settlements of ancient Sri Lanka were located outside the present-day Tamil districts; the largest concentrations of stone inscriptions, Buddhist monuments, and major irrigation projects named after Sinhalese rulers are confined to the

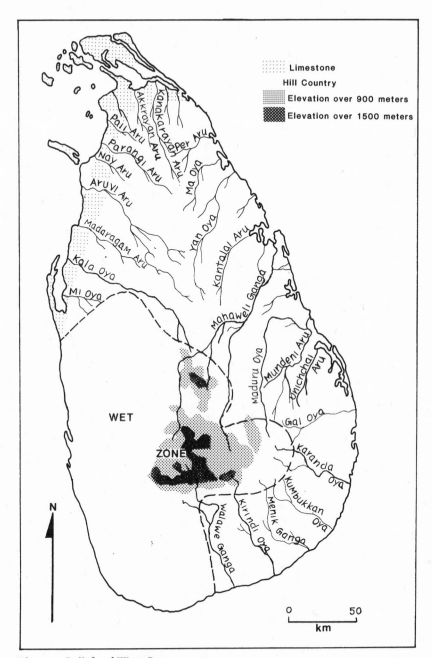

Figure 2. Relief and Water Resources

well-watered river valleys of the Anuradhapura, Kurunegala, and Polonnaruwa districts of northern Sri Lanka.[6] These Dry Zone settlers developed a very productive agricultural system by using advanced technology to irrigate crops via a series of tanks, anicuts, and channels. With the support of benevolent rulers, the settlers harvested enormous quantities of rice to sustain a population of more than two million in the Dry Zone.[7] This highly developed civilization collapsed in the thirteenth century A.D. as a result of environmental and nonenvironmental factors, including the Chola invasions from South India.

Following the collapse of the Sinhalese kingdom, the Sinhalese population abandoned the Dry Zone districts known as Nuwara Kalawiya and Tamankaduwa and drifted toward the Wet Zone in the southwest. Tamils, too, abandoned their original settlements and relocated in the Jaffna Peninsula and in the more favorable coastal sites in the Northern and Eastern provinces. As a result of the movement of the Sinhalese from the Dry Zone to the Wet Zone, Tamils became the only ethnic community to occupy the northern and eastern parts of Sri Lanka. By the fourteenth century A.D., the Tamil kingdom extended its suzerainty over a large part of northern Sri Lanka and the large number of Tamils who had migrated from South India settled in different parts of the present-day Tamil districts. The Tamil settlements of the northern and eastern parts of the island were completely isolated from the rest of the country. It was in the relative isolation of the Tamil districts that the Sri Lankan Tamils developed the sense of collective identity based on language, culture, and territory that is a prerequisite of nationality. Thus, Tamil claims to an ancestral or traditional homeland are based on more than 700 years of uninterrupted settlement in a territorially demarcated area of Sri Lanka where towns, villages, and natural and manmade features are known by Tamil-derived names of ancient origin. Sinhalese extremist nationalists, however, contend that the Tamils have no right to recognize these districts as their traditional homeland since the whole of Sri Lanka belongs to the Sinhalese, who were forcefully driven out of the northern parts of the island by Tamils.

The Fall of the Ancient Sinhalese Civilization and the Abandonment of the Dry Zone

Sinhalese hostility toward Tamils is partly attributed to events that transpired more than seven centuries ago when South Indian invaders, according to Sinhalese traditions, destroyed the ancient Sinhalese civilization of the Rajarata. As noted in chapter 1, this is a popular view held by the majority of the Sinhalese that has been used effectively by Sinhalese extremist nationalists to justify Sinhalese colonization of the predominantly Tamil districts and to deny basic rights to the minority. Even the *Ceylon Year Book,* published by the Department of Census and Statistics, supported this view, stating, "Incursions of marauders from the neighboring sub-continent, recurring century after century, eventually destroyed the irrigation works which alone made fertile and invaluable the arid lands known as the Dry Zone."[8] Contrary to the belief that Tamils forced the large Sinhalese population to relocate to the southwest, there are convincing suggestions that the decline and fall of the Sinhalese civilization was due to a host of factors, including invasions, some of which were encouraged by rivalries within royal households, civil wars and internal dissensions, climatic change resulting in decreased amounts of precipitation, intellectual and aesthetic exhaustion, social disintegration, decreasing soil fertility after centuries of use without fertilization, siltation of tanks, malaria epidemics, and the inability of weak governments to control and mobilize the people in order to repair and maintain the irrigation systems in working order.[9] While it is true that all of these factors were responsible for collapse of the civilization, the contribution of the climatic factor toward the civilization's eclipse cannot be overlooked.

It has been suggested that to cite climatic change as a major cause for the sudden fall of the civilization is "so simple, but not often applicable in the absence of direct or convincing evidence."[10] However, it is not improbable for the region to have experienced a series of years with either abnormally low or high amounts of rainfall due to the failure of the monsoon or to the high frequency of intensive cyclones. These abnormal weather conditions need not be associated with climatic change. Even in recent years, the failure of the northeast monsoon to deliver adequate water to irrigation tanks has resulted in poor harvests; the floods of December 1956 and January 1957 destroyed many irrigation systems and disrupted agricultural activities.[11] It took almost two years for the Irrigation Department to repair the extensive damage caused to major and minor irrigation systems by these floods. Moreover, a prolonged drought, lasting for several years, could have adversely affected a large portion of the Dry Zone, while the Jaffna Peninsula could have weathered the adverse effects of the severe drought because of its unique environmental characteristics. Although the annual effective dry period in the peninsula is the longest of all the settled areas in the Dry Zone, prolonged droughts would not deplete the reservoir of underground water and hinder agricultural activities. This unique character of the environment has bestowed upon the peninsula the capacity to sustain a large population, continuously. Apparently, the Tamil people had to flee the Vanni like their Sinhalese counterparts, but they found refuge in the Jaffna Peninsula to the north. The population of the Jaffna Peninsula grew rapidly, and when the first census was taken in 1871, it had the highest population density, 251 persons per square kilometer, in the Dry Zone (see Table 4).

The census of 1871 also indicated that the island of Mannar off the western coast of Sri Lanka, including the narrow coastal stretch along the mainland, and the Puttalam coast had the next highest densities of 11 and 8 persons per square kilometer, respectively (see Table 4). These areas were not depopulated after the thirteenth century, unlike the rest of the Dry Zone, because of their unique soil characteristics. The regosols are excessively drained and impede surface flow of water, but soil moisture is held a few feet below the surface and is accessible for human consumption. Many of the settlers in the Mannar area were apparently fishermen who relied on this source of water supply for domestic use and on other regions for rice. The Batticaloa coastal stretch of sandbars on the eastern side of the island is another region in the Dry Zone that had a high population density in 1871. This

Table 4. Population Densities of Selected Regions in the Dry Zone for the Years 1871, 1931, and 1946

	Population			Density (persons per sq. km)		
	1871	1931	1946	1871	1931	1946
Jaffna Peninsula	241,454	347,283	420,115	251	367	444
Mannar Coast	21,063	25,137	31,471	8	10	12
Puttalam Coast	24,551	35,078	42,669	11	15	18
Vanni	28,753	32,413	36,115	5	6	7
Trincomalee Coast	19,449	37,492	68,635	7	14	26
Batticaloa coastal sandbars					212	247
Tamankaduwa[a]	4,770	7,909	12,907	1	3	6

Source: B. H. Farmer, *Pioneer Peasant Colonization in Ceylon*, pp. 6–14.

[a]The portion of the Dry Zone with abandoned tanks and ruins of the ancient capital, Polonnaruwa. Such low densities were recorded for the Nuwara Kalawiya region with its ancient capital, Anuradhapura. Tamankaduwa and Nuwara Kalawiya are Sinhalese districts.

high density is attributed to a combination of rich alluvial soils for paddy cultivation, availability of water from shallow wells, and reliable precipitation during the Maha or rainy season rainfall, compared to the rest of the Dry Zone. Except for the Trincomalee coast, where regosols are common, the hinterland of the Dry Zone was almost completely empty in the nineteenth century.[12] Other areas in the Dry Zone, such as the Vanni, the Eastern, North-Central, and Northwest provinces, had low population densities in the nineteenth century. These are the areas where underground water resources for domestic and agricultural uses are limited.

Had the disaster that befell the Sinhalese settlements been in the form of floods from intense cyclones, the results could have been devastating to areas with dense networks of irrigation channels and tanks. Areas like the Jaffna Peninsula, where falling rain is not retained on the surface because of the peninsula's underground rocks and topography, would not have been as vulnerable. There are no prominent relief features and rivers in the peninsula to impound water behind dams. In contrast, the underlying metamorphic rocks and the topography of the mainland are suitable for the construction of dams and for retaining water in tanks at many locations. Therefore, considering that in many places the ratio of tanks to cultivated area was almost 1:1, exceptionally heavy rains could have breached dams and caused havoc to agriculture and settlements on the mainland. The probability of high waters breaching the dams is great because the tanks were laid in a steplike manner along valleys and the failure of dams upstream would have threatened others downstream because of increasing discharge. The nature of damage incurred from flooding depends primarily on the quantity of water discharged by streams in different regions. Some of the rivers draining the North-Central Province have their source in the Wet Zone, and during periods of excessive rainfall more water is discharged by streams flowing through what are the Sinhalese areas than through the Vanni. This might have spared the Tamil settlements from being marooned or destroyed by floods. Damage to irrigation systems and settlements could have been particularly severe in the Sinhalese areas known as Nuwara Kalawiya and Tamankaduwa, because the Mi Oya, the Kala Oya, Aruvi Aru, the Mahaweli Ganga, Yan Oya, and Maduru Oya discharge large quantities of water in these areas, compared to other regions in the Dry Zone. Nuwara Kalawiya was the region surrounding the ancient capital, Anuradhapura, and the portion of the Dry

Zone with the abandoned tanks and ruins of the ancient capital Polonnaruwa was known as Tamankaduwa.

Once the floods receded, the tanks and canals, which were heavily silted and extensively breached, could not be restored by those surviving the floods. Prior to this period, recurring floods, perhaps not destructive enough to decimate the population, had on many occasions destroyed irrigation works, but many were restored because rulers were able to organize a massive labor force to accomplish this major undertaking.[13] Moreover, the pools of stagnant water resulting from the breaching of bunds and dams became breeding areas for the malaria-carrying vector *Anopheles culifacies*. The final stage in the depopulation of the Sinhalese settlements in the Dry Zone occurred when the Dry Zone became infested with malaria. The absence of tanks and canals in the Jaffna Peninsula spared the inhabitants there from malaria.

Tamil Districts as the Traditional Homeland of the Tamils

With the establishment of the Kingdom of Jaffna, the northern part of the island as well as a large portion of the Batticaloa and Trincomalee districts were almost entirely populated by Tamils. Very little land that extends from the hill country to the coast, including the Batticaloa District (which is also referred to as the Bintenne), was occupied by Sinhalese.[14] Even as late as 1871, the population of the Bintenne was fewer than 32,500, of whom the major portion were Tamils.[15] It was in the Kingdom of Jaffna that the Tamils of Sri Lankan origin developed the customs and traditions that distinguish them from the Tamils of South India. While it is true that the origins of the "undisputed antiquity of the Tamil cultural traditions which has always been a source of pride" to the Tamils of the island are in South India, Sri Lanka Tamils did not identify themselves politically with Tamil Nadu.[16] Indeed, Sri Lanka was divided into two nations and three kingdoms at the beginning of the sixteenth century, and the Sri Lankan Tamils lived as a distinct nationality in their traditional homelands in the northern and eastern parts of Sri Lanka.[17]

This division was maintained by the Portuguese and the Dutch, who, when they occupied Sri Lanka in the sixteenth and seventeenth centuries, administered the three states separately. The Dutch, in particular, regarded Tamils as an ethnic group with a linguistic, cultural, and territorial identity of their own. They codified Tamil customs and traditions relating to property rights, inheritance, and marriage in order to administer the traditional Tamil areas.[18] The British, however, abolished the separate system of administration for low-country Sinhalese, Kandyan-Sinhalese of the hill country, and Tamils on the grounds that it perpetuated the division of the country along ethnic lines. Although the two communities were brought together under a unitary state, they never shed their separate identities, which had evolved in diverse geographical regions over seven centuries. It was in the Wet Zone, which was rapidly developed by the British for commercial purposes, where Sinhalese and Tamils came into direct contact with each other for the first time. Tamils, concerned about the problems of overcrowding, landlessness, and the lack of employment opportunities in their water-deficient homeland, which was neglected by the British, sought employment in the Sinhalese areas of the Wet Zone (see Figure 3). Therefore, the Sinhalese-dominated Wet Zone became the focus of competition between Sinhalese and Tamils for employment. Tamils, by virtue of their proficiency in the English language, competed successfully with the Sinhalese and acquired a disproportionately high percentage of employment in the government services and in the professions. However, they continued to adhere to their traditional values and culture wherever they settled outside their homeland, returning to their place of birth in northern and eastern Sri Lanka after retirement. Consequently, the two communities did not mingle freely with each other and behaved as though members of separate nationalities. Even before independence, underlying intergroup prejudices and cultural revival movements had aroused communal self-consciousness among the members of each community, but Sinhalese leaders did not advocate the enactment of laws that were specifically designed to discriminate against the Sri Lankan Tamils.

The beginnings of Sinhalese nationalism can be traced to the 1930s when leaders of the two communities began to mistrust each other as political reforms were introduced by the British to grant greater Sri Lankan representation in the State Council. Prior to 1931, communal representation made it feasible for the minorities to safeguard their interests against majority domination, but this concession was abolished in 1931. The Donoughmore Commission abolished communal representation in 1931, even though it was fully aware that there were two distinct communities that were suspicious of each other and that the majority community was determined to eliminate communal representation in order to weaken the political power of minorities. The Soulbury Commission did not revive communal representation in 1946, but it was aware of the need to safeguard the rights of all national minorities, especially the Tamils, against discrimination by the Sinhalese majority. Therefore, it provided for adequate representation for minorities from the sparsely populated Tamil provinces by delimiting electorates according to area and population. The area provision did furnish adequate representation to Tamils and Muslims from the predominantly Tamil-speaking areas until the 1950s, but this and other constitutional provisions that guaranteed fundamental rights to minorities were ineffective in preventing the Sinhalese-dominated parliament of independent Sri Lanka from enacting legislative measures that did not recognize Tamils as a distinct nationality within the state of Sri Lanka. Therefore, it was only in the mid-1950s, following the passage of the Sinhala only legislation without any provisions for the reasonable use of Tamil, that the Tamils began to give serious consideration to the questions of Tamil nationality and homeland. By this time, "underlying group prejudices accentuated by awakened memories of past conflicts [had] aroused communal consciousness and antagonism" between the communities.[19]

Demands for the recognition of Tamils as a distinct nationality and the identification of their districts as the Tamil homeland have been rejected by many Sinhalese leaders for various reasons: First, they consider Sri Lanka as the homeland of one nationality—the Sinhala Buddhists—since the island was originally settled by Sinhalese and bequeathed to them by Buddha. Accordingly, they do not recognize the Tamils as a distinct nationality in the nation of Sri Lanka regardless of their status as a separate nationality for more than seven hundred years, in a well-defined territory on the island. Many Sinhalese nationalists fail to distinguish between the concepts of "nation" and "nationality," although history has shown that two or more nationalities can live peacefully in a multinational nation, such as Switzerland. Even in India, the homelands of major nationalities have been recognized by the creation of ethnically based states. Second, Sinhalese extremist nationalists claim that the nation of Sri Lanka has always been unified under one ruler, even though history shows that the island was fragmented into several kingdoms, including the Jaffna kingdom, prior to the nineteenth century. Finally, Sinhalese are of the opinion that Tamils have no right to object to the settlement of Sinhalese people in Tamil districts since Tamils, who had access to jobs in the South, had settled in large numbers in Sinhalese districts, although Tamil settlements were not sponsored by the government or established in specific areas in the South in order to change the demographic composition of Sinhalese districts. Tamils used their rights as private citizens to secure jobs and purchase property in both Tamil and Sinhalese districts.

The concept of a traditional Tamil homeland was not rejected by all the Sinhalese leaders, however, although none of them was successful in overcoming the opposition from Sinhalese extremists to carry out the promises they made to the Tamil people. Indeed, S. W. R. D. Bandaranaike recognized the concept of the traditional Tamil homeland when he was willing to devolve administrative powers to regional councils in the Northern and Eastern provinces, under the provisions of the Bandaranaike-Chelvanayakam Pact of 1957 (see Appendix I). The proposed regional councils in Tamil provinces were to be granted powers for selecting allottees to colonization schemes that would be established in Tamil districts. The pact also included provisions that recognized Tamils as a distinct nationality and Tamil provinces as the traditional homeland by permitting the use of Tamil for administrative purposes in the areas to be administered by separate regional councils. Likewise, the concept of a traditional homeland was recognized by Dudley Senanayake when he agreed, under the provisions of the Senanayake-Chelvanayakam Pact of 1965, to specify the priorities that would be observed by district councils of the Northern and Eastern provinces when granting lands to allottees under colonization schemes (see Appendix II). These provisions were intended to reduce the number of Sinhalese who would be settled in Tamil districts under government-sponsored colonization schemes. Dudley Senanayake could not enact the pact into law, but his government was compelled to formulate the Tamil Language (Special Provisions) Regulations of 1966 in order to administer the predominantly Tamil provinces. Indeed, these language regulations, which are currently in force, acknowledge that the Northern and Eastern provinces are distinctly Tamil areas and that they cannot be administered unless special provisions are formulated to transact all government and public businesses and maintain all records in Tamil. Had the provisions of either the Bandaranaike-Chelvanayakam Pact or the Senanayake-Chelvanayakam Pact been enacted into law, the policy of settling large numbers of Sinhalese people in Tamil districts would have been automatically discontinued. Instead, the policy of colonizing Tamil districts with Sinhalese peasants goes on unabated, and the ethnic composition of these districts, especially in the Eastern Province, has changed radically since the mid-1950s. Moreover, the government formulated a plan in the 1980s to settle more Sinhalese in Tamil districts in order to reflect the nationwide population ratio of 75 percent Sinhalese and 25 percent minorities.

The Government's Colonization Policy

It is not the purpose of this discussion to outline the history of peasant colonization in the Dry Zone but to explore the nature and purpose of the overall policy of government-aided colonization in Sri Lanka. Peasant colonization schemes are sponsored by the government to settle peasants away from their native villages on crown lands in the Dry Zone. During the colonial period, large areas designated as the property of the crown were granted to the highest bidder, but since the 1930s, crown lands have been mapped out and developed in the Dry Zone for the benefit of peasant colonists. Soil and engineering surveys are conducted at the planning stage of a colony before allotments are blocked out and channels and roads are constructed through the coordinated efforts of the departments of Land Development and Irrigation. Colonization schemes are associated with major river basin projects, such as the Gal Oya scheme, or with projects involving the restoration of old irrigation tanks, such as the Kantalai Tank, although not all are provided with irrigation facilities (see Figure 3).

Peasant colonists, who are selected from the list of applicants, are allotted a lowland lot on which to cultivate paddy and a highland lot with a house. While colonists are selected from applicants on the basis of need, Tamil politicians have claimed that preference was given to Sinhalese over Tamils in the selection of allottees for colonization schemes that are located in Tamil districts. The size of the lot varied from one to three acres of highland and two to five acres of paddy land. In the past, the government provided assistance to the colonists for clearing forest, ridging, fencing, construction of toilets, and construction of wells. In new projects associated with major river basin projects, peasants are settled on land with irrigation facilities. Lowlands are even machine-cleared, stumped, ridged, and rippled by the Land Development Department. Settlers are also given addi-

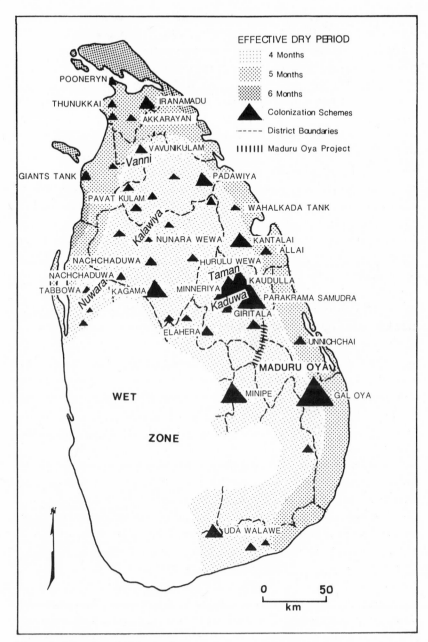

Figure 3. Climate and Colonization

tional allowance for a temporary structure, seed paddy, cash for the purchase of implements, and eighteen months of food aid.

On paper, the major objectives of government-aided colonization of the Dry Zone are to relieve the pressure of population from densely populated areas and to increase domestic food production. There is a necessity to relieve the population pressure on limited agricultural land both in the Wet Zone, where the Sinhalese are concentrated, as well as in some of the Dry Zone districts, where a substantial number of Tamils have been landless for centuries. This landlessness is due both to the dense population and the lack of water to expand agriculture. The people in the densely populated Dry Zone districts face acute problems because of the lack of water and the absence of other avenues of employment, yet preferential treatment has been given to the peasants of the Wet Zone in the allocation of land and water resources. It is well documented that a high percentage of the Tamils of the Jaffna and Batticaloa districts was unemployed and landless, compared to peasants of other Dry Zone districts, when government-aided land colonization began in the 1930s, yet the government showed little urgency in developing the Vanni in order to alleviate the problems of the Jaffna peasants.[20] While the major objectives of state-aided colonization were to ameliorate the conditions of the peasantry and to increase domestic food production, it was apparent from the outset that the government had other motives in pursuing an aggressive policy of moving a large number of Sinhalese families from the Wet Zone to the Dry Zone. Some of the newly appointed Ceylonese ministers to the State Council in the 1930s made these motives clear when they envisioned the recreation of the glories of the Sinhalese civilization of the Rajarata through planned colonization of the Dry Zone and restoration of the irrigation works.

Restoration of ancient irrigation works and resettlement were undertaken in colonial times prior to the 1930s in Batticaloa, Trincomalee, Mannar, Anuradhapura, Polonnaruwa, Puttalam, and Hambantota districts but major efforts to transfer peasants from the Wet Zone to Dry Zone districts considered by Tamils to be their traditional homeland did not take place until later. Except for the Tabbowa and Malay colonies, the Dry Zone was not colonized in 1931, but by the year 1953 twenty-seven peasant colonies had been established in this water-deficient region.[21] The only colonization schemes that helped to ease, even in a minor way, the problem of unemployment and overcrowding in the Tamil-dominated districts were the Iranamadu colonies of Paranthan and Kilinochchi in the Jaffna District and the Unnichchai colony in the Batticaloa District, which were established in 1936 and 1950, respectively (see Table 5 and Figure 3). From the very beginning, colonization schemes in the Eastern Province were not designed to alleviate the overcrowding and unemployment problems in the Tamil districts but were intended to change the ethnic composition of the province, since the allottees were largely Sinhalese rather than Tamils. This was clearly demonstrated when the number of Sinhalese colonists selected for settlement in the Allai, Kantalai, and Gal Oya colonies established in the early 1950s exceeded the number of Tamil peasants selected from the local district. Of the 47,931.2 hectares of land alienated to 16,532 allottees, between 1931 and 1953, the Tamils received only 17.4 percent of the total allotments.[22]

Between 1953 and 1960 the number of families settled in colonization schemes, excluding the Gal Oya and Uda Walawe projects, increased from 16,532 to 37,908, an increase of 129 percent in fewer than ten years. More "crown land," located along the western and southern portions of the Eastern and Northern provinces, respectively, was alienated to Sinhalese peasants under the Village Expansion Scheme. Peasants from Sinhalese districts were settled in new Village Expansion Schemes that involved the restoration or reconstruction of tanks in portions of Tamil districts that are adjacent to present-day Sinhalese population centers in the Polonnaruwa and Anuradhapura districts. Colonization schemes involve the settlement of peasants away from their native villages, while "village expansion" involves the settlement of peasants on land near their native village. In the Kantalai and Padawiya colonies in Trincomalee District, for example, Kantalai Tank was reconstructed and its water supply aug-

Table 5. Peasant Colonization in the Northern and Eastern Provinces at the End of 1953

	Total	Sinhalese	Tamils	Tamils as a % of Sinhalese
Northern Province	656	0	656	100
Eastern Province	5,199	2,976	2,223	75
Whole Island	16,532	2,976	2,879	17

Source: B. H. Farmer, *Pioneer Peasant Colonization in Ceylon*, pp. 108–209.

mented from the Amban Ganga in 1959. These improvements in the Kantalai scheme contributed to the expansion of the area under paddy and sugar cane farming and to the settlement of a large number of Sinhalese peasants and Sinhalese sugar cane factory workers in the Trincomalee District. At the end of 1963, Vavuniya, Trincomalee, Batticaloa, and Puttalam districts had 46.7 percent of all the peasants settled in the Dry Zone under the Village Expansion Scheme (see Table 6). It is estimated that the total investment in irrigation and land development from 1932 to 1964 was approximately US $156 million, most of it concentrated on major schemes involving Sinhalese settlements in both Sinhalese and Tamil districts.

Of the twenty-seven colonies established in the Dry Zone before 1953, Gal Oya in Amparai District and the Parakrama Samudra in Polonnaruwa District were the largest in terms of allottees and investment; no single development scheme of the magnitude of these two has ever been planned or developed in the Northern Province. More than 15,000 people, most of whom are Sinhalese, were also permanently settled as peasants and industrial workers in the Gal Oya Valley in the early 1960s. Seasonal employment was made available to approximately 10,000 additional people when the project was completed.[23] Before the development of the Gal Oya River project, the population of the Batticaloa District was predominantly Tamil and the present-day Amparai Electorate District formed part of the Batticaloa District. The settlement of large numbers of Sinhalese peasants

Table 6. Alienation of Land to Peasants for Village Expansion in the Dry Zone, 1961–1962/1963

Districts	End of 1961–1962	End of 1962–1963	% of Total Allottees in 1962/1963	Total Area (hectares)	% of Total Area
Jaffna	4,502	4,779	2.9	3,741.4	2.8
Mannar	4,794	4,880	3.0	4,404.7	3.3
Vavuniya	17,564	17,597	11.0	14,851.9	11.1
Batticaloa	20,102	19,897	12.5	17,185.4	12.8
Trincomalee	12,928	15,763	9.9	31,618.4	23.7
Puttalam	18,246	21,324	13.3	13,380.8	10.1
Anuradhapura	38,637	39,513	25.0	21,514.8	16.0
Polonnaruwa	6,318	6,560	4.1	7,642.2	5.7
Hambantota	28,771	29,125	18.3	19,440.7	14.5
Total		159,438		134,230.3	

Source: Department of Census and Statistics, *Ceylon Year Book*, 1963 and 1966.

in the Gal Oya Basin made it feasible for the government to create a separate electoral district for the Sinhalese and increase Sinhalese representation in the parliament. Indeed, the Amparai Electoral District is represented by a Sinhalese member of parliament (see Figure 1). Amparai was the site of the first communal riots. These riots occurred one year after the publication of B. H. Farmer's *Pioneer Peasant Colonization in Ceylon,* in which Farmer had optimistically stated, "Communalism causes relatively little trouble in the colonization schemes, in spite of the marked division within the national population. . . ."[24]

The restoration of the Padawiya Tank on the Ma Oya River, the Kantalai Tank on the Kantalai River, the Parakrama Samudra on the Mahaweli Ganga, and other major reservoirs on the Yan Oya, and the Aruvi Aru (Malwatu Oya) have resulted in the settlement of many thousands of Sinhalese colonists in the predominantly Tamil areas of the Northern and Eastern provinces. The number of families settled under colonization schemes (excluding the Gal Oya and Uda Walawe river basin projects) went from 16,532 in 1953 to as much as 60,000 by 1968, an increase of 263 percent. In addition to these legalized settlements, there was considerable encroachment on crown land by retail traders and laborers all along the lower reaches of the Mahaweli Ganga in the Eastern Province.[25] The government has not been successful in evicting these squatters since the 1950s, and in recent years it has even permitted Sinhalese squatters to live and conduct business on crown lands in the Eastern Province.[26] Yet, Tamil squatters are not shown the same tolerance and are often evicted by the army and police from major irrigation and colonization projects located in Tamil districts.

Government Investments in River Basin Development Projects

It is estimated that the number of landless families settled in the Dry Zone colonization schemes by the mid-1970s could be anywhere from 80,000 to 160,000 people. Another 600,000 landless peasants were settled under the Village Expansion Scheme.[27] Since 1977, major emphasis has been placed on river basin development projects, and more than 34,480 families had been settled under the Accelerated Mahaweli Development Program by 1983.[28] The Accelerated Mahaweli Development Program involves the diversion of water from the Mahaweli Ganga, which has its source of water supply from the Wet

Zone of the hill country, to the Dry Zone rivers, such as the Maduru Oya. This plan is designed to expand the area under irrigated agriculture and peasant settlements in the Dry Zone. This does not include the thousands of additional people who have found employment in such nonfarming activities as irrigation, manufacturing, and generating hydro-electric power.[29] It is estimated that 303,192 hectares of land had been brought under cultivation under the scheme by 1983 and more than one-third of this area is under irrigated crops, particularly rice. The yield of paddy under the Mahaweli Development Program was as high as 5,131 kilograms per hectare during the 1982–1983 rainy season. Moreover, approximately US $730 million have been spent on the Mahaweli Ganga Diversion Project by the end of 1983 and it has been estimated that an additional sum of US $1.5 billion would be spent on this and related projects before completion.[30]

Large areas have also been irrigated and thousands of families settled under the Uda Walawe project. The Uda Walawe project involves the impounding of the waters of the Walawe Ganga that flow through the Moneragala and Hambantota districts in southern Sri Lanka. This project is intended to bring large areas of land under paddy, sugar cane, cotton, citrus, and vegetables and also increase the supply of water to areas that are already under paddy. Between 1981 and 1983 more than 50,000 hectares were brought into cultivation and approximately 19,000 families were settled under this project.[31] Most of the benefits of this massive investment will accrue to the thousands of Sinhalese who are already settled on existing projects or to those who will be settled in new colonization schemes such as the Maduru Oya. The Maduru Oya scheme involves the diversion of the waters of the Mahaweli Ganga into the Maduru Oya River, which flows through Amparai and along the border between the Polonnaruwa and Batticaloa districts before it empties into the sea north of Kalkudah in the Batticaloa District. It is designed to extend the area under paddy cultivation in the Amparai and Polonnaruwa districts. The surplus water from the Mahaweli Ganga will largely benefit the settlers in the Elahera, Minneriya, Giritala, Kaudulla, Kantalai, and Padawiya schemes (see Figure 3). The Maduru Oya River project, which is part of the Mahaweli Ganga Diversion Project, like the Kantalai, Allai, Padawiya, and Gal Oya projects, is one of the five major irrigation projects designed specifically to benefit the Sinhalese. The cost of this project is estimated to be $6.4 million and, at full development, 100,000 people, most of them Sinhalese, are expected to move into this colony. While these massive irrigation and land development projects, involving large sums of money, are designed to improve the economic conditions of the Sinhalese districts and Sinhalese peasantry, no steps have been taken by Sinhala governments to improve the economic conditions of the people in the predominantly Tamil areas.

The Extent of Sinhalese Colonization of Tamil Districts

Statistical data on the number of people who have moved from non-Tamil districts to Tamil districts from 1953 to 1983 are not available and thus it is necessary to use an indirect method of estimation to determine the extent of colonization. To derive these estimates, the actual growth of population for Tamil districts, as presented by the Sri Lankan government in the Census of Population, was compared with their projected growth of population if the population growth rate of these districts was similar to that of the island as a whole (see Table 7). The actual population growth of Tamil districts, except for Jaffna District, was larger than the projected growth because, in addition to natural increases, large numbers of people have been settled in these districts under government-sponsored colonization schemes. Although definite conclusions cannot be made on the actual number of people who have migrated from Sinhalese districts into the Tamil districts, these estimates furnish vital information on the nature of Sinhalese colonization in these districts since the 1950s.

The actual growth rate of population in the Jaffna District was below the projected growth rate by 69,146 people, suggesting that a substantial number of people continued to seek employment elsewhere in Sri Lanka or abroad. In other Tamil districts, actual growth has always been greater than the potential growth and the gap between the actual and projected has widened dramatically since the 1960s (see Figure 4). It is particularly interesting to note that the difference between the actual and projected population in the Vavuniya District was 49,344 before the boundaries of the Vavuniya District were redrawn in 1979. When the population of the newly created Mullaitivu and Vavuniya districts are combined, the difference is as high as 116,049, with much of the difference coming from the annexation of population centers from Anuradhapura District. The annexation of a small portion of the Mannar District to the newly created Mullaitivu District merely redistributed the Tamil population

Table 7. Actual Versus Projected Population Increases in Tamil Districts, 1953–1983

Districts	1953	1963	1971	1983	Difference between Actual[a] and Projected (1983)
Jaffna					−69,146 (1)
Actual	491,148	612,955	701,603	868,000	
Projected		644,320	772,539	937,146	
Mannar					29,636 (2)
Actual	43,689	60,095	77,780	113,000	
Projected		57,235	68,624	83,364	
Vavuniya (1953–1978)[b]					49,344 (3)
Actual	35,112	68,712	95,243	111,000	
Projected		45,996	55,149	61,656	
Vavuniya and Mullaitivu (1953–1983)					116,049 (4)
Actual	35,112	68,712	95,243	183,000	
Projected		45,966	55,149	66,951	
Trincomalee					113,881 (5)
Actual	83,917	137,878	188,245	274,000	
Projected		109,931	131,807	160,119	
Batticaloa and Amparai (1953–1983)					246,882 (6)
Actual	270,493	409,122	529,326	763,000	
Projected		354,345	424,859	516,118	
Batticaloa (1963–1983)					65,030 (7)
Actual		197,022	256,672	352,000	
Projected			236,229	286,970	
Amparai (1963–1983)					102,067 (8)
Actual		212,100	272,605	411,000	
Projected			254,308	308,933	
Total Difference between Actual and Predicted:					
i. (1) + (2) + (3) + (5) + (7) + (8)					290,812
ii. (1) + (2) + (4) + (5) + (6)					432,302

Source: Central Bank of Ceylon, *Review of the Economy;* Department of Census and Statistics, *Ceylon Year Book;* Department of Census and Statistics, *Statistical Pocket Book of the Democratic Socialist Republic of Sri Lanka.*

[a]The rate of population increase for the whole nation was as follows: 1953–1963 = 31%; 1963–1971 = 19.9%; and 1971–1983 = 21.48%.

[b]The population of Vavuniya cannot be computed for 1979–1983 because it was redrawn after 1978.

of these districts, but the annexation of a portion of the Anuradhapura District to the newly created Vavuniya District involved the addition of a large number of Sinhalese to the population of a Tamil district. With the establishment of the district councils in 1980, the southern boundary of the Vavuniya District reverted to its original position. Trincomalee District, which has been a region of aggressive colonization by Sinhalese peasants, shows a difference of more than 113,881 people. Finally, if the population figures of Batticaloa and Amparai (which became separate districts in the 1960s), representing the original Batticaloa District, are combined, the difference is more than 246,880 people. Even when the Batticaloa and Amparai districts are considered separately, the figures are 65,030 and 102,067, respectively. The widening gap between the actual and projected population figures in the districts of the Eastern Province demonstrates that a large number of Sinhalese colonists from the non-Tamil provinces has been systematically resettled in this province via government-aided colonization and village expansion schemes. If these estimates are considered for the Tamil districts, at least 432,302 additional people have been added to the population of the Tamil districts through modification of the boundaries of some of these districts and through colonization schemes between 1953 and 1981. This does not take into consideration the large number of Sinhalese who were settled in the Eastern Province prior to 1953.

It is possible to estimate the number of Sinhalese who were resettled in the predominantly Tamil districts by comparing the actual versus projected population increases of Sinhalese in the Eastern and Northern provinces (see Table 8). Since Sinhalese colonization of Tamil districts began prior to 1953, the number of people added to the Trincomalee, Amparai, and Vavuniya districts would be larger than the figures presented in Table 8. Indeed, the whole region from the central hills to the east coast, referred to as the Bintenne, and the Trincomalee coast had populations of only 39,043 and 19,449, respectively, in 1931.[32] My estimates are that more than 165,000 Sinhalese have been added to the population of the Eastern and Northern provinces through colonization schemes between 1953 and 1981. During the same period approximately 84,000 Tamils from the non-Tamil districts were settled in the two provinces. Indeed, if the number of Sinhalese who were settled in the Tamil districts prior to 1953 were included, the figure would be much larger, considering the fact that an estimated 90,000 colonists and their families were settled in the Dry Zone at the end of 1953.[33]

The question is often posed as to why Tamils have objected to the settlement of landless peasants in the Tamil districts where there are more stretches of uninhabited land for establishing colonization schemes than in any other areas in the Dry Zone. This question can

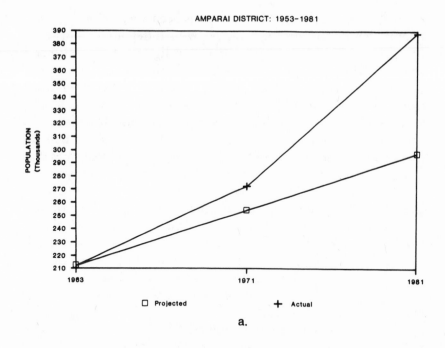

a.

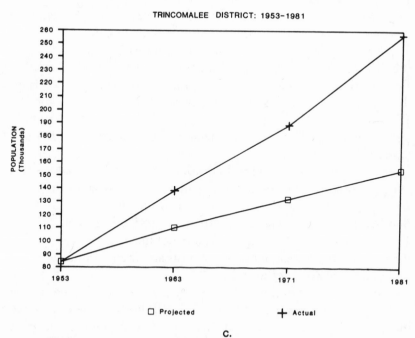

c.

Figure 4. Projected versus Actual Population Growth for Selected Districts

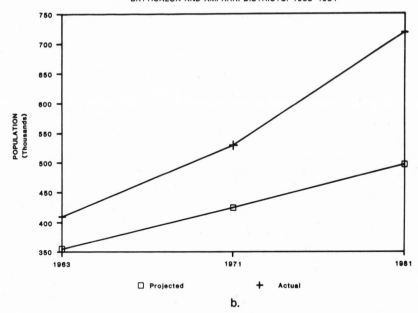

b.

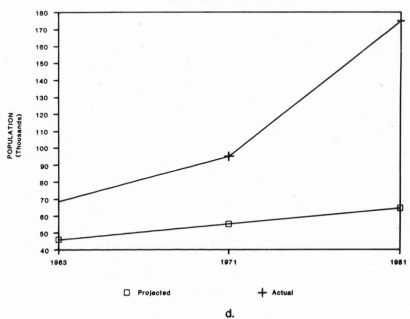

d.

Table 8. Actual Versus Projected Population Increases of Sinhalese in the Eastern and Northern Provinces, 1953–1981

Districts	1953	1963	1971	1981	Difference between Actual[a] and Projected (1981)
Jaffna					−6,231 (1)
Actual	5,902	6,130	20,402	4,615	
Projected		7,731	9,270	10,846	
Mannar					4,857 (2)
Actual	2,097	2,404		8,710	
Projected		2,747	3,293	3,853	
Vavuniya and Mullaitivu					8,920 (3)
Actual	5,934	12,039		19,824	
Projected		7,773	9,320	10,904	
Trincomalee					58,274 (4)
Actual	15,237	39,985	55,308	86,341	
Projected	`	20,007	23,989	28,067	
Batticaloa and Amparai					99,852 (5)
Actual	31,107	67,420	94,150	157,017	
Projected		40,750	48,859	57,165	
Total Difference between Actual and Predicted:					
i. Sinhalese					165,672
ii. Tamils (excluding Muslims and Indian Tamils)					84,425
iii. Sinhalese and Tamils					250,097

Source: Central Bank of Ceylon, *Review of the Economy;* Department of Census and Statistics, *Ceylon Year Book;* Department of Census and Statistics, *Statistical Pocket Book of the Democratic Socialist Republic of Sri Lanka.*

[a]The rate of population increase for the whole nation was as follows: 1953–1963 = 31%; 1963–1971 = 19.9%; and 1971–1981 = 17.0%.

only be satisfactorily answered if the areal size of each district in the Dry Zone is compared with the actual population increases that have occurred since 1953 (see Table 9). It is clear from Table 9 that the highest rate of population increase and the highest population density are recorded for the Jaffna District. Although Tamils from Jaffna have, in the past, lived and found employment in Sinhalese areas, the population has continued to grow in the district, accompanied by overcrowding, unemployment, and food shortage problems. The government, however, has not taken steps to assist the Jaffna Tamils by settling them in those colonization schemes that were established in the Tamil districts of Vavuniya, Trincomalee, Batticaloa, and Amparai. On the contrary, some of these schemes were largely settled by Sinhalese peasants form the North-Central Province and from the

Table 9. The Number of People Added to a Square Kilometer of Area in Selected
Dry Zone Districts from 1953 to 1983

District	Area (in square kilometers) 1983		Density of Population (person per square kilometer) 1983	Number of Persons Added to a Square Kilometer of Area 1953–1983
Amparai	4,539.2		91	43.8[b]
Batticaloa	2,464.6		143	62.9[b]
Amparai and Batticaloa	7,003.8		109	70.3
Jaffna	2,072.5		419	181.8
Mannar	2,002.1		56	32.1
Vavuniya	3,664.64	(1978)	30	20.7[c]
Vavuniya	2,645.2	(1983)	39	
Mullaitivu	1,966.1	(1983)	41	
Trincomalee	2,618.2		105	72.6
Anuradhapura[a]	7,129.2		87	48.0[b]
Polonnaruwa[a]	3,403.8		82	48.1[b]
Anuradhapura and Polonnaruwa[a]	10,533.0		85	48.1

Source: Department of Census and Statistics, *Ceylon Year Book,* 1963 and 1966; Department of Census and Statistics, *Statistical Pocket Book of the Democratic Socialistic Republic of Sri Lanka,* 1980 and 1984; Central Bank of Ceylon, *Review of the Economy,* 1979 and 1983.

[a]Sinhalese districts with very few Tamils.
[b]Computed for the period 1963–1983.
[c]Computed for the period 1953–1983 (before the creation of Mullaitivu District).

Wet Zone. Jaffna Tamils could not colonize Mannar and Mullaitivu districts in large numbers because there were no major projects like the Kantalai or those in Amparai District to absorb them. Even Vavuniya District, which has registered the smallest increase in population between 1953 and 1978, was not developed to accommodate the overflowing population from the Jaffna District. Only a few minor irrigation projects were established in Vavuniya to assist a small number of Tamil and Sinhalese settlers. Since 1978, however, the area of Vavuniya District has been expanded to include a substantial number of Sinhalese from the Anuradhapura District, and the Tamils can no longer rely on this district to solve their population and agrarian problems. Vavuniya's original southern boundary was restored in 1980. Problems relating to overcrowding and lack of irrigation facilities to expand agriculture have also plagued the Tamils of Batticaloa District for centuries, yet they were not given preference in the selection of colonists for the Amparai colonization scheme. Instead, the Amparai region became the focus of rapid colonization by Sinhalese peasants, and what was once a no-man's land had a population density of 91 persons per square kilometer in 1983. The highest population increase per square kilometer has occurred in the Trincomalee District where a large number of Sinhalese from other districts have been resettled through colonization and village expansion schemes. Even though the Anuradhapura and Polonnaruwa districts are much larger and are less densely populated than the Trincomalee District, this Tamil district was specifically selected for peasant colonization.

An analysis of the information furnished in Tables 7, 8, and 9 demonstrates that the Tamils are justified in criticizing the manner in which the policy of government-aided colonization has been pursued since the 1950s. There is, and has been, sufficient land, especially in the larger districts of Anuradhapura and Polonnaruwa, to settle landless peasants from the Wet Zone, yet Tamil districts of smaller size and higher density were selected for colonization by Sinhalese peasants. Instead of caring for the needs of the local population of the Tamil provinces, the government brought in Sinhalese peasants in large numbers to settle in colonization and village expansion schemes, which were established deliberately in Tamil areas.

The Development of Water Resources in the Dry Zone

The physical environment, particularly the climate, imposes serious limitations on the development of water resources and agriculture in the Dry Zone. Nowhere is the land 100 meters above sea level, and it slopes very gradually from the central hill country toward the coast as evident by the flow of rivers (see Figure 2). Old, resistant metamorphic rocks lie under the Dry Zone except for the Jaffna Peninsula and a narrow strip of the northwestern coast, which are composed of limestone.[34] The limestone is exposed in many locations on the peninsula and buried under a thick layer of sand on the mainland. On the mainland, rivers flow in broad valleys between low ridges giving the landscape an undulating character and, wherever the topography is suitable, rivers have been dammed to irrigate crops. Although the Jaffna Peninsula is devoid of rivers because of the presence of joints in the limestone bedrock, the limestone holds a vast reservoir of underground water, while the impermeable crystalline rocks of the mainland yield very little ground water. It is the underground water resources that have contributed to the survival of the Tamil settlements in the Dry Zone since the thirteenth century and to the development of one of the most intensively cultivated and settled areas on the island. On the mainland, agriculture and settlements are almost exclusively dependent on surface water stored behind bunds in large tanks along river valleys. Agricultural activity is, however, hampered because many of the rivers discharge very little water during the prolonged dry period when evapotranspiration rates are high.

Indeed, the most critical factor limiting agricultural productivity in the Dry Zone is the quantity of available soil moisture.[35] Soils are mainly recharged with moisture from October to December, when the northeast monsoon, as well as tropical cyclones, supply approximately between 1,016 to 1,524 millimeters of rainfall. The Mannar and the Hambantota districts receive the least quantities of annual precipitation, but, as a whole, the Tamil areas are hotter, drier, experience a longer period of water deficit, and warrant more irrigated water than the Sinhalese districts for successful agriculture. In fact, the regional variations in agricultural productivity in the Dry Zone can be explained with reference to the quantity of rainfall as well as to the length and intensity of the prolonged dry period. It is also clear, based on available climatological data, that the highest annual and monthly average temperatures in the Dry Zone are recorded in the Tamil areas where meteorological drought lasts for seven to eight months of the year. The longest effective dry period, lasting for approximately seven months and occurring with a probability of 100 percent, has been recorded in the Jaffna Peninsula; the effective dry period is on the whole longer in the Tamil districts, compared to the Sinhalese districts of the Dry Zone (see Figure 3).[36] Manfred Domros, who utilized the Papadakis formula to compute the water balance for selected stations in Sri Lanka, emphasizes that the "water deficit starts in March and April (e.g., Batticaloa), or even in February (e.g., Jaffna and Mannar): these areas also experience an eight month-long, continuous period of water deficit" (see Table 10).[37] Even the driest Sinhalese Dry Zone districts, such as Puttalam and Hambantota, have fewer months of water deficit than all of the Tamil districts. Notwithstanding the fact that agricultural development in the Tamil districts is hampered by the paucity of water resources, major irrigation projects continue to be located in Sinhalese districts.

Indeed, the economic development of the Tamil areas, outside of the Jaffna Peninsula, is seriously hindered by the lack of adequate supplies of irrigated water to cultivate rice and secondary food crops. It is imperative, given the high density of population in the penin-

Table 10. Climatic Parameters for Selected Dry Zone Stations

	Anura-dhapura	Batticaloa	Mannar	Jaffna	Trincomalee	Puttalam	Kurunegala
(TE)[a]	27.3	27.4	27.8	27.6	28.0	27.3	27.0
PE[b]	1680.0	1713.0	1793.0	1728.0	1763.0	1705.0	1683.0
PRE[c]	1446.0	1756.0	1011.0	1352.0	1646.0	1126.0	2155.0
D[d]	357.0	480.0	782.0	645.0	473.0	579.0	26.0
Dry[e]	04.0	05.0	06.0	06.0	05.0	04.0	03.0

Source: C. W. Thornthwaite and Associates, "Average Climatic Water Balance Data of the Continents, Part II. Asia," *Publications in Climatology,* pp. 56–58; Manfred Domros, *Agroclimate of Ceylon,* pp. 77–124.

[a] Mean annual temperature (in celsius).
[b] Annual potential evapotranspiration using Thornthwaite's formula (in millimeters).
[c] Annual precipitation (in millimeters).
[d] Soil moisture deficit as defined by the formula: potential evapotranspiration minus actual evapotranspiration in millimeters.
[e] Average duration (in months) of effective dry period.

sula and the lack of employment opportunities for Tamils in the private and public sectors, that major irrigation projects be initiated in the predominantly Tamil areas. The Tamils, however, lack the resources and the machinery to augment the supply of water to northern rivers in order to solve their agrarian problems without government assistance. Table 11, giving mean annual yields of water from river basins in the Dry Zone, demonstrates the dilemma the Tamils face in striving to develop agriculture.[38]

As the information on the annual discharge of water from river basins in different parts of the Dry Zone clearly shows, Tamil settlements are confined to areas where the supply of surface water is relatively inadequate. Of the approximately twenty streams that drain exclusively in the Tamil areas in the Northern Province, only Kanakarayan Aru and the Parangi Aru basins discharge, individually, more than 125 million cubic meters of water, annually, into the ocean; most of the basins discharge between 10 to 40 million cubic meters of water annually. The total river basin discharge from the Tamil area of the Northern Province is less than 750 million cubic meters, annually. In contrast, Kala Oya and Moderagam Oya, which originate and drain through the Sinhalese districts of the North-Western and North-Central provinces, discharge more than 515 million cubic meters of water. The basin of the Aruvi Aru, which includes both Tamil and Sinhalese districts, discharges almost 285 million cubic meters of water annually. The Aruvi Aru, nevertheless, is extensively tapped at its upper reaches to fill the Nuwara Wewa, Turuwila, and Nachchaduwa tanks in the Sinhalese district of Anuradhapura. Only a small portion of the total discharge of Aruvi Aru is used for irrigating paddy in the Vavuniya and Mannar districts. The Yan Oya and Ma Oya rivers discharge approximately 890 million cubic meters of water annually from their basins and, although they drain into the sea via the Northern and Eastern provinces, a large portion of this discharge is stored in reservoirs, such as Huruluweva, Wahalakada, and Padawiya tanks for the benefit of Sinhalese peasants resettled in colonization schemes. The Gal Oya Basin, and the recently inaugurated Maduru Oya Basin, which have become the focus of Sinhalese colonization of the Eastern Province, discharge more than 650 million cubic meters of water. The Unnichchai Basin of the Eastern Province, where most of the settlers are Tamils, discharges only 85 million cubic meters of water. Finally, large quantities of water from the Mahaweli Ganga Basin have been used effectively to augment the supply of water in the river basins of the North-Central and Eastern provinces. With these additional supplies of water, agricultural productivity has been increased and paddy cultivation extended to new areas for the benefit of Sinhalese peasants.

Table 11. Mean Annual Discharge from River Basins in the Dry Zone

River Basins	Million Cubic Meters	Major Contributions
Mahaweli Ganga[a]	4,933	Parakrama Samudra, Minneriya, and Kadulla tanks (existing) in Polonnaruwa District; augmenting water supply to existing tanks in Anuradhapura and Trincomalee (only Kantalai) districts; Mahaweli Project will extend irrigation facilities to Maduru Oya region (area of new peasant colonization benefiting Sinhalese) and supply additional water to existing tanks in Sinhalese districts. If the whole project were to be carried out according to the master plan, many of the tanks in the newly created Vavuniya District will have additional water to increase rice production. However, the original plan to augment the supply of water of rivers that flow into the Jaffna lagoon (creating a fresh-water lagoon) has been left out. The Mahaweli Ganga Project has been designed primarily to assist Sinhalese peasants of Sinhalese and Tamil districts.

continued

Table 11. (continued)

River Basins	Million Cubic Meters	Major Contributions
Maduru Oya[a]	518	Proposed Mahaweli Ganga Project will provide adequate water to extend paddy cultivation. Sinhalese residents from Polonnaruwa and other districts are to be settled in colonization and village expansion schemes.
Yan Oya[a]	368	Hurulu Wewa and Wahalkade tanks in Anuradhapura District.
Kala Oya[a]	313	Kala Wewa and Kurunchikulam in Anuradhapura District.
Aruvi Aru	285	Nuwara Wewa, Hurulu Wewa, Nachchaduwa, and Mahagalkaduwala tanks in the Anuradhapura District; Pavatkulam in Vavuniya District; Giant's Tank and Paraiyanalankulam in Mannar District.
Moderamgam Aru[a]	204	Nikaya Wewa in Anuradhapura District.
Karagarayan Aru	180	Irranamadu Tank in Jaffna District.
Mi Oya[a]	170	Tabbowa Wewa in Puttalam District.
Gal Oya[a]	148	Senanayaka Samudra in Amparai District.
Parangi Aru	141	Paddy in the downstream section.
Kantalai[a]	100	Kanatalai in Trincomalee District but benefits Sinhalese colonists (Elahera-Minneriya-Yoda Ela canal augments water supply from Mahaweli).
Unnichchai	86	Unnichchai Tank in Batticaloa District.
Nay Aru	84	Irra-Illuppalakkulam in Mannar District.
Pali Aru	82	Iraniyankulam in Jaffna District.
Mandekal Aru	56	Batticaloa District (no important tank).
Pankulam Aru	39	Pankulam in Trincomalee District.
Ma Oya[a]	37	Padawiya Tank in Vavuniya District (Sinhalese colonization), additional water from Mahaweli Ganga Project.
Akkarayan Aru	37	Akkarayan Kulam benefits Jaffna and Mullaitivu districts.
Mundel Aru	28	Benefits Amparai and Batticaloa districts.
Pallavarayan Aru	27	Jaffna District (minor tanks).
Kal Aru	23	Upper reaches in Anuradhapura District and downstream in Mannar District.
Nethali Aru	22	Jaffna District (no important tank).

Source: Department of Census and Statistics, *Ceylon Year Book;* Central Bank of Ceylon, *Review of the Economy;* S. Arumugam, *Water Resources of Ceylon;* R. L. Brohier, "Underground Water Supply of Northern Ceylon," pp. 39–42; R. L. Brohier, "The Jaffna Peninsula Lagoon Scheme," pp. 212–213; S. Selvanayagam, "Agrarian Problems and Prospects of Developing the Jaffna Region of Ceylon"; Manfred Domros, *The Agroclimate of Ceylon*, pp. 201–211; B. L. C. Johnson and M. LeM. Scrivenor, *Sri Lanka: Land, and Economy*, pp. 58–71.

[a]Benefits Sinhalese districts and Sinhalese settlements in Tamil districts.

The government continues to invest large sums of money on the Mahaweli Ganga Project to augment the supply of water and extend paddy cultivation in Sinhalese areas, while the Tamil areas continue to be neglected. It is the scarcity of irrigated water that restricts the expansion of rice cultivation and limits yields in Tamil districts, relative to Sinhalese districts, and many Tamils are convinced that Sinhala governments are deliberately unwilling to remedy this situation. They thus find it necessary to demand the devolution of substantial legislative and fiscal powers to Tamil areas so that the governmental units in these areas will have the authority to initiate major irrigation and colonization projects for the benefit of the local residents. As yet no substantial governmental powers have been devolved to Tamil areas and the Tamil districts continue to lag behind Sinhalese districts in rice production. Many new irrigation projects in the Dry Zone continue to be associated with the resettlement of Sinhalese peasants in the Dry Zone, while many of the Tamils of the water-deficient districts, such as Jaffna and Batticaloa, have been neglected.

Agricultural Development

Nowhere in the Dry Zone are the local people so dependent on agriculture as are the residents of Jaffna and Batticaloa districts. The people of the two districts have for centuries sustained a viable agricultural system in order to support a large population with limited resources. By the year 1962, the percentage of land devoted to cultivation in the Jaffna and the Batticaloa districts was as high as 27.4 and 18.05, respectively, and additional land could not be brought under cultivation to meet the needs of the increasing population because of the lack of water.[39] From the mid-1940s, the people of the two districts have pinned their hopes on the government to initiate major irrigation and colonization projects, to resettle landless peasants, and to increase rice production.

Prior to the 1950s, most of the intensively cultivated lands in the Dry Zone, particularly in the Jaffna and Batticaloa districts, was developed almost entirely by the local people without any assistance from the government. To their dismay, most of the major government-sponsored irrigation projects in both Sinhalese and Tamil districts were primarily designed to resettle Sinhalese peasants (see Figure 3). If the major objective of the colonization and irrigation projects was to relieve pressure of population on agricultural land, major schemes should also have been initiated to resettle Tamil peasants. Colonization schemes intended to resettle Sinhalese peasants from the Wet Zone could have been largely restricted to Sinhalese districts, especially given that the population densities per acre of agricultural land area were only 0.16 and 0.14 in Anuradhapura and Polonnaruwa districts, respectively, in 1963.[40] In contrast, the population densities per acre of agricultural land area in the Jaffna and Batticaloa districts were as high as 0.99 in the Jaffna District and 0.32 in the Batticaloa District, respectively, in the same year.

According to statistical data relating to the extent of area sown to rice on an annual basis for the years 1980/1981, 1981/1982, and 1982/1983, the Tamil districts in the Northern Province ranked at the bottom of the list of all the Dry Zone districts (see Table 12 and Figures 5 and 6). Between 1963 and 1983, the greatest increases in the area sown to rice were recorded in the Amparai and Trincomalee districts where large numbers of Sinhalese were settled in colonization schemes.

The Jaffna District had a population of 868,000 and a density of 419 persons per square kilometer in 1983, yet the area sown to rice was only two-thirds of the area devoted to rice in the Anuradhapura District, which had a population of 622,000 people and a density of only 87 persons per square kilometer (see Table 13). The population densities in the Mullaitivu, Mannar, and Vavuniya districts are small enough to accommodate some of the landless and unemployed people from the Jaffna District under government-sponsored irrigation and colonization schemes. Unfortunately, few major government-sponsored irrigation and colonization schemes have been established in the Northern and Eastern provinces in recent years. Most of the new irrigation schemes are minor projects that are barely adequate to supply supplementary water for crops grown during the rainy season. Indeed, the water that is applied to previously rain-fed land does not even guarantee one season of water supply during years of abnormally low rainfall. It is true that the extent of the area sown with paddy in Tamil areas has increased as a result of the development of minor irrigation schemes, but the yields are not as high as those cultivated under major irrigation projects where there is better control of water supply.[41]

Yields of rice have increased dramatically in Sri Lanka with the introduction of hybrid seeds as part of the Green Revolution. How-

Table 12. Changes in Gross Extent of Area Sown and Yield Per Hectare of Rice in
Dry Zone Districts, 1961/1963 to 1981/1983[a]

	Annual Gross Extent of Area Sown				Yield Per Hectare 1981/1983 (kilograms)	
	1961/1963 (hectares)	1981/1983 (hectares)	% under Yala 1981/1983	Change from 1963–1983 Maha + Yala (hectares)	Maha	Yala
Sinhalese Districts						
Polonnaruwa	37,340	54,802	41	17,462	4,572	3,815
Anuradhapura	53,932	52,790	11	−1,142	3,217	3,558
Hambantota	26,923	31,745	42	4,819	3,984	3,886
Moneragala	1,750	13,477	22	11,727	3,324	3,174
Total				32,866		
Tamil Districts with Major Colonization Schemes						
Amparai	50,109	75,607	36	25,498	4,163	4,320
Trincomalee	23,330	40,001	26	16,671	2,812	3,786
Vavuniya[b]	22,103	24,720	4	2,617	2,366	3,336
Total				44,786		
Tamil Districts						
Batticaloa	34,584	54,873	18	20,389	2,703	3,347
Jaffna	33,013	35,546	13	2,533	2,336	4,033
Mannar	14,014	16,372	2	2,358	2,977	2,996
Total				25,280		

Source: Department of Census and Statistics, *Ceylon Year Book,* 1963, 1966, and 1967. Central
Bank of Ceylon, *Review of the Economy,* 1978, 1981, 1982, and 1983.
[a]The values are averaged for three consecutive years: 1961, 1962, and 1963, as well as 1981,
1982, and 1983. Only those districts entirely in the Dry Zone are included.
[b]The latest values for Vavuniya do not apply to the period 1981–1983 but to the year 1978 when
the district was redrawn.

ever, these increases were recorded only in areas where adequate water
was made available in the form of irrigation, in such districts as Trincomalee and Amparai. In particular, supplementary irrigation during
the Maha or rainy season contributed to high yields of rice in the
Polonnaruwa, Amparai, and Anuradhapura districts from 1981 to
1983 (see Table 14). Except for the Mannar District, the percentage of
sown land under irrigation was much greater in the Sinhalese districts
than in the Tamil districts in 1979/1980. Therefore, while most of the
Sinhalese districts recorded yields ranging between 3,200 to 4,570
kilograms per hectare during the Maha season, when most of the
paddy lands are under cultivation, all other districts recorded less
than 3,000 kilograms per hectare in 1981/1983. The Jaffna District
was at the bottom of the list with 2,336 kilograms per hectare.

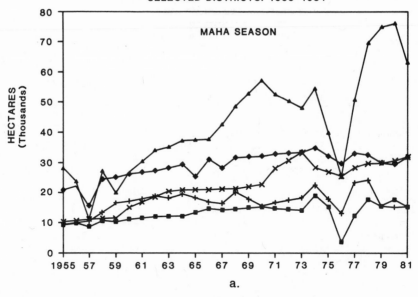

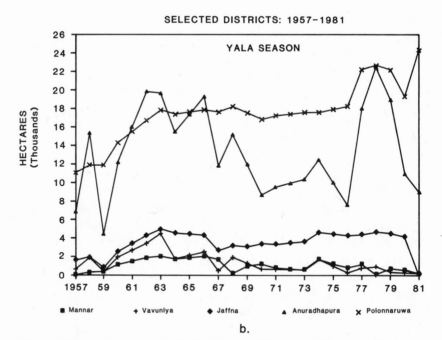

Figure 5. Extent of Area under Paddy (Mannar, Vavuniya, Jaffna, Anuradhapura, and Polonnaruwa)

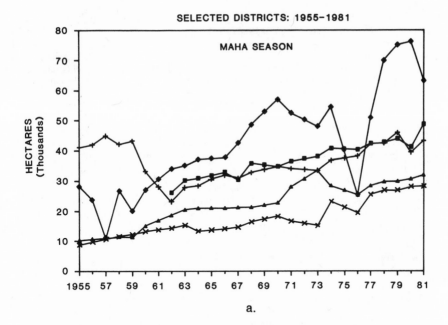

SELECTED DISTRICTS: 1955–1981

MAHA SEASON

a.

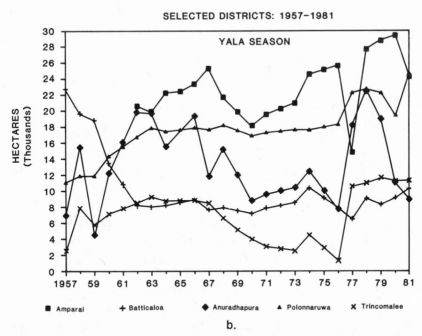

SELECTED DISTRICTS: 1957–1981

YALA SEASON

■ Amparai   + Batticaloa   ◆ Anuradhapura   ▲ Polonnaruwa   X Trincomalee

b.

Figure 6. Extent of Area under Paddy (Amparai, Batticaloa, Anuradhapura, Polonnaruwa, and Trincomalee)

Table 13. Changes in the Annual Per Capita Production of Rice in Dry Zone
Districts, 1961/1963 to 1981/1983[a]

	Population[b] (thousands)		% Change	Density (per square km)	Production Per Capita (kilograms)	
	1963	1983	1963–1983	1983	1963	1983
Sinhalese Districts						
Polonnaruwa	114	278	143.8	82	870	790
Anuradhapura	280	622	122.1	87	387	268
Hambantota	275	449	63.2	173	197	270
Moneragala	132	298	125.7	53	34	144
Tamil Districts[b] with Major Colonization Schemes						
Amparai	212	411	93.8	88	450	754
Trincomalee[c]	138	274	98.6	105	336	432
Vavuniya[d]	—	102	—	39	—	335
Tamil Districts						
Batticaloa	197	352	78.6	143	317	426
Jaffna	613	868	41.5	419	82	104
Mannar	60	113	88.3	56	528	419
Mullaitivu[d]	—	81	—	41	—	490

Source: Department of Census and Statistics, *Ceylon Year Book,* 1963, 1966, and 1967. Central
Bank of Ceylon, *Review of the Economy,* 1978, 1981, 1982, and 1983 (Provisional estimates for
1983 population see Table 54).

[a]The figures for annual per capita production of rice are computed by using assumptions and
procedures presented by Barbara Harriss, "Paddy and Rice Situation in Sri Lanka," in B. H.
Farmer, ed., *Green Revolution,* pp. 20–30, note 12.
[b]Provision for 1983.
[c]The percentage of Sinhalese increased from 18.2 to 33.6 in the Trincomalee District between
1953–1981. In the Amparai District the percentage of Sinhalese increased from less than 25
prior to 1963 to more than 38 in 1981. The percentage of Sinhalese population in the Vavuniya
District in 1981 was 16.6.
[d]These two districts were carved out of the original Vavuniya District in 1978.

Obviously, Tamil districts lag far behind the Sinhalese districts in the
production of rice.

The regional variations in agricultural productivity in the Dry Zone
can be best expressed by comparing the annual per capita production
of rice, on a district basis. Indeed, great disparity exists between the
Tamil and Sinhalese districts in their capacity to support the local
populations.[42] In 1963, the highest and the lowest per capita pro-
ducers of rice were Polonnaruwa and Moneragala districts, respectively, but, by 1983, Jaffna District was at the bottom of the list (see
Table 13). The position of Jaffna District as a self-sustaining region
has deteriorated in recent years because the area under irrigation
remains small compared to the size of its population (see Table 14).

Table 14. Size of Land Holdings and Percentage of Sown Area
under Irrigation in the Dry Zone (Maha 1979/1980)

	% of Sown Area Irrigated	Average Size of Holdings (hectares)
Sinhalese Districts		
Polonnaruwa	95.3	4.0
Anuradhapura	92.7	4.1
Hambantota	92.5	3.0
Moneragala	63.2	3.9
Tamil Districts		
Trincomalee	56.6	3.1
Vavuniya	83.4	5.7
Batticaloa	30.4	2.7
Jaffna	31.6	1.3
Mannar	94.7	3.7

Source: Department of Census and Statistics, Ministry of Planning Implementations, *Socio-Economic Indicators of Sri Lanka.*

The per capita production of rice in the Jaffna District was only 104
kilograms in 1983, while it was more than 268 kilograms in most of
the districts. Moreover, the per capita production of rice in the Northern Province in 1983 was only 182 kilograms, while it was 433 and
625 kilograms in the North-Central and the Eastern provinces,
respectively. Therefore, the Northern Province, especially the Jaffna
District, lags behind other regions in the production of rice and in
the capacity of the local population to rely on locally produced rice
for survival. The Jaffna District has become increasingly dependent
on other districts for rice as its population soars because of natural
increase and the influx of refugees from the rest of the island, where
employment opportunities for Tamils in the public and private sectors have become almost nonexistent. In the view of many Tamils,
this dependency has been deliberately engineered by successive governments in order to weaken the minority's economic and political
stronghold over their traditional areas.

For Sri Lanka Tamils, the ethnic problem is closely linked to the
political and economic issues on which the communities differ. Politically, the Tamils believe that they have as much right as the Sinhalese
to consider the island their legitimate home, by virtue of their long
tenure on the island. However, the prospects for Tamils living and
working in the Sinhalese areas are limited, given the policy of dis-

crimination and the acts of violence that have been perpetrated against them since 1956. Therefore, to ensure their freedom and survival, the Tamils desire to preserve their homeland and institutions. Indeed, Tamil areas have served as a refuge for those who have been adversely affected by anti-Tamil riots in the past. The Tamils are deeply concerned about the gradual encroachment of Sinhalese settlements into Tamil areas and dread that they will become a minority in their own homeland. Tamils fear that, given the record of successive governments, their districts will continue to be economically neglected. They are convinced, however, that if substantial powers are devolved to Tamil areas, the issues of economic development of Tamil areas, the need for Tamils to work in Sinhalese areas, and the problem of discrimination will subside. Nevertheless, any proposals that do not recognize the right of the Tamil population to preserve the integrity of their areas will be rejected by militants and moderates alike. Apparently, increasing numbers of Tamils strongly believe that they have the right to self-determination since they possess many characteristics that contribute to nationhood. Tamils have "a shared historical experience, a continuous linguistic and cultural tradition, a common way of life, the result of a traditional system of beliefs and values dominated by Saivaism and, most important of all, a defined territory as homeland."[43]

Education, Employment, Economic Development of Tamil Districts, and Electoral Representation

TAMILS of the moderate persuasion and Tamil militants may differ with each other on the tactics with which to resist Sinhalese domination, but there is a large measure of agreement among them on the issues of cultural identity, the right of self-determination, the territorial integrity of Tamil areas, and citizenship rights for Tamils of Indian origin. The laws and regulations of successive Sinhala governments have discriminated against the Tamils in higher education, employment, and development of Tamil districts. While some Tamils still believe that Tamil demands can be met by establishing a federal form of government and others are strongly convinced that a negotiated settlement to the ethnic problem is no longer feasible and that the Tamils have to establish an independent state, the Tamil people as a whole are determined to obtain substantial concessions from the government.

In the 1950s and 1960s, when Tamil leaders indicated their disapproval of the use of Sinhala for administrative purposes in Tamil areas by staging peaceful demonstrations, they did not receive the full backing of the Tamil people, partly because some Tamils were confident that they might ultimately overcome the language barrier to employment by mastering the Sinhala language. Tamils living in rural areas may even have been grateful to the government for providing an opportunity for their children to be educated in their mother tongue for the first time in many centuries. Education in most schools was conducted in the English language, and it was difficult for children from rural areas to master a foreign language in order to secure employment. Children from urban areas, on the other hand, had adequate opportunities to become proficient in the

English language and to secure employment in the civil service or to gain admission to universities. It was now possible for children from rural areas to be educated in their own tongue and compete successfully with those children from the urban areas for jobs. It was also feasible for children educated in the Tamil medium to secure government employment merely by becoming proficient in Sinhala. Unfortunately, with the passage of time, it became apparent to the Tamils that the Sinhala Only Act was primarily contrived to exclude them from certain categories of jobs. Administrative regulations were even issued stipulating that Tamil children could not be educated in the Sinhala language on grounds that Sinhala is not the language of their parents. Nevertheless, it was not until the early 1970s, when the government issued discriminatory regulations curtailing the number of Tamil students selected for certain faculties in the universities, that Tamil youths began to challenge their leaders and to demand more militant action to secure Tamil rights. As we have seen, they insisted on drastic action, which came in the form of a demand for the establishment of a separate Tamil state to be called Eelam.

Discrimination in Education

The problem of discrimination in education cannot be adequately analyzed without some background information on why Sri Lankan Tamils rely on education rather than on land for their livelihood in this agricultural country. For centuries the Tamils of northern Sri Lanka managed to live geographically isolated from the rest of the island by making effective use of the resources of the water-deficient environment of this region. Seasonal rains and plentiful supplies of underground water have been ingeniously channeled onto paddy fields and onto carefully prepared garden plots of subsidiary food crops and tobacco. Given the ecological constraints of the local environment, however, the agricultural resources have become limited in relation to the needs of the rapidly increasing population. In the Batticaloa and Jaffna districts in particular, the inhabitants face severe agrarian problems, such as the small size of the holdings, the large size of peasant families, fluctuating and unreliable income, the high cost of farming, and lack of adequate credit.[1]

The Jaffna region, which includes the Jaffna Peninsula and the eleven nearby islands, is the cultural hearth of the Tamils of Sri Lanka. In 1981, approximately 75 percent of the Sri Lankan Tamil population of the northern provinces or 40.6 percent of the Sri Lankan Tamil population of the island resided in the region. Although resources are limited, the population of the region has increased rapidly, from 241,451 in 1871 to nearly 800,000 in 1983.[2] Agricultural productivity has not kept pace with the population growth in the region, especially in the Jaffna District, because most of the suitable agricultural land has been under cultivation for hundreds of years; crop yields have been low until very recently. It is estimated that 40 percent of the region's 1,151.8 square kilometers is sandy, alkaline, and consists of rocky waste. The population density in the effectively occupied areas of agriculture, settlement, and other uses was almost as high as 1,180 persons per square kilometer, while the density in the Jaffna municipality would have been at least 2,580 persons per square kilometer in 1983. The capacity of the local environment to support the increasing population began to diminish in the nineteenth century. Jaffna Tamils had no recourse but to seek employment outside the region. Migration to other Dry Zone districts was not feasible since the development of the Dry Zone did not effectively get under way until well into the twentieth century when a few colonization schemes were established.

The major option open to them was to leave the peninsula and secure employment in the public service of the colonial government. Opportunities to acquire proficiency in the English language had been made available to Tamil youths by Christian missionaries, who established a large number of schools in the Jaffna region. Roman Catholic missionaries arrived on the island with the Portuguese in the sixteenth century and established Catholic schools in the coastal areas throughout the island. The Church of England came to the island with the British in the nineteenth century, but it was the English Methodist and the American Congregationalist Church missionaries who had the greatest impact on the spread of Christianity and English education in the Jaffna Peninsula. Many of the Protestants on the island are Jaffna Tamils who were converted by American missionaries. In the Jaffna region, the Catholic Church, the Anglican Church, the Congregationalist Church, and the Methodist Church operated dozens of primary schools and a large number of secondary schools in which the medium of instruction was in the English language.[3] The Christian missionaries received financial aid from the colonial government to provide education in English for those who could not afford it. The colonial government had to support and encourage mission schools in order to create a supply of people who were literate in English and capable of running the civil administration of the country. The Jaffna region supplied a large number of English educated men who were willing to work as clerks in the public service. Since English education was the only means to secure employment in the public service and in other professions, Jaffna Tamils did not object to the establishment of Christian schools in the Jaffna Peninsula. The Sinhalese of the Wet Zone did not face the same adverse economic conditions that the Tamils of the Jaffna region did. Moreover, there were clear indications that the Buddhist revivalist movement of the nineteenth century was somewhat militant and "was never wholly without political overtones."[4] Therefore, Christian missionaries did not receive from the Sinhalese people the same welcome extended to them by the Tamils of Jaffna for the establishment of large numbers of English-language schools in Sinhalese-dominated districts.

This does not imply that the number of Tamils attending schools in the North was greater than that in the other provinces, but the number of Tamils employed in the public service was proportionally greater in relation to the actual size of the population it represented. More Tamils sought work at various levels of the government service and in the professions, including medicine, engineering, and law because of the lack of opportunities in the Jaffna region. This reasoning was effectively expressed by A. Sivanandan when he stated, "The industry of a people who had worked an ungiving land was now given over to education, and the government service, into which education could take them. Education was land."[5] Tamil children were pressured by their parents to master English, mathematics, and science subjects as a means to secure employment that brought fame, high status, and monetary benefits to the family. In fact, "Tamil children were good in figures and their parents goaded them in their academic work for fear of unemployment or hard work as the price of failure."[6]

There is no denying that Tamils who were educated in the English medium took advantage of the favorable treatment accorded them by the British to secure promotions to high positions in the civil service and to receive professional university degrees. Nevertheless, this does not suggest that Tamils were appointed to high positions in the public service if they were less qualified than Sinhalese applicants for these jobs. Sinhalese as well as Tamils were denied access to the public service and were assigned to low-paying minor positions if they lacked proficiency in the English language. A few of the English-educated and more adventurous Tamils who were denied employment in the government service emigrated to Malaysia between 1860 to 1925.[7] Many of those who worked elsewhere on the island or in Malaysia returned to the Jaffna region upon retirement, bringing with them substantial sums of money to purchase land, build homes, educate their grandchildren, and furnish needed capital for business ventures. With the enactment of the Sinhala only legislation, many Tamils had to take early retirement and thus to rely more heavily on the meager resources of their traditional homeland.

One would have thought that once Sinhala was made the official language of the country grievances against the Tamils would gradually be dropped, but the situation worsened as the number of Sinhalese seeking public service employment increased. The introduction of Sinhala as the official language, the change in the medium of instruction in schools, and the establishment of a number of regional and Buddhist universities enabled a large number of Sinhalese to gain admission to universities and to qualify for jobs in the public service. On the other hand, the introduction of Sinhala as the official language drastically reduced the number of Tamils employed in the public service and increased the number of unemployed Tamil high school graduates. Moreover, these unemployed youths with high school diplomas found that admission to certain faculties in the universities was closed to them because of government-imposed restrictions.

Until 1969, admissions to universities were based on the results of the final examination at the high school level (General Certificate of Education Advanced Level Class). Both Sinhalese and Tamil students were required to take the same GCE Advanced Level Examination, but Sinhalese and Tamil students took the examination in the medium in which they were educated. The medium of instruction for those seeking admission to the arts faculty changed from English to Sinhala and Tamil in the 1960s. It was only in 1970 that the first batch of students seeking admission to science faculties were permitted to take the General Certificate of Education (Advanced Level) examination in Sinhala and Tamil. Students do not automatically qualify for admission to the university even if they perform well in the examination. Since the number of places available for admission to different fields of study is limited due to the lack of facilities, the final selection is based on open competition whereby only those students scoring above a certain percentile rank in a combination of subjects are selected.

The United Front Party came to power in 1970 at a time when many prominent Sinhalese claimed that the two-language policy was not effective enough in increasing the number of Sinhalese students admitted to science programs in universities. As long as university admissions were based strictly on merit, they argued, the Tamils would have the advantage and many deserving Sinhalese students would be excluded from universities. In addition, it was rumored that out of 160 students admitted to the faculty of engineering of the University of Ceylon at Peradeniya, Kandy, in 1970, a hundred were Tamil-medium students. This aroused communal feelings on campus and the "complaints of unfair selection, though unsubstantiated, fell on receptive ears and a lower qualifying mark was set for Sinhalese-medium candidates seeking admission to science based courses so that a 'politically accepted' proportion of Sinhalese candidates could be selected."[8]

Indeed, the United Front government of Mrs. Bandaranaike decided that it was difficult to evaluate the relative performance of students who were educated in the Sinhala medium with those who were educated in the Tamil medium, especially when Tamil students were performing exceptionally well in the science disciplines compared to the Sinhalese students. Sinhalese students had also sought admission in large numbers to science faculties, but many of them could not compete successfully with Tamil students in open competitive examinations, even when the medium of instruction was in English. In order to admit more Sinhalese students to the science faculties, the government reduced the minimum requirements necessary for them to secure admission to these faculties (Table 15). The minimum requirements for Tamil students seeking admission to science faculties were raised relative to those required for Sinhalese students. In justification of this argument, they decided to identify different sets of minimum marks that students educated in the different media would have to score to be admitted to the different fields of study in the university. Since Tamil students have traditionally sought admission to the science faculties because employment opportunities are limited for those graduating in the arts disciplines, yet the government decided that a greater number of Tamil students could be admitted by lowering the minimum standards for admission to the arts faculty.

Table 15. University Admissions Based on
          Minimum Marks, 1971

Course of Study	Medium	Minimum Marks
Arts	Sinhalese	187
	Tamils	170
Engineering	Sinhalese	227
	Tamils	250
Medicine and	Sinhalese	229
Dentistry	Tamils	250
Bio-Science	Sinhalese	175
	Tamils	181
Physical Sciences	Sinhalese	183
	Tamils	204

Source: C. R. de Silva, "The Impact of Nationalism on
Education: The Schools Take-Over (1961) and the University Admissions Crisis 1970–1975," in Michael Roberts,
ed., *Collective Identities, Nationalism, and Protests in
Modern Sri Lanka*, pp. 486.

In the early 1970s, some Sinhalese scholars and politicians complained that Tamil students were overrepresented in universities,
especially in the sciences and engineering. When English was the
medium of instruction in the universities, examiners could not be
accused of favoring Tamil students in certain subjects, relative to a
large majority of Sinhalese students, since both Sinhalese and Tamil
examiners were using a language not their own. When the students
seeking admission to universities began to be evaluated in both the
Sinhala and Tamil media by Sinhalese and Tamil examiners, complaints of favoritism were raised. Sinhala and Tamil were adopted as
the media of instruction in the science faculties in 1970 in order to
assist students from rural areas to follow university courses in professional fields, such as engineering and medicine. Complaints of favoritism became more intense as the number of Sinhalese students
desiring to enter science and engineering faculties increased dramatically in the 1970s.

This increase in the number of Sinhalese students seeking admission to science faculties was brought about by a gradual expansion of
science in secondary education. Moreover, the great majority of high
school graduates preferred to pursue science degrees, since most of
those who had graduated with arts degrees in the 1960s were unem-

ployed. Instead of increasing the funding for higher education to meet the growing demand for science degrees at the national and regional levels, however, Mrs. Bandaranaike's government decided to change the system of selecting students for admission to the universities, which was based on "open competition."

Some scholars and politicians in the majority community justified such a change on grounds that Sinhalese students could not compete with Tamil students in professional fields as long as the Tamil districts had more schools, better educational opportunities, and smaller class sizes.[9] They also claimed that the ability of Tamil students to score better marks than Sinhalese students in science subjects was attributable to the availability of better laboratory facilities in Tamil districts. On the contrary, a regional analysis of available data on the percentage of the population enrolled in schools and colleges for the 1978/1979 academic year demonstrates the following: (1) Over 21 percent of the illiterate population of Tamil districts have no schooling compared to 23 percent for the island as a whole. (2) The highest literacy rates on the island are found in the Wet Zone districts with predominantly Sinhalese populations, and include Colombo, Gampaha, Kalutara, and Matara districts (see Table 16). (3) The percentage of population attending primary and secondary schools in the Tamil districts was below the national average. Only 6.67 percent of the estate population had secondary schooling. Despite this low level, the government adopted no measures to develop special ethnic quotas for Indian Tamils.[10] (4) A higher percentage of the population of the Tamil districts had passed the General Certificate of Education (GCE) Ordinary Level examination, relative to other areas, but the figure for High School Certificate or GCE Advanced Level examination for Tamil districts was below the national average.[11] Finally, contrary to popular belief, the percentage of the population with undergraduate degrees for Tamil districts was less than one-half of the national average. Moreover, both urban and rural areas of Sinhalese districts tended to fare better than the Tamil districts in the size of the undergraduate population and in the number of persons who had passed degree examinations. In fact, except for the category of those who had passed the GCE (OL), the rest of the figures for Tamil districts are below the national average. Thus it can be seen that Tamil districts did not offer more educational opportunities, relative to those of Sinhalese districts. Moreover, the percentage of the Tamil population in Tamil districts did not have greater access to university education

Table 16. Analysis of Population with Different Levels of Education, 1978/1979, by Region

Educational Level	Estate	Zone I (a)	Zone II (b)	Zone III (c)	Zone IV (d)	Zone V (e)	All Island
		(in percentage of population in each region)					
No Schooling (illiterate)	43.58	19.47	25.38	21.60	27.10	19.08	23.40
No Schooling (literate)	1.08	0.69	0.70	2.97	0.83	1.25	0.97
Primary	47.39	36.70	42.36	37.22	40.94	32.41	38.92
Secondary	6.67	31.04	23.72	25.81	22.81	31.76	26.43
Passed SSC/GCE (OL)	1.28	10.23	6.58	11.53	7.24	13.11	8.64
Passed GCE (AL)	0.00	1.19	0.64	0.79	0.66	1.36	0.88
Undergraduate	0.00	0.21	0.12	0.05	0.10	0.16	0.14
Passed degree	0.00	0.36	0.42	0.18	0.30	0.65	0.34
Other	0.00	0.13	0.08	0.10	0.02	0.02	0.08

Source: Editorial Notes, "Notes and Documents: Human Rights Violations and Ethnic Violence in Sri Lanka," p. 149.

(a) Zone I: Wet Zone districts with predominantly Sinhalese population, including Colombo District (excluding the Colombo Municipality), Gampaha, Kalutara, Galle, and Matara districts; (b) Zone II: Dry Zone districts with predominantly Sinhalese population, including Hambantota, Moneragala, Amparai, Polonnaruwa, Anuradhapura, and Puttalam districts; (c) Zone III: Dry Zone districts with predominantly Tamil population, including Jaffna, Mannar, Vavuniya, Trincomalee, and Batticaloa districts; (d) Zone IV: Wet Zone largely highland districts with predominantly Sinhalese population but including the estate population of Indian Tamils. This region includes Kandy, Matale, Nuwara Eliya, Badulla, Ratnapura, Kegalle, and Kurunegale districts; (e) Colombo municipality.

compared to Sinhalese districts. The level of educational attainment among the Tamils was less than that of the low-country Sinhalese, but slightly better than that of the Kandyan Sinhalese.[12]

There was, however, no justification for introducing a lower university entrance qualifying mark for Sinhalese-medium students seeking admission to certain faculties since no discrepancies were uncovered in the grading standards between media. Even before the standardization scheme replaced the minimum marks scheme, the percentage of Tamils in universities had begun to decline because of the change in the medium of instruction in certain faculties. Sri Lankan Tamils, who constituted 10 percent of the population, were overrepresented in 1948 when they held 31 percent of the places in the university, but this percentage had dropped to less than 16 percent by 1970.[13] By 1970, Sri Lankan Tamils together with Indian

Tamils were underrepresented in the universities, since they constituted 21.6 percent of the population, but held only 16 percent of the places.[14]

To the disappointment of some Sinhalese extremists, this new system of selecting students to universities did not reduce the number of Tamils gaining admission to some of the prestigious faculties and Sinhalese schools in backward rural areas continued to lag behind urban areas in their ability to assist students to secure entrance to science faculties. In order to rectify the disparity existing among Tamil students, Sinhalese students, urban areas, and rural-backward areas, many plans involving various combinations of standardization and district quotas were experimented with between 1973 and 1976. In 1973, the government introduced a new procedure by which university admission came to be determined according to standardized marks for different media, as well as for different subjects. Under this procedure marks in the two media were reduced to a uniform scale. The rationale for adopting this scheme was that Tamil students have adequate opportunities to attend schools that are well equipped to impart instructions in science courses, and thus it was appropriate to reduce the marks they score in the General Certificate of Education Examination (Advanced Level) to a level that corresponds to the marks they would have scored if they had attended Sinhalese schools that are poorly equipped and staffed to teach science subjects. The uniform scale was determined in such a manner that the number of students qualifying in each medium would be proportional to the number taking the examination in each medium.

This system appealed to certain sections of the Sinhalese population since it dramatically increased the percentage of Sinhalese entering the faculties of engineering and medicine, but it did not satisfy the Sinhalese politicians who represent the less developed, rural districts, especially the Kandyan areas. They complained that students in these districts did not have the educational facilities to compete with students from urban areas. In order to satisfy this constituency, the government introduced the District Quota System in 1974 and used it concurrently with the Standardization System introduced in 1973. Under the District Quota System some seats in the universities were set aside to be allocated to different districts according to the percentage of population in each district. The quota was not applied uniformly to all subjects and more places were allocated for science subjects.

The greatest negative impact of all these experiments was felt by the Tamils rather than by the affluent Sinhalese of the rural and urban areas. Sinhalese historian C. R. de Silva, commenting on the impact of standardization and district quota systems on the comparative strength of ethnic communities in universities, states that "ethnically there is little doubt that the major blow fell on Ceylon Tamils."[15] The Indian Tamils have not gained by standardization even though "they have the poorest schooling facilities on the island."[16] The percentage of Tamils entering engineering courses fell from 48.3 percent in 1970 to 16.3 percent in 1974 (see Table 17). Likewise, the percentage of Tamils admitted to the faculty of medicine declined from 48 percent in 1970 to 26.2 percent during the same period. On the whole, admission of Tamil students to science-oriented courses dropped from 35.5 percent in 1970 to less than 21 percent in 1973. De Silva also noted that, on the other hand, "the Sinhalese emerged

Table 17. Changes in the Ethnic Composition of Candidates Admitted to the Different Faculties in Sri Lankan Universities between 1970 and 1983

	Arts	Physical Biological Architecture	Engineering	Medicine and Dental	Agriculture and Veterinary	Law
	Sinhalese and Tamils[a] (percentages)					
1970	89.1	69.7	51.7	49.2	39.2	57.7
	(6.9)	(27.6)	(48.3)	(48.0)	(53.6)	(34.6)
1971	89.7	68.0	55.9	51.7	59.4	54.2
	(7.0)	(28.6)	(40.8)	(43.0)	(34.4)	(33.4)
1972	92.7	67.0	62.4	53.7	59.6	85.8
	(4.7)	(31.2)	(34.7)	(41.8)	(38.5)	(10.2)
1973	91.8	73.1	73.1	57.5	54.9	77.3
	(5.9)	(23.6)	(24.4)	(38.4)	(42.2)	(18.1)
1974	86.0	75.1	78.8	69.9	80.9	[a]
	(10.0)	(22.0)	(16.3)	(26.2)	(15.2)	[a]
1981	82.8	63.5[c]	67.2	72.7[d]	—	73.0
	(13.3)	(31.8)	(28.1)	(23.1)		(16.2)
1983	77.1	73.4[c]	66.4	72.8[d]	—	78.1
	(16.4)	(23.1)	(28.1)	(22.1)		(11.5)

Source: C. R. de Silva, "The Impact of Nationalism on Education: The Schools Take-Over (1961) and the University Admissions Crisis 1970–1975," in Michael Roberts, ed., *Collective Identities, Nationalism, and Protests in Modern Sri Lanka*, pp. 494–495; Editorial Notes, "Notes and Documents: Human Rights Violations in Sri Lanka," p. 146.

[a]Percentage of Tamils in each category presented within parentheses.
[b]The values for law and arts are combined.
[c]This only applies to physical sciences.
[d]This only applies to medicine.

as the main beneficiaries. Their share of admissions to science-based faculties rose from 75.4 percent in 1974 and to over 80 percent (estimate) in 1975."[17] On the other hand, Tamil students' share of admissions to the science-based faculties fell from 35 percent in 1970 to 19.3 percent in 1983, whereas the total share of Sinhalese admissions was at 75 percent in the same year. The Sinhalese share of admissions in the fields of physical sciences, biological sciences, engineering, medicine, and law was 73.4, 70.3, 66.4, 72.8, and 75 percent, respectively, in 1983.[18] Thus the popularly held notion that Tamils on the average account for 50 percent of all students admitted to the faculties of science, engineering, medicine and law is not true; Sinhalese have always had at least 60 percent of the university admissions in these fields and in recent years their representation in these fields has approached and even surpassed their proportion of the population at large in Sri Lanka.

Until 1974, Tamil undergraduates were educated on the two campuses of the national university, one in Colombo and the other in Peradeniya. Sinhalese undergraduates were also educated at this national university, as well as at two other institutions of higher learning that were elevated from the position of Buddhist seminaries into Vidyodaya and Vidyalankara universities in the late 1950s. There was, however, more competition from students to enter the national university because it offered undergraduate education in all the sciences and professional fields. Since the university could not accommodate all the students who qualified in the General Certificate of Education (Advanced Level) examinations, admission was based on an open competitive examination. Both Sinhalese and Tamil students competed with each other for the limited places in the university. As long as the procedure for admitting students to the national university was based on open competition, Tamil students had no problems filling a large number of the allotted places in the different fields of study, except in the arts. With the introduction of the Standardization and the District Quota systems, large numbers of deserving Tamil students were intentionally kept out.

By 1974, Sinhalese leaders became aware that the introduction of the Standardization and District Quota systems had alienated the Tamil community as a whole and that there was an urgent need to appease them. One way was to establish a campus of the University of Ceylon in Jaffna, which they had demanded since the 1960s, so that more Tamils could gain admission to the university. Therefore, after a period of rapid decline in the number of students admitted to professional fields in universities, there was a slight improvement in the proportion of Tamils entering engineering, science, and medical courses after the establishment of a makeshift Jaffna Campus in 1974. Tamil students were gradually squeezed out of the main campuses where facilities for studying in the professional fields were excellent.

The standardization scheme was modified in 1976, when it was decided that 70 percent of students would be chosen on the basis of their marks and 30 percent on the basis of district quotas. The government eventually abolished the system of standardizing marks for admission to universities, but a comparison of the figures for 1974 and 1983 suggest that the percentage of Tamils admitted to the engineering faculty has improved while the percentage of students selected to the faculty of medicine continues to decline.[19] The number of Sinhalese students entering the faculties of engineering and medicine has increased since the middle 1970s when additional campuses were established. Moreover, "the damage done by discriminatory measures against the minorities is considerable and suspicion between the Sinhalese and the Tamils is unlikely to die away even if the university admissions issue is resolved to the satisfaction of both parties."[20] The system of "standardization" with its district quotas is considered by the Tamils to be one of the most discriminatory of the regulations designed to restrict the educational opportunities of the Tamil community, a community that places a high premium on education. It was the issue of university admissions, more than any other factor, that compelled unemployed and educated Tamil youths to clamor for the establishment of a separate Tamil state.

Discrimination in Employment

While regulations dealing with the standardization of marks were intended to trim the competitive advantage Tamil students had with regard to university admissions, the Sinhala only legislation by requiring a knowledge of Sinhala among the qualifications for various jobs eliminated Tamil competition on a larger scale because the administrative regulations of the Act that stipulated that children must be educated in the language of the parents was "in practice a denial of Sinhala media education to Tamils."[21] Students who were educated in the Tamil medium were denied access to public service jobs, and unemployment among the GCE Ordinary Level Certificate holders was at a deplorable state in the late 1960s. High unemployment, however, was not limited to Tamil youths, since as many as 80.2 percent of those who had passed the GCE Ordinary Level examination and 96.3 percent of those who had passed the GCE Advanced Level examination in Sri Lanka were unemployed in the middle 1970s.[22] The unemployment rate among Tamil males who had successfully passed the GCE Advanced Level was as high as 41 percent, while it was only 29 percent for Sinhalese males in 1983, according to the *Labor Force and Socio-Economic Survey* published by the Ministry of Plan Implementation and the Department of Census and Statistics.[23]

The language regulations further aggravated the problem of unemployment among the Tamils, especially because a significantly higher percentage of Tamil youths had passed the GCE Ordinary Level examination in comparison to Sinhalese youths by 1979 (see Table 15). Discriminatory laws and regulations had already reduced the number of Tamils employed in government services. Prior to independence, 30 percent of those employed in the government service in Sri Lanka were Tamils, but by 1975 the figure had dipped to nearly 6 percent.[24] It is true that Sinhala governments may have been justified in reducing the number of Tamils holding government jobs in order to rectify the imbalance in ethnic representation in the public service, but this need not have implied that the Tamils should be virtually shut out from government services and the Sinhalese overrepresented (see Table 18).

The recruitment of Tamils to the administrative service, the teach-

Table 18. Ethnic Representation in Public and Corporation Sector
        Employment in 1980

Categories	State Sector (corporations excluded)		Public Sector (state and corporations)	
	Sinhalese	Tamils	Sinhalese	Tamils
Professional and Technical	82	12	82	13
Administrative and Managerial	81	16	83	14
All Categories	84	12	85	11

Source: Department of Census and Statistics and Ministry of Planning Implementation, *Census of Public and Corporation Sector Employment, 1980,* and Editorial Notes, "Notes and Documents," pp. 141–142.

ing profession, and the public-sector corporations had also declined by the 1970s. Among the hundred persons selected for administrative services in 1973, only four were Tamils and two were Moors (Muslims). Moreover, of the 23,000 persons appointed to the teaching profession between 1971 and 1974, only 1,867 were Tamils and 2,507 were Moors.[25] According to Satchi Ponnampalam, the recruitment of 1,867 Tamil teachers in this period was not adequate to compensate for the 3,500 Tamil teachers who would have retired during these three years.[26] The number of Tamils recruited to the police department, the army, and naval forces also declined precipitously; of a total of 10,000 persons who became members of the armed forces between 1977 and 1980, only 220 were Tamils (see Table 19).[27] According to many Tamils, the government has systematically excluded Tamils from the armed forces in order to be able to impose its will on the Tamil people. Atrocities committed by the security forces in the Tamil areas, under the pretext of maintaining law and order, could have been avoided if a substantial number of the army personnel were Tamils. Tamils dominated certain sections of the public sector jobs in the past, particularly in the fields of accountancy and engineering, but this situation has changed in recent years. Indeed, the figures released by the Department of Census and Statistics and the

Table 19. Tamils' Share of Government Service Jobs for Selected Years[a]

Categories (%)	1956	1965	1970	1980
Administrative Service (a)	30	20	5	
Administrative and Managerial (b)				16[b]
Professional and Technical (c)	60	30	10	12[b]
Clerical Service (a)	50	30	5	
Army, Navy and Police (e)	40	20		4.0
Teachers				10.7
Prima Flour Mill				
Plants in Tamil area (d)				19.2
All Categories (b)				12.0[b]

Source: (a) W. Scharz, *Tamils of Sri Lanka*, p. 13; (b) Editorial Notes, "Notes and Documents," pp. 141–142; (c) Schwarz, *Tamils of Sri Lanka*, and A. Sivanandan, "Sri Lanka: Racism and the Politics of Underdevelopment"; (d) Angelito Peries, "Historical Background to the Genocide of Tamils in Sri Lanka," pp. 19–24; (e) Peries, "Historical Background," and Sivanandan, "Sri Lanka."

[a]Information obtained by combining data from different sources because no single source provides data for the whole period, 1956 to 1970.
[b]This figure applies merely to state sector but if this was combined with the public sector corporations, figures are 13, 14, and 11 percent, respectively.

Ministry of Plan Implementation indicate that the percentage of Sinhalese in all categories of employment in the state sector in 1980 was as high as 84 percent compared to 12 percent for the Tamils (see Table 18).[28] The Sinhalese comprise 74 percent of the population but hold 82 percent of the jobs in professional and technical fields and 83 percent of the jobs in the administrative and managerial categories in the state and public sectors. The Sri Lankan Tamils, who comprise 12.6 percent of the population, had 13 percent of professional and technical positions and 14 percent of administrative and managerial positions in 1980. The 1983 estimates of public sector employment reveal that while the Sinhalese share of employment in this sector was 85 percent, the Tamil share was only 11 percent.[29] This figure of 11 percent has been drastically reduced since the anti-Tamil riots of 1983.

Discrimination in Public-Sector Employment

Public-sector corporations include a large number of labor-intensive industries that have been established in various parts of the island with foreign aid. Although state-run industries were set up during World War II in Sri Lanka, no large-scale industries were developed in the Tamil areas prior to 1950. The decision to locate a major industry, such as the Kankesanthurai cement factory in the Jaffna District, in a particular region was dictated entirely by the presence of large quantities of the basic raw materials, such as limestone and clay, in close proximity to each other. Prior to the establishment of the Kankesanthurai cement factory in 1950, plywood, leather, ceramic, and glass factories were opened in Sinhalese areas where abundant supplies of raw materials are available. Similarly, the Paranthan chemical factory, which manufactures DDT and caustic soda, was located in the Jaffna District because there was an urgent need to eradicate malaria before colonization schemes could be planned in the Dry Zone. This factory, which became operational in 1955, is ideally situated both in relation to the supplies of raw material from the salterns at Elephant Pass and to markets via road and rail. The production of salt at Elephant Pass became a government-run industry in 1957. Another major industry established in Tamil areas prior to the 1960s is the paper factory at Valaichchenai. The reason for locating this industry in the Batticaloa District was the availability of paddy straw, water, and illuk grass in the vicinity of the factory. The only other factory located in predominantly Tamil areas is the mineral sands factory at Pulmoddai.

Only four state-run industries, excluding the salt operation at Elephant Pass, have been established in predominantly Tamil areas since independence. These factories were set up during the early days of independence when the Tamil Congress extended its cooperation to the government, and G. G. Ponnampalam, a Jaffna Tamil, was the Minister of Housing and Industries. All the other government-run industries have been located in either Sinhalese districts or in Tamil districts where Sinhalese have been settled in colonization schemes. In particular, labor intensive sugar cane plantations and sugar cane factories were established at Kantalai and Gal Oya to provide employment to the large number of Sinhalese who settled in the districts under colonization schemes. Although the productive capacities of the cement and paper factories have been increased to meet the growing demand for cement and paper products, these improvements have been accomplished with minimum capital investment and without having to employ a large number of Tamil workers (see Table 20).

A comparative analysis of the employment and capital investment figures on government-run industries for 1965/1966 and 1982 demonstrates that Tamil areas have been discriminated against in the allocation of resources for industrial development. Of the approximately

Table 20. Government-Sponsored Industries in Sri Lanka, 1965–1982

Industry[a]	Capital Investment (Millions of Rupees)		% of Total (1982)	Employment		% of Total (1982)
	1965/1966	1982		1965	1982	
National Milk Board	14.7	221.4	3.4	1,116	1,738	2.5
Ceylon Oil and Fats	21.9	165.2	2.6	550	1,083	1.6
Sugar[a,b]	87.1	546.6	8.6	1,104	7,269	10.5
Flour[a,b] Milling	(11.1)	(69.8)	(1.0)	63	600	0.9
Salt[a]	2.1	68.6	1.0	953	1,485	2.2
Tobacco[b]	3.8	30.6	0.4	112	939	1.4
Distillery[b]	3.9	104.7	1.6	77	1,919	2.8
Textiles	50.3	465.9	7.3	1,212	8,816	12.8
Wellawatte[b] Spinning		73.1	1.1		2,322	3.4
Leather	5.2	44.2	0.6	550	1,070	1.5

continued

Table 20. (continued)

Industry[a]	Capital Investment (Millions of Rupees) 1965/1966	1982	% of Total (1982)	Employment 1965	1982	% of Total (1982)
Plywood	2.8	170.3	2.6	685	3,547	5.2
Timber[b]	10.1	62.7	1.0	1,228	2,119	3.1
Paper[a]	29.0	894.9	14.0	1,005	4,562	6.6
Printing[b]	3.6	79.1	1.2	92	555	0.8
Chemicals[a]	12.3	47.8	0.6	242	543	0.7
Petroleum[b]	183.2	811.9	12.8	378	5,944	8.7
Fertilizer[c]	7.2	2.4	0.3	90	975	1.4
Tire[b]	55.0	173.7	2.7	650	1,959	2.8
Rubber[b]	(10.7)	(47.8)	(0.7)	145	(326)	(0.4)
British/Ceylon Corporation		65.1	1.0		1,264	1.9
Colombo Gas and Water		21.8	0.3		332	0.5
Ceylon Oxygen		101.9	1.6		389	0.6
Ceramics	8.1	485.3	7.6	324	6,161	8.9
Cement[a]	61.4	1,117.0	17.6	1,016	6,614	9.6
Mineral Sands[a]	11.0	169.1	2.7	600	570	0.8
Mining and Minerals		121.1	1.9		2,370	3.4
Steel[b] (Endaramulla)	115.9	313.7	4.9	596	2,305	3.3
Hardware	15.1	46.5	0.6	290	1,385	2.1
Total	725.5	6,406.6	100.0	13,078	68,835	100.0

Source: D. R. Snodgrass, *Ceylon: An Export Economy in Transition,* pp. 394–396; R. R. Nyrop et al., *Area Handbook for Ceylon,* pp. 355–363; B. L. C. Johnson and M. LeM. Scrivenor, *Sri Lanka: Land, People and Economy,* pp. 121–128; and Central Bank of Ceylon, *Review of the Economy* (1969), pp. 50–87; (1970), pp. 64–65; (1981), p. 61; (1982), p. 63.

[a]Located in Tamil areas: one of three cement factories; one of three sugar cane factories, but located in Sinhalese-dominated Kantalai colonization scheme; the only mineral sands industries; one of the many salterns; the only chemical industry; the only paper manufacturing factory; and one of the two flour mills. Excluding the flour mill, all of them were constructed in the 1950s. Of the approximately 40 major government-sponsored industrial units, only 6 are located in Tamil-dominated areas. More than 20 were established between 1960 and 1980.

[b]Data for the years 1965/1966 and 1982 are not available and data for other years have been substituted as follows: Sugar—capital, 1969/1970, and employment, 1966/1967; Flour—employment, 1967/1968, and capital, 1981; Distillery—capital, 1973, and employment, 1966/1967; Tobacco—capital, 1972; Wellawatte mills—capital, 1981; Timber—capital and employment, 1968/1969; Printing—capital and employment, 1969/1970; Tire—capital and employment, 1967/1968; Rubber—capital, 1981, and employment, 1980; Steel—capital and employment, 1966/1967.

[c]The capital investment for fertilizer is underestimated according to the information for 1981 and since the capital investment figures for Flour and Rubber are for the year 1981, they are not included to derive the total investment or the percentages.

13,000 people who were employed in state industrial enterprises in 1965/1966, more than 3,000 or 23 percent were employed in the five industries located in predominantly Tamil areas (see Table 20). Between 1965/1966 and 1982, the number of people employed in state-run enterprises located in the predominantly Tamil areas increased from 3,000 to only 8,800 or less than 12.8 percent of the employees in twenty-eight major industries throughout the country. During the same period, the total number of people employed in state-run industries rose from approximately 13,000 to 68,835, a whopping increase of 429 percent. This increase was accomplished through an investment of Rs. 5.6 billion between 1965/1966 and 1981, with most of the capital investment designated for improving economic conditions in Sinhalese districts. Not a single labor-intensive industry similar to the textile industries in Veyangoda, Tulhiriya, Mettegama, Pugoda, and Minneriya was ever planned for the Tamil districts, even though the Jaffna District has the highest level of unemployment in the country.

Moreover, capital investment to improve the productive capacities of existing industries has been limited to those industries located in Sinhalese districts. It was this preferential treatment that contributed to the meteoric rise of the Puttalam District as the leading producer of cement in Sri Lanka. This was accomplished by rerouting Murungan clay, which was originally designated for the exclusive use of the Kankesanthurai factory in Jaffna, to the Puttalam factory. The net result is that in 1982, the productive capacity and production of cement in Puttalam was 440,000 and 333,555 metric tons, respectively. In contrast, the productive capacity and production of the Kankesanthurai factory in the same year were 298,000 and 225,772 metric tons, respectively, despite the fact that the Kankesanthurai factory has the better location for cement production.

Even when the advantages for locating an industry in a Tamil district were ideal, the government was not necessarily interested in proceeding with the project. For example, in the 1960s the World Bank recommended that the Thunukkai-Pooneryn region in the Jaffna District was ideal for establishing a large sugar cane plantation and a factory. Instead of following up on this recommendation, the government expanded the area under sugar cane at less suited sites, particularly at the Walawe Ganga River Basin project. In addition, whenever new industries were established in Tamil districts, the local population was not exclusively selected to work in such enterprises. Special mention might be made of the procedure adopted by the Ministry of Planning and Plan Implementation of selecting workers for the Japanese-financed Pima Flour Mill in Trincomalee. Of the 451 persons selected to work in this mill, 379 were Sinhalese; Tamils, who constituted nearly 35 percent of the population of the Trincomalee District, received only 72 positions. Thus the Sinhalese, who constitute less than 34 percent of the population of the district, had more than 84 percent of the positions in the mill. It is estimated that of the 189,000 persons selected to work in public-sector corporations during the period 1956 to 1970, 99 percent were Sinhalese.[30]

Discrimination in Private-Sector Employment

Opportunities for the Tamils to find employment in the private sector are also limited, since industrial enterprises sponsored by foreign aid have not been established in Tamil districts. Government regulations prohibit the establishment of certain categories of industries outside the "Free Trade Zone," which is located around the city of Colombo. Many successful labor intensive industries were financed and operated in the Free Trade Zone by Tamils before they were destroyed by mob violence in 1983. There is no reason why these people, with Free Trade Zone regulation, could not establish similar enterprises in the Tamil districts. Transportation links between the Tamil districts and the rest of the island are adequate to distribute manufactured products from the Tamil districts to the other areas of the island and abroad. Fish, onions, tobacco, and paprika have been shipped from the Tamil areas to Sinhalese districts by road and rail without any difficulty until very recently. Even a large portion of the fish caught off the coast of the Jaffna Peninsula are trucked to Colombo for export. Agricultural and manufactured products, however, cannot be exported directly to foreign countries from the Jaffna Peninsula since the Kankesanthurai Harbor on its northern coast has not been developed by the government. Whether the decision not to improve the Kankesanthurai Harbor was motivated by political reasons is not certain, but conditions for expanding the fishing industry, as well as market-oriented industries, would have improved if successive governments had followed through with the recommendation of the World Bank to develop the harbor. Instead, it was decided to improve the Trincomalee port. Moreover, the improvements at Trincomalee were contemplated only after it was made certain that large numbers of Sinhalese civilians had been settled and a large contingent of military and naval personnel had been stationed in the Trincomalee District.

Since published information on employment in the private sector is unavailable, the number of people registered with the Employees Provident Fund (EPF) for two different periods has been used to estimate these figures on a regional basis.[31] Although all the employees who made at least one contribution to the Employees Provident Fund have not registered with it, the data presented in Table 21 provide some indication of the employment opportunities available in the private sector in different regions. There is clear evidence that employment opportunities in the private sector are largely confined to Colombo and its suburban areas where more than 20 percent of the population is concentrated. Elsewhere, there seems to be a close relationship between the number of people registered with the EPF and the population of the districts. Kandy, Kurunegala, Galle, Kalutara, and Jaffna are the most populated districts, with at least 5.6 percent of the population registered with the EPF in each district. Each of these populated districts, except Jaffna, had a share of at least 2.69 percent of all those who were employed in the manufacturing sector in 1977 (see Table 21). Jaffna District's share was only 1.90 percent, clearly demonstrating that this district has been neglected. The government has not established state-run industries or assisted individuals in establishing private-run industries in the Jaffna District since independence. In 1978, the Northern Province, which is made up of the districts of Jaffna, Mannar, Mullaitivu, and Vavuniya, comprised more than 7 percent of the island's population and yet only 2.4 percent of all persons employed in manufacturing activities in the private sector resided there. Moreover, Vavuniya and Trincomalee districts had the lowest percentage of employees in manufacturing for the year 1977. Employment data for Amparai District have not been reported, indicating the possibility that its figures are combined with that of Batticaloa. Thus, it may be seen that employment opportunities for people living in the predominantly Tamil areas are available neither in the agricultural sector nor in the industrial sector.

Tamils were, however, successful in trade and businesses that were established outside the Northern and Eastern provinces. Because of this fact there is a widely held opinion among the Sinhalese that a handful of Tamils dominate the private sector of the economy. While this may not be true, many Tamils from the North had to seek employment in the private sector, particularly in retail trade, busi-

Table 21. Number of Employees Registered under the Employees Provident Fund on a District Basis, 1967 and 1977

District	Manufacturing 1967	Manufacturing 1977	Nonagricultural 1977	Manufacturing % of Total 1967	Manufacturing % of Total 1977	Population % of Total 1978
Colombo (Municipal Council area)		198,033	496,796		46.36	
Colombo	(111,692)	89,363	170,339	69.44	20.92	20.95
Kalutara	4,654	15,012	37,144	2.90	3.51	5.69
Kandy	4,917	11,479	59,852	3.06	2.69	9.07
Matale	1,362	4,339	12,234	0.85	1.02	2.49
Nuwara Eliya	368	1,739	15,263	0.23	0.41	3.30
Galle	5,318	12,602	38,865	3.31	2.95	5.74
Matara	1,944	6,036	22,092	1.21	1.41	4.65
Jaffna	3,058	8,116	24,727	1.90	1.90	5.65
Mannar	127	1,813	3,300	0.08	0.42	0.64
Vavuniya	98	335	2,461	0.06	0.08	0.78
Batticaloa	639	21,554	32,625	0.40	5.05	4.34
Trincomalee	335	723	19,055	0.21	0.17	1.57
Puttalam	12,067	23,367	33,141	7.50	5.47	3.08
Anuradhapura	455	950	8,475	0.28	0.22	3.24
Polonnaruwa	474	916	5,363	0.29	0.21	1.33
Badulla	1,527	3,376	27,689	0.95	0.79	6.29
Ratnapura	585	4,166	19,333	0.36	0.98	5.21
Kegalle	1,007	6,270	22,037	0.63	1.47	5.06
Hambantota	346	1,131	5,620	0.21	0.26	2.74
Kurunegala	9,866	15,844	40,855	6.13	3.71	8.18
Total	160,839	427,164	1,091,913	100.00	100.00	96.18[a]

Source: Central Bank of Ceylon, *Review of the Economy,* 1969 and 1978.

[a]Moneragala and Amparai had 1.60 and 2.22 percent of the total population, respectively. Employment figures were not furnished for these two districts.

ness, and industries, because of limited opportunities at home. Of course, Tamils would not have been successful in business and trade if they had not possessed entrepreneurial skills and the willingness to take risks. A few of them succeeded in establishing large-scale business enterprises that had Sinhalese as well as Tamil shareholders and directors. It is estimated that the percentages of Tamils who held posts as directors, chairmen, and partners/proprietors in Sri Lankan commercial companies for the period 1979 to 1981 were 18.62, 20.96, and 20.54 percent, respectively.[32] Moreover, many of the Tamil-owned labor intensive industries that were located in the Free Trade Zone employed thousands of Sinhalese inhabitants of the South rather than Tamils from the North, where thousands of educated youths are unemployed. Outside the capital city of Colombo, many Tamils succeeded in establishing retail trade on a minor scale at locations where such services were nonexistent; wherever such services were already available the Tamils competed successfully with Sinhalese retail traders. Contrary to the opinion held by some Sinhalese, it was not the motive of Tamil retailers to exploit and deceive the local people. After all, Tamil retailers had conducted business with Sinhalese villagers for more than a century. In the past, they had provided basic necessities to isolated villages but in recent years they found themselves branded as exploiters. Many of these Tamil retailers, businessmen, and industrialists have been forced, under tragic circumstances, to flee to the North. The predominantly Tamil areas, however, can no longer absorb the influx of more people because economic development of these areas has been deliberately neglected by the government.

Economic Development in Tamil Districts

Once Sri Lanka became independent, the government sought to deal with the problems of unemployment, landlessness, scarcity of food, and lack of water for irrigating crops through investments in irrigation and Dry Zone development projects. A major aim was to provide opportunities for local farmers to grow food. Prior to 1977, there were many restrictions on the importation of food products that would compete with local products. It was the practice of all governments since independence to purchase food items from farmers at higher prices and sell them to the consumers at lower prices through various guaranteed price schemes.

The open economic policy, which was initiated by the present government in 1977, removed all the restrictions that were imposed by successive governments on the imports of agricultural and manufactured products from foreign countries. This policy has devastated the market-oriented farming economy of Tamil districts, especially in the Jaffna Peninsula, where a large section of farming population depends for its livelihood on the sale of chillies (paprika), onions (shallots), and tobacco throughout the island.[33] The imposition of restrictions on the imports of onions and chillies, the introduction of guaranteed price supports for these crops, and the availability of cheap credit, as well as storage and marketing facilities, had made Sri Lanka self-sufficient in onions and chillies from the 1960s. The Jaffna region constitutes only a tiny fraction of the island, yet it produces a great share of the island's onions and chillies. The Jaffna Peninsula produced more than 15 percent of the island's chillies although the area planted with chillies in the peninsula was only 7.8 percent of the total area devoted to chillie cultivation on the island. By the early 1970s, the Jaffna District produced more than 83 percent of the island's domestic requirements for onions while the peninsula, which had 43 percent of the total area devoted to onion cultivation on the island, produced more than 50 percent of the nation's onion crop. The successful cultivation of onions and chillies, as well as tobacco, raised farm income and encouraged farmers to modernize agriculture.

In the late 1970s, when the United National Party government lifted the ban on the imports of onions and chillies from India, the economic prosperity enjoyed by the Jaffna farmers began to crumble. Farmers were forced to cut onion production drastically because the government imported large quantities of onions in order to establish a buffer stock of cheaper onions. These cheaper onions were sold in the South during the off-season when the price of Jaffna onions was high. The buffer stock program and import practices resulted in temporary shortages, temporary gluts, and spoilage of large quantities of onions from time to time. Tamil farmers considered this import policy to be deliberately designed to discriminate against them. They believe that the government is apathetic to the needs of the northern farmers and that the import policy is one more discriminatory measure designed to stifle the economic development of Tamil areas.

Agricultural development involving the expansion of the acreage under irrigation, improving crop yields by modernizing agriculture, and assisting farmers to market their crops under favorable guaranteed price schemes can ameliorate only some of the agrarian problems of landlessness, small holdings, unreliable income, and unemployment in rural parts of the Tamil districts. Agriculture alone cannot absorb all of the unemployed in the rural areas nor can it raise the standard of living of the people substantially. Nonagricultural resources will have to be tapped and labor intensive industries established in Tamil areas with adequate facilities to market finished products if the situation is to be improved. Unfortunately, the region lacks most of the minerals essential for the development of heavy industries. The only minerals found in large quantities in the Jaffna region suitable for industrial use are limestone, which became the basis for the establishment of the first cement factory on the island at Kankesanthurai, and salt. Although the industries in the Jaffna District for producing cement, salt, and chemicals, including the production of fertilizer at the Paranthan chemical factory, could have been expanded, no government since their inception in the 1950s has been willing to invest large capital to accomplish this. The cement factory at Kankesanthurai employed approximately 1,500 in 1980, an increase of less than 500 employees since 1965 (see Table 20). The saltern at Elephant Pass employed, at most, 500 persons per year. The Paranthan chemical factory employed 543 persons, an increase of 300 since 1965. Since the 1950s, however, no other major industries have been established in the region. In 1965, these three industries employed 11 percent of all those working in government-sponsored industries on the island, but by 1982 this figure had plunged to 3.6 percent. In 1982, government-sponsored textile industries in various parts of the country, including the spinning mill at Wellawatte in the Colombo District, employed more than 11,135 workers, but the Jaffna region did not have any such labor-intensive industries. It is true there are several privately owned handloom and powerloom centers in the region producing high-quality textiles, but most of these are operated on a small scale for the local market with minimum capital. Garment manufacturing at the Layden Mill in Jaffna town employed approximately 300 people in 1980. Most of the industries are small-scale operations employing few workers.

Small- and large-scale industries could play a vital role in reducing unemployment in the Jaffna region, if the government would issue permits to operate them, facilitate the influx of foreign capital into the region, develop the Kankesanthurai Harbor to facilitate the transport of manufactured products to foreign nations and the import of raw materials, and provide tax and other incentives to entrepreneurs, as is done in the Free Trade Zone. Many successful labor-intensive industries were financed and operated in the Free Trade Zone by Tamils until they were destroyed by mob violence in 1983; there is no reason why these very people cannot establish such industries in the northern region to reduce the severe unemployment problem. Moreover, many foreign-owned companies would be more than willing to take advantage of the cheap labor, as they have done in Singapore, to set up labor-intensive industries in the region, if the government were willing to permit them.

The prospects for developing a highly profitable fishing industry in the region are promising, since the continental shelf around the Jaffna region and on the Pedro Bank provide an ideal environment for fish breeding. Unfortunately, the fishing community does not have the funds to purchase large fishing boats, trawlers, and modern nets to improve the catch. To modernize fishing operations, the Kanke-santhurai Harbor and other small fishing ports, such as Myliddy and Point Pedro, will have to be developed and equipped with facilities to refrigerate fish on a large scale. The government has neglected these ports, however, and even discouraged the successful operations of the Ceylon-Norway Development Foundation. At one time, this privately funded project employed approximately 1,250 persons at Karainagar and Jaffna town to build boats, repair nets, and process fish.[34] By 1976, this project had become a profitable operation, with the profits going toward community development in Karainagar. Unless the government is inclined toward encouraging such privately funded and government-sponsored projects in the region, the economy of this part of the country will continue to deteriorate.

The use of the natural resources of the island largely to benefit the Sinhalese community is a result of the lack of Tamil representation in decision-making bodies.[35] In 1956, when they were excluded from the executive branch of government, elected representatives of the Tamil community lost the ability to secure tangible benefits for their constituents. Even in parliament, Tamil representatives failed to secure the support of its members to improve the economic well-being of the Tamil people. Moreover, the TULF, the only party that truly represented the Tamil people, and whose members were non-militant, was proscribed in 1983. This situation is likely to continue unless substantial administrative, legislative, and fiscal powers are granted to the Tamil community.

Colonization, Electoral Gerrymandering, and Electoral Representation

The resettlement of Sinhalese peasants in Tamil areas through colonization schemes is the issue that Tamil leaders have always insisted must be resolved before any accord can be reached on other issues. The colonization policies of Sinhala governments, according to the Tamils, have been designed to transfer political control of the Tamil districts to the Sinhalese. The Tamils naturally desire to preserve electoral control over their districts in order to safeguard their language, preserve their culture, live and move freely without apprehension, and improve the depressed state of the regional economy.

Colonization schemes that brought Sinhalese peasants into Tamil provinces contributed to an unprecedented growth of population in these areas during the last three decades. In the years 1953 to 1981 the population growth in the Tamil districts, excluding the Jaffna District, ranged from 145 to 394 percent, whereas the islandwide population growth was approximately 85 percent during the same period (see Table 22). The Vavuniya District in the Northern Province, which is contiguous to the Sinhalese district of Anuradhapura and which has been the focus of major colonization and village expansion projects, recorded a population increase of 394 percent during the same period. Trincomalee District and the combined districts of Amparai and Batticaloa have also been the focus of aggressive colonization by Sinhalese peasants, and population growth in these two districts has been as much as 192 and 166 percent, respectively, during this period. The Sinhalese population in the Eastern Province increased by 424 percent between 1953 and 1981.

Table 22. Distribution of Ethnic Communities in Predominantly Tamil Districts, 1953–1981

Districts	Ethnic Community	1953	1981	Population increase 1953–1981	Population increase (%) 1953–1981
	Tamils	477,586	812,247	334,661	70
	Sinhalese	5,902	4,615	−1,287	−22
Jaffna	Moors	6,394	13,757	7,363	115
	Others	1,967	493	−1,474	−75
	Total	491,848	831,112	339,264	69
	Tamils	28,223	68,178	39,955	141
	Sinhalese	2,097	8,710	6,613	315
Mannar	Moors	10,879	28,464	17,585	161
	Others	2,490	1,558	932	−37
	Total	43,689	106,910	63,221	145
	Tamils	25,913	142,803	116,890	451
Vavuniya	Sinhalese	5,934	19,824	13,890	334
and	Moors	2,844	10,417	7,573	366
Mullaitivu	Others	421	372	49	12
	Total	35,112	173,416	138,304	394
	Tamils		73,133		
	Sinhalese		15,541		
Vavuniya[a]	Moors		6,640		
	Others		255		
	Total		95,904		

continued

Table 22. (continued)

Districts	Ethnic Community	1953	1981	Population increase 1953–1981	Population increase (%) 1953–1981
	Tamils	37,511	93,510	55,999	149
	Sinhalese	15,273	86,341	71,068	465
Trincomalee	Moors	27,777	74,403	46,626	167
	Others	3,357	2,536	−821	−24
	Total	87,917	256,790	168,873	192
	Tamils	130,377	317,941	187,564	143
Batticaloa	Sinhalese	31,107	157,017	125,910	405
and	Moors	106,033	240,798	134,765	127
Amparai	Others	2,975	3,929	954	32
	Total	270,493	719,685	449,192	166
	Tamils		238,216		
	Sinhalese		10,646		
Batticaloa[a]	Moors		79,317		
	Others		2,720		
	Total		330,899		
	Tamils		79,725		
	Sinhalese		146,371		
Amparai[a]	Moors		161,481		
	Others		1,209		
	Total		388,786		
	Tamils	531,722	1,023,228	491,506	92
Northern	Sinhalese	13,933	33,148	19,215	137
Province	Moors	20,117	52,638	32,521	162
	Others	4,878	2,423	2,455	50
	Total	570,650	1,111,437	540,788	94
	Tamils	167,888	411,451	243,563	145
Eastern	Sinhalese	46,380	243,358	196,978	425
Province	Moors	133,410	315,201	181,791	136
	Others	6,332	6,465	133	2
	Total	354,010	976,475	622,465	175
	Tamils	699,610	1,434,679	735,069	105
Tamil	Sinhalese	60,313	276,507	216,193	358
Districts	Moors	153,527	367,839	213,912	139
	Others	11,210	8,888	−2,322	−21
	Total	924,660	2,087,912	1,168,165	127

Source: Robert N. Kearney, *Communalism and Language in the Politics of Ceylon,* p. 8; Editorial Notes, "Notes and Documents: Human Rights Violations and Ethnic Violence in Sri Lanka," p. 140.

[a]Vavuniya District was redrawn to include a portion of Anuradhapura District in 1979 and a portion of the Vavuniya and Mannar districts were combined to form the Mullaitivu District. Amparai District was carved out of the Batticaloa District in 1960 and hence the year 1953 cannot be used to determine its ethnic composition.

In the 1940s, Amparai was a sparsely populated portion of the Batticaloa District, but the Gal Oya River Basin Development project and government-sponsored colonization scheme of the 1950s contributed to the rapid growth of its population. By 1960, the area had been sufficiently colonized to warrant its status as a separate district. Its population grew by more than 83 percent between 1963 and 1981 and by as much as 22 percent between 1971 and 1980. To the Tamils, the state-sponsored colonization of Batticaloa District by Sinhalese settlers and the subsequent creation of Amparai District were contrived by Sinhala governments to weaken the Tamil stronghold in their traditional homeland. Sinhalese colonization of the Batticaloa District contributed to communal tension, and it is no surprise that Amparai District witnessed the first of the many communal disturbances that have plagued Sri Lanka since 1958. Amparai, Batticaloa, Mannar, and Trincomalee districts, which are targeted for Sinhalese colonization, registered the highest population increases between 1971–1981. During the same period, the overall increase for the island was 17 percent; the districts of Amparai, Batticaloa, Mannar, Trincomalee, and Vavuniya registered increases as high as 42.6, 28.9, 44.3, 36.4, and 59.3 percent, respectively.[36] The overall population of the combined Northern and Eastern provinces grew by 126 percent between 1953 and 1981, whereas the Sinhalese population increased by 358 percent; the Tamil population grew by 105 percent (see Table 22).

This resettlement of Sinhalese peasants in Tamil areas has drastically altered the ethnic composition of the Tamil districts; at least 165,670 Sinhalese were added to the population of the Northern and Eastern provinces in fewer than thirty years (see Table 8). This explains why the Sinhalese population increased dramatically from fewer than 46,500 in 1953 to as many as 243,000 in 1981, an increase of 424 percent. In contrast, the Tamil and Moor populations increased by only 145 and 136 percent, respectively, during the same period. Trincomalee District witnessed the highest level of growth for the Sinhalese population, due exclusively to colonization. The Sinhalese population in this district was approximately 15,270 in 1953, but by 1981 it had swelled to 86,280, an increase of 465 percent. In terms of actual numbers, Amparai District has the largest number of Sinhalese; the size of the Tamil population is only half that of the Sinhalese.

State-sponsored colonization schemes and gerrymandering have resulted in more political leverage for the Sinhalese living in some Tamil districts (see Table 23 and Figure 7). Sinhala governments have often redrawn and altered the size of districts in Tamil areas in order to facilitate greater representation of Sinhalese in the legislature. The size and number of districts in the Northern Province have been modified by gerrymandering, and Tamils are fearful they will soon become a minority in their own homeland. In order to create the Mullaitivu and Vavuniya districts, the combined area of Jaffna and Mannar was reduced from 4,920.32 to 4,074.6 square kilometers, a decrease of 845.72 square kilometers. In contrast, the combined size of Vavuniya and Mullaitivu districts has increased from 3,664.64 to 4611.3 square kilometers, an increase of 946.66 square kilometers.

Table 23. Ethnic Distribution and Parliamentary Representation in Sri Lanka, 1946–1977[a]

Year	Ethnic Community[b]	Population	% of Total	Elected M.P.'s	Weightage
1946	Sinhalese	4,621,507	69.2	68	71.0%
	Tamils	1,514,320	17.3	20	21.0%
	Muslims	408,823	6.2	6	6.3%
	Total	6,658,339		95 (Burghers 1)	
1953	Sinhalese	5,616,705	69.3	75	78.0%
	Tamils	1,818,801	22.9	13	13.6~
	Muslims	511,425	6.3	6	6.3%
	Total	8,097,895		95 (Burghers 1)	
1971	Sinhalese	9,146,679	71.9	123	81.0%
	Tamils	2,611,935	20.5	19	12.5%
	Muslims	853,707	6.7	8	5.3%
	Total	12,711,143		151 (Burghers 1)	
1977	Sinhalese	10,204,000	73.30	137	81.5%
	Tamils	2,644,000	19.00	21	12.5%
	Muslims	983,000	7.00	10	5.9%
	Total[b]	14,850,000		168	

Source: Department of Census and Statistics, *Statistical Pocket Book of the Democratic Socialist Republic of Sri Lanka,* 1981, 1982, 1983, and 1984; Robert N. Kearney, *The Politics of Ceylon (Sri Lanka),* p. 47; Robert N. Kearney, "Politics and Modernization," in T. Fernando and R. N. Kearney, eds., *Modern Sri Lanka: A Society in Transition,* pp. 57–81; Satchi Ponnampalam, *Sri Lanka: National Conflict and the Liberation Struggle,* p. 193; Walter Schwarz, *The Tamils of Sri Lanka,* pp. 13–14; Angelito Peries, "Historical Background of Genocide of Thamils in Sri Lanka," p. 14.

[a]The United National Party extended the tenure of parliament until 1989 by means of a referendum conducted in 1982.
[b]Includes Indian Tamils.

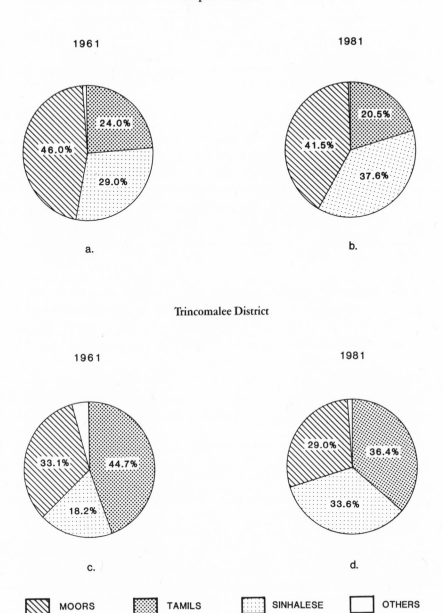

Figure 7. Major Commmunities in Amparai and Trincomalee Districts

This increase was accomplished by annexing portions of the Sinhalese Nuwaragam Plata North and Hurulu Plata North divisions of the Anuradhapura District (see Figure 8). The original southern boundary of Vavuniya District was restored in 1980. This annexation transferred the Padawiya colony from Anuradhapura District to Vavuniya District and raised the Sinhalese population of the district from 11.4 to 16.6 percent. Likewise, the percentage of Sinhalese residing within the original boundaries of the Batticaloa District was only 28 percent of the total population in 1981. In 1960, before the Amparai District was carved out, Tamils had represented approximately 48 percent of the population of the Batticaloa District. In 1981, Tamils comprised only 20 percent of the population of the new Amparai District and the Sinhalese 37.6 percent. The political leverage of the Sinhalese in the Eastern Province was further enhanced by the creation of two electoral districts that correspond to the Assistant Government Agent divisions where Sinhalese have been settled since the 1950s (see Figure 1). The Amparai Electoral District and the Seruwila constituency of the Trincomalee District are represented by Sinhalese members of parliament. Most of the Sinhalese population of the Trincomalee District is concentrated in the Seruwila Electoral District, which comprises the Assistant Government Agent divisions of Seruwila, Gomarankadawala, Morawewa, and Kantalai, where most of the Sinhalese reside.

In providing for electorates to be determined according to area and population the Soulbury Constitution of 1946 provided for adequate representation for minorities: one seat for every 1,000 square miles and one seat for every 75,000 inhabitants. Since twenty-five seats or 26.3 percent of the ninety-five seats in the legislature were allocated according to area, the minorities of the Northern and Eastern provinces were assigned 8.4 percent of the seats in the House of Representatives even before the seats were allocated according to population. The area provision did furnish adequate representation and protection against majority domination of the legislature until the 1970s. However, the population of the country almost doubled between 1946 and 1970, and the number of seats in the House of Representatives was accordingly increased to 151. The eight seats that were allocated according to area to the minorities of the Northern and Eastern provinces account, at the present time, for only 5.3 percent of all the seats in the legislature. Thus, the strength of the Tamils and the Muslims in the legislature has declined relative to that of the Sinhalese

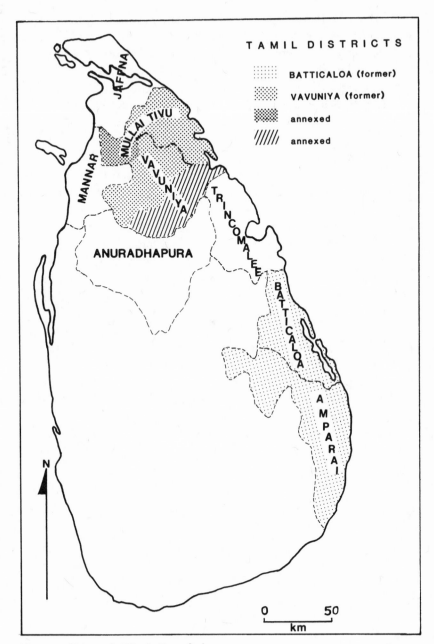

Figure 8. Changes in District Boundaries

(see Table 23). In 1977, the Sri Lankan Tamils and the Indian Tamils, who accounted for 20.5 percent of the total population of the country, had only 12.5 percent of the seats in the House of Representatives. On the other hand, the Sinhalese, who accounted for 73.3 percent of the population, were allotted 81 percent of the seats in 1977. The United National Party, which won 140 out of 168 parliamentary seats in 1977, extended the tenure of parliament until 1989 by means of a referendum.

The overrepresentation of the Sinhalese in the legislature is due partly to the disfranchisement of Tamils of Indian origin. The Indian Tamils elected seven representatives to the House of Representatives in 1946, but since 1949 only one has been elected to represent them in the legislature. They were not represented in the legislature between 1956 and 1976. In 1977, Indian Tamils constituted more than 6 percent of the total population but had only one elected representative in parliament. Indians have lived and worked in the hill country for nearly two centuries, but they have been deprived of their political rights. Yet, the thousands of disfranchised Indians are counted for purposes of electoral delimitations, so that more Sinhalese are elected from the hill country to parliament. Since these members of parliament are elected by a Sinhalese electorate they do not have to represent the interests of the Sri Lankan Indians. The Sri Lankan Tamils and the Tamils of Indian origin, as one group, constituted 18.1 percent of the total population, but had only 12.5 percent representation in the 1981 legislature. Therefore, while the Sinhalese comprised 73.98 percent of the total population in 1981, they enjoyed more than 81.5 percent representation. By denying voting rights to Indian Tamils, more seats have been created for members of the Sinhalese community than their population would warrant. Therefore, it is not surprising that one observer, commenting on the problems facing the Tamil minority in Sri Lanka, stated that "Ceylon, perhaps, is the only country in the world which has given weightage in representation to the majority community in the legislature at the expense of the minority."[37] Indeed, "the weightage introduced in favor of minority groups was now turned into weightage favoring the majority group. It is now possible for one of the major Sinhalese political parties to ignore the Tamil minority and still win an absolute majority in parliament."[38]

CHAPTER 5

The Tamil Move toward Eelam

DURING the nineteenth century, the British abandoned the separate systems of administration for Tamil and Sinhalese areas that the Dutch and Portuguese had employed and replaced them with a highly centralized unified form of government. Under this centralized government all decisions relating to the administration of provinces and the allocation of resources for development of rural districts were concentrated with the bureaucracy in Colombo, the capital of Sri Lanka. Plans for the economic development of the country were based upon generalized schemes that were applicable to the island as a whole, especially to the developed parts of the southwest rather than to the outlying rural districts. Officials and planners at the district level, who were knowledgeable of the local problems and environment, were rarely consulted or trusted when economic development plans were prepared for their districts. These practices contributed to the unbalanced development of regions, with most of the outlying districts lagging behind Colombo and other districts in the southwest.

When Sri Lanka became independent in 1948, local politicians and bureaucrats continued to deemphasize the devolution of specific decision-making powers to governing bodies at the district and provincial levels. Sri Lankan politicians and bureaucrats even compelled the Donoughmore Commission to abandon its recommendation for the establishment of provincial councils designed to decentralize administrative functions to provinces in the 1930s. It is also possible that Sinhalese communal pressure may have influenced the decision of the Donoughmore Commissioners not to pursue their recommendation on the devolution of administrative functions to provincial councils.[1] Apparently, the British were not concerned about developing backward-rural areas nor genuinely interested in safeguarding the rights of the Tamils. The Choksy Commission of 1956 recommended the establishment of regional councils but the United National Party was reluctant to carry out the recommendations for fear that it would turn Sinhalese extremists against them.[2] Had the recommendation of the commission to devolve specific decision-making functions to provinces been carried out, many of the controversies over Tamil rights, colonization, and regional autonomy might have been minimized and even avoided.

Demands for a Tamil Linguistic State within a Federal Union

Tamil demands for decentralization of administration began with the formation of the Federal Party under the leadership of S. J. V. Chelvanayakam in 1948. However, the Federal Party had to wait until the elections of 1956, when it received a clear mandate from the Tamil people, to devise a strategy for the creation of a semi-autonomous Tamil state within the framework of a "Federal Union of Ceylon." Indeed, the Federal Party would have limited its demands to the devolution of specific administrative functions to the Northern and Eastern provinces had the problems facing the Tamils been limited to discrimination in employment and in the allocation of resources for the economic development of Tamil areas. However, with the enactment of the Sinhala only legislation, plus state-sponsored Sinhalese colonization of Tamil districts, the Federal Party demanded the establishment of a Tamil linguistic state to be called "Thamil Arasu" within a federal union.

For Tamils, the desire to use their mother tongue for administrative purposes does not merely reflect their political sentiment but also indicates their linguistic competence. For over three centuries, when Sri Lanka was under British, Dutch, and Portuguese rule, more than 90 percent of the Tamil population three years and older were at the mercy of a few unscrupulous translators and others who were proficient in Portuguese, Dutch, and English to communicate with the government. Only a very small percentage of the population was proficient in these languages and thus able to work for their colonial masters. There is little doubt that Tamils were eager to become free from British domination; they wanted to educate their children and to communicate with the government in their mother tongue. To their disappointment, Sinhala was made the only official language of independent Sri Lanka and the Tamils continued to be aliens in their own land. Within ten years of independence, Tamils were debarred from using their mother tongue to secure employment and their leaders were largely excluded from the executive branch of government. They were denied funds to develop the economy of their districts and were deprived of their right to preserve their traditional homeland. To demonstrate their disapproval of discriminatory laws, they staged peaceful demonstrations, some of which were ignored while others were broken up by security forces. Indeed, since 1958 Tamils have been verbally threatened by Sinhalese extremists and, on occasion, targets of mob violence.

When the Tamils failed to secure any political concessions from Sinhala governments, they began to demand the establishment of a federal system of government. They claimed that a federal system of government would safeguard their language, preserve their traditional homeland, and permit them to live peacefully with the Sinhalese in a united Sri Lanka. Federalism, according to some Tamils, is the only solution to the ethnic problem. As they see it, Sri Lanka "can either become the Switzerland of the East—by following the middle path of negotiation, conciliation, and goodwill—or the Lebanon of South Asia. . . ."[3] They were prepared to accept a federal system of government with Sinhala as the official language but in which Tamil would be the language of administration and the medium of instruction in the Northern and Eastern provinces. A federal system of government, according to the Tamil federalists, would ensure employment opportunities for Tamil-speaking people in Tamil districts while at the same time exclude those Tamils who are not competent in the Sinhala language from securing employment in Sinhalese-dominated areas and in the central government. A federal system of government also appealed to the Tamils because it would deter the planned colonization of Tamil areas by Sinhalese.

Sinhalese extremists are, however, opposed to the granting of regional autonomy to Tamil areas because they claim it would lay the foundation for the revival of the Tamil kingdom of precolonial times. They believe it would pave the way for complete independence, although this claim cannot be substantiated with actual facts. Regional problems associated with multilinguistic societies have been solved by establishing a federal form of government in such large countries as Canada and in small countries such as Switzerland. Indeed, federal systems of government in these countries have served to allay the fears of minorities, averted national disintegration, and contributed to economic prosperity. To assure the Sinhalese that the Tamils will remain an integral part of Sri Lankan society, the Federal Party emphasized that the decision-making powers of the governing body in the Tamil state would be limited to lands, agriculture, fisheries, industries, education, and health. Federalists have always stressed that if the rights of Tamils were guaranteed, they would cooperate with the Sinhalese to develop a strong national economy. Such goodwill, they claim, could not be secured without the establishment of a federal system of government that would guarantee the Tamils the use of their language for administrative purposes, preserve their culture, provide employment opportunities for Tamils, and develop the Tamil areas according to the economic needs of the inhabitants without interference from the Sinhala government.[4] Federalists did not demand political independence but they had wanted some measure of economic independence.

There is no substance to Sinhalese claims that Tamils would seek foreign assistance to subjugate the Sinhalese once regional autonomy is granted under a federal set-up, since defense, foreign affairs, currency, transportation, and other essential services related to national security would be under the control of the central government. Instead of educating the public on the merits of federalism for multi-linguistic societies, Sinhalese leaders criticized Tamil demands as a ploy to create a separate state for them in the North. Even Tamil leaders did not educate the Tamil electorate on the concept of federalism, and many Tamils equated the decentralization of specific decision-making power to the Tamil provinces with the establishment of a Tamil kingdom or Thamil Arasu, which was the name of the Federal Party. Nevertheless, if the federalists had been serious about establishing an independent sovereign state for the Tamils, they would not have persisted in negotiating with Sinhalese leaders on issues pertaining to decentralization of administration to provincial councils. Indeed, Tamil leaders have consistently expressed their willingness to negotiate with governments to settle this ethnic problem to the mutual benefit of both communities. Some Sinhalese politicians, however, have been less willing to negotiate with the Tamil leadership on the ethnic issue than to "educate" the Sinhalese masses about the wrong reasons why regional autonomy should not be granted to Tamils. They have not communicated to the Sinhalese masses that the sharing of governmental power by authorities at the provincial level, under a federal system of government, would be limited to specific functions involving regional or rural development. Instead, they have, for their own political reasons, manipulated the regional autonomy issue and obstructed the government from granting even minimum concessions to the Tamils.

Regional Councils as an Alternative to Federalism

One of the most significant political concessions ever offered to the Tamils came in 1957 when Prime Minister Bandaranaike and Federal Party leader Chelvanayakam signed the Bandaranaike-Chelvanayakam Pact (see Appendix I).[5] In negotiating this settlement the federalists departed from their original plan for the creation of a semi-autonomous linguistic state within a federal union, while the Sinhala government granted limited concessions to Tamils on the sensitive issue of colonization of Tamil districts. Tamils consider the colonization issue to be the most serious of the problems facing them, since maintaining their traditional homeland is a prerequisite for the preservation of the Tamil language, for providing employment opportunities to Tamils, and for Tamils to live without fear in their own land. The Tamil federalists also sought concessions for Tamils in Sinhala areas, while being aware that Sinhala was the the only official language of Sri Lanka. They were satisfied that Tamil was to be made the language of administration in the Northern and Eastern provinces. It was already apparent that the federalists were no longer demanding that Tamil should have parity of status with Sinhala as an official language as long as Tamil was recognized as the language of a national minority. Federalists had insisted all along that Tamil should have the official status of a national language.

The main provisions of the pact were:

(a) Tamil should be recognized as the language of a national minority.

(b) Tamil should be the language of administration in the Northern and Eastern provinces while Sinhala would continue as the only official language of Sri Lanka, including the Northern and Eastern provinces.

(c) The Northern Province would form one single region and be served by one regional council while the Eastern Province should be divided into two or more regional council areas with prior approval of parliament.

(d) Two or more council regions could amalgamate even across provincial boundaries or one region could divide itself. "Regions could collaborate for common purposes" with prior approval of parliament.

(e) Council members would be elected directly by the people of the respective council areas. Electorates would be carved out by a Delimitation Commission.

(f) Regional councils would have authority over agriculture, lands, and land development, colonization, education, social services, fisheries, roads, electricity, and cooperatives. The council could not initiate major laws but would have the powers to make by-laws, similar to those granted to municipal councils.

(g) Regional councils would have the power to select those allotted to colonization schemes and also to appoint personnel to direct these projects.

(h) Block grants would be allotted to regional councils by the central government based upon an agreed formula. The regional councils would have the financial powers of taxation.

The provisions of the Bandaranaike-Chelvanayakam Pact were a marked departure from the concessions the federalists had demanded from the government on the issues of language and colonization. Foregoing their original position, they dropped their demands for parity of status for Sinhala and Tamil throughout the island. Instead, Tamil would be used for administration in the Northern and Eastern provinces, provided this did not conflict with the "Sinhala only" provision. They also accepted the status of Tamil "as a language of a national minority" instead of insisting upon the status of "national language." The Federal Party's proposal that Tamil provinces should have substantial legislative powers was dropped and instead substantial administrative powers were to be granted to regional councils. Although Sinhalese colonization of Tamil areas would be minimized under the proposed agreement, it would still be under the direct control of the Land Ministry in Colombo. The federalists thus sacrificed many of their original demands for the sake of reaching an honorable settlement with Sinhalese leaders.

The agreement was never enacted into law because of pressure from both Sinhalese extremists and the United National Party, which accused Bandaranaike of attempting to divide the country on a racial basis. It became apparent, once again, that Sinhalese politicians were willing to manipulate the ethnic issue at the risk of endangering the political stability of the country and its national unity, as long as it contributed to the political advantage of the party they represented. Contrary to Sinhalese claims, the proposed regional councils were merely glorified municipal councils and would not have had any powers to make laws or to contribute to the reestablishment of the Tamil kingdom in the North. Since the signing of the Bandaranaike-Chelvanayakam Pact in 1957, no other Sinhalese government has offered the Tamils concessions that included the provisions set out in the pact, and the Tamils, for their part, have been unwilling to accept any agreement that does not incorporate its major provisions, especially that of the regional councils.

Between 1960 and 1977, no significant progress was made toward devolution of administrative power to the provinces. Sinhalese leaders were reluctant to consider decentralization of administrative functions to governmental bodies at the provincial or regional levels. Instead, most of the subsequent discussions on devolution of administrative functions were restricted to district councils rather than regional councils. Srimavo Bandaranaike's Sri Lanka Freedom Party government (1960–1965), Dudley Senanayake's National Government (1965–1970), and Srimavo Bandaranaike's United Front (1970–1977) were all unwilling to revive the Bandaranaike-Chelvanayakam Pact as a means of devolving minimum administrative functions to governing bodies at the district level (see Appendix I).

Demands for an Independent, Sovereign State

S. W. R. D. Bandaranaike's government had granted some concessions to the Tamils in 1958 regarding the use of their language for administrative purposes in the Northern and Eastern provinces, according to the provisions of the Tamil Language (Special Provisions) Act No. 28.[6] These language concessions were, however, modified or ignored when Mrs. Bandaranaike's Sri Lanka Freedom Party enforced new regulations making Sinhala both the official language and the language of administration in the Tamil provinces. When the SLFP was defeated in the general elections of 1965, the coalition National Government was successful in enacting appropriate regulations for the use of Tamil for administrative purposes and as a medium of instruction in the Northern and Eastern provinces, according to the provisions of the Tamil Language (Special Provisions) Regulations, 1966 (see Appendix III).[7] No progress was made, however, toward resolving the issues of economic development in Tamil areas, cessation of colonization in Tamil areas, and devolution of administrative power to district councils.

The Tamils suffered a major setback to the progress they had made toward securing language concessions from the National Government when Srimavo Bandaranaike's United Front came to power. The United Front introduced the new constitution of 1972, which reaffirmed the position of Sinhala as the only official language of Sri Lanka without making any reference to the status of Tamil as a national language or as the language of administration in the Northern and Eastern provinces. The new constitution did not incorporate any safeguards guaranteeing the rights of minorities. It not only became difficult for Tamils to administer the Northern and Eastern provinces in Tamil, but they also found it increasingly unsafe to live in the Sinhalese-dominated South. By the mid-1970s, the Tamils had lost confidence in the ability of Sinhala governments to redress their grievances. In 1976, the Tamil United Liberation Front issued its manifesto demanding the creation of an independent Tamil state:

> . . . what is the alternative now left to the nation that has lost its rights to its language, rights to its citizenship, rights to its religion and continues day by day to lose its traditional homeland to Sinhalese colonization? What is the alternative now left to a nation that has lost its opportunities to higher education through "standardisation" and its equality of opportunities in the sphere of employment? What is the alternative to a nation that lies helpless as it is being assaulted, looted and killed by hooligans instigated by the ruling race and by the security forces of the state? Where else is an alternative to the Tamil nation that gropes in the dark for its identity and finds itself driven to the brink of devastation?
>
> There is only one alternative and that is to proclaim with the stamp of finality and fortitude that we alone shall rule over our land our forefathers ruled. . . . Hence the TULF seeks in the General Elections the mandate to the Tamil nation to establish an independent, sovereign, secular, socialist state of Tamil Eelam that includes all the geographically contiguous areas that have been the traditional homeland of the Tamil-speaking people in the country.[8]

The TULF manifesto also stated that Eelam would be ultimately established "either by peaceful means or by direct action or struggle." Despite this vow TULF members, for the most part, continued to negotiate with the government in hopes of finding a solution to the ethnic problem. In all of these negotiations TULF members claimed that Sinhala governments had deliberately neglected the economic development of the Tamil-majority areas. They stressed that the governments had ignored Tamil demands for a greater share of the national growth and that Tamil districts, particularly Jaffna, have consistently lagged behind many Sinhalese districts in the amount of capital invested in large-scale development projects. The TULF maintained its willingness to negotiate with the government on the issue of decentralization of administrative and legislative functions to regional councils even after the 1977 parliamentary elections when the UNP was returned to power and TULF candidates enjoyed a huge victory that demonstrated the extent to which the Tamil community supported its demands. TULF members stressed that in order to achieve a more balanced regional development of the island, the national government should be willing to decentralize specific decision-making functions to provincial governments.

The Integrated Rural (District) Development Program of 1976

Since 1957, successive governments have failed to introduce appropriate legislation to decentralize administrative functions to provinces or districts in order to encourage them to initiate development projects. However, Mrs. Bandaranaike's United Front government initiated the Integrated Rural (District) Development Program (IRDP) of 1976 "in an attempt towards the achievement of a more balanced regional development in Sri Lanka."[9] Programs and projects initiated under IRDP have been vigorously pursued by the United National Party government because the World Bank and other international funding agencies will grant loans for projects involving rural development schemes as long as there is some measure of decentralization of administrative functions to districts. The IRDP did not, however, involve any decentralization of administrative functions to districts as envisaged by Tamil leaders. Tamil leaders had hoped that many of the rural districts in the Northern and Eastern provinces could be developed by the establishment of district councils, especially when rural development plans can be initiated at the district level, but the United Front and the UNP governments had refused to accept Tamil proposals. Instead, the UNP government adopted the IRDP to develop rural districts. It was disappointing to the Tamils to know that while the United Front and the UNP governments were reluctant to decentralize administrative functions to regional councils, they devised alternative plans to develop rural districts, although such plans did not originate at the regional level.

The UNP government is required to follow the guidelines set by the World Bank and other international funding agencies in order to finance rural development projects under the Integrated Rural Development Program. The IRDP permits planners, administrators, and members of parliament at the district and provincial levels, who are better informed than the bureaucrats at the national level, to identify the specific problems facing their areas and to devise appropriate strategies to solve them.[10] Decentralization of administrative functions to local bodies is deemed a prerequisite for the success of rural development projects, and the government accomplished this by establishing a "decentralized budget, the appointment of district Political Authorities, followed by the appointment of District Ministers," and by enhancing the "role played by Members of Parliament in Government's administrative and development activities at the district level."[11] Indeed, the Sri Lankan government would not expect to receive financial support from outside funding agencies for its rural development projects without having devised appropriate administrative arrangements for elected members of parliament to have some voice in the development of their respective areas. Even the type of rural development projects initiated by the government under the Integrated Rural Development Program are those that the World Bank and other funding agencies or countries are willing to support projects that would improve agricultural productivity; increase the supply of irrigated water for crops; set up processing facilities for agricultural commodities such as canned fruits, vegetables, and fish; establish small- and medium-scale industries to process edible oils, manufacture sugar, fertilizer, textiles, small farm implements, and cement; and improve education, health, and infrastructure in rural areas.[12] The World Bank, for example, is favorably disposed toward granting funds for rural development schemes which are designed to raise productivity of rural farmers.[13] Following the recommendations of funding agencies, Sri Lankan governments were successful in financing many projects at the district level between 1979 and 1982.

Since the inception of the IRDP, large sums of capital, most of it in the form of grants from foreign sources, have been invested in the development of Sinhalese districts.[14] Integrated Rural Development Programs were implemented in the Sinhalese districts of Kurunegala (1979), Matara (1979), Hambantota (1979), Nuwara Eliya (1980),

Matale (1981), Puttalam (1981), and Badulla (1982). The first IRDP project was implemented in the Kurunegala District in 1979 to improve its infrastructure, rural electrification, water supply, education, and health at a cost of Rs. 465 million. This project is also associated with irrigation and water management to improve paddy production. Approximately Rs. 200 million for this project was funded through the International Development Association (IDA) of the World Bank. Between 1976 and 1981 similar development plans were initiated for:

(1) Matara District at a total cost of Rs. 75 million from a grant from the Government of Sweden;

(2) Hambantota District at a total cost of Rs. 147 million from a grant from the Government of Norway, a project that also involved the restoration of the Kirama-Oya irrigation scheme;

(3) Nuwara Eliya District at a cost not specified but with funds committed by the Netherlands government for the preparation of a rural development program and its implementation;

(4) Puttalam District at a total cost of Rs. 300 million, from a plan developed and evaluated by the World Bank;

(5) Matale District at an approximate cost of Rs. 780 million, more than Rs. 250 million of which was provided by the World Bank; and

(6) Badulla District at a cost of Rs. 369.5 million with funds from IFAD and SIDA.[15]

Almost Rs. 2 billion were targeted for developing rural districts under the IRDP projects during the period 1979 to 1982, yet, no single project was implemented in Tamil districts until 1984 when Mannar and Vavuniya districts were brought under this program. Indeed, many IRDP and major river basin projects have been financed from foreign sources involving large sums of money to improve Sinhalese districts. It is true that the United States had a water project in Point Pedro in the Jaffna Peninsula, but "the foreign aid utilization in the Jaffna District for the period 1977–1982 was almost nil."[16] Therefore, while the Integrated Rural Development Program has the approval of the World Bank and other countries that are funneling large sums of money toward rural development at the district level in Sri Lanka, no effort was made by the UNP government to improve the depressed economy of rural districts in Tamil areas, particularly in Jaffna. Rather than merely promising to redress the grievances of the Tamils, as pledged in its election manifesto of 1976, and even before appointing a presidential commission to deal with those grievances, the UNP government should have initiated development projects in Tamil areas under the IRDP. The Jaffna District should have been one of the first districts to be developed under the program, since it is one of the few districts that has not benefited from agricultural investment programs since the 1950s.

District Development Councils

The United National Party conceded in 1977 that some of the Tamil grievances were justified and that appropriate measures would be adopted to resolve these problems. Based on the recommendations of the Presidential Commission, appointed in 1979 to inquire into these grievances, the District Development Councils Act No. 35 was enacted in September 1980 defining the composition, structure, powers, and responsibilities of the proposed district councils.[17] Provisions were made to establish one District Development Council (DDC) in each of the island's twenty-four administrative districts. The DDCs are composed of: (1) a district minister who is a member of parliament of the governing party but does not necessarily represent the people of the district where he serves as minister; (2) members elected to the council every four years and members of parliament of the district (the number of members elected directly to the council would not normally exceed the number of members of parliament representing the district); and (3) an executive committee comprised of the chairman of the council, the district minister, and two appointed members selected by the district minister in consultation with the chairman and with the approval of the president.[18] The chairman of the council will represent the party that receives the highest number of votes in the district council elections and is therefore chosen directly by the people.

The DDC scheme is basically an economic plan intended to end discriminatory government policies that have blocked the development of rural agricultural districts. The law-making functions of the councils are limited, even though they have the power to prepare plans for agricultural and industrial development for their respective districts. The councils also have control over the location of industries and the selection of workers who are to be employed in major economic enterprises. They may collect and levy local taxes according to local needs. They exercise control over the planning and maintenance of schools and provide improved educational opportunities to more students in rural districts. They are democratically constituted, members of the council and their chairmen being elected directly by the people of the district. The district minister is, however, appointed by the president and is responsible only to him or her. On paper, specific administrative functions have been transferred to district governments so that the people of all twenty-four districts can upgrade their economy by developing agricultural and industrial projects.

Some consider the legislative and executive functions of the DDCs as reflecting the "roles of both cabinet and parliament at the central government level";[19] and the elected members of the council, the chairman of the council, and the district minister have powers and responsibilities that correspond to those performed by the members of parliament, the prime minister, and the president, respectively. The structure and associated administrative arrangements of the DDCs may have been partially intended to satisfy prospective foreign donors, such as the International Monetary Fund and the World Bank, which have stressed the need to decentralize specific decision-making functions to provincial governments in order to develop rural areas.[20] The DDC plan is the only agreement negotiated between a Sinhala government and Tamil leaders within the last quarter century that became law, because the DDCs were not meant to resolve the language and colonization issues, which were conveniently set aside.

The TULF and the Tamil people hoped that the DDC plan would solve some of the pressing problems facing them. The TULF believed that the DDCs would provide a means to deal with the lack of employment, food, and basic manufactured items in Tamil districts. Even with their limited administrative functions and restricted powers the DDCs can, nevertheless, in consultation with the relevant ministries in Colombo, prepare annual development plans involving "agriculture, food, land use, settlement, animal husbandry, small and medium industries, health, education, etc."[21] Funds for DDCs are generated from rates and taxes that are subject to parliamentary approval. Funds were derived from "fines, proceeds from sales, property revenues, funds allocated by parliament (currently fixed at the number of MPs in a district multiplied by Rs. 2,500,000), separate grants allocated by the appropriate ministers, loans, donations, and direct assistance of one kind or another."[22] To finance development projects, the DDCs can raise taxes locally, receive allocations from the center, obtain loans within Sri Lanka, and even "negotiate loans directly with external lenders, with the approval of the Minister of Finance and Foreign Affairs."[23]

The establishment of the District Development Councils, as anticipated, did not solve the problems of language and colonization; it was never meant to. The TULF assumed that the constitutional provisions for the use of Tamil as a language of administration in the Northern and Eastern provinces would also be effectively implemented with the establishment of district councils. To their disappointment the DDCs did not solve the problems of language, colonization, and development of Tamil areas.[24] Using the existing structure of the administrative districts, both the DDCs and the IRDP were designed to encourage balanced regional development at the district level rather than to implement the provisions of the Tamil Language (Special Provisions) Regulations of 1966 and to halt Sinhalese colonization of Tamil districts. While it is true that the DDCs are democratically constituted, this does not mean that the decision-making authority has been truly devolved to district councils or that development plans need not be approved by the relevant ministries. It is equally true that while the initiation and implementation of development plans are at the district level, the council's power to implement projects can be restricted if there is a lack of funds or if a council's decision conflicts with that of the district minister. The DDCs could have been used effectively to develop Tamil districts had the district ministers and others, who were chosen to administer the DDCs, cooperated with the chairmen and members of the councils. Moreover, some of the Tamil leaders, who demanded a greater degree of regional autonomy for Tamil areas, were opposed to their functioning and did not cooperate with the government to carry out the DDC plan. A district minister, who was chosen from the ruling party by the president, was not directly responsible to the people of other districts, especially of the Tamil districts and often succeeded in blocking any plans that were contrary to the government's policies or which gave undue economic advantage to a Tamil district.

In reality the DDC plan is an administrative arrangement designed to transfer government functions from the central government to the districts. The district minister has to abide by the decisions of his governing party on issues relating to colonization and can thus block any decisions made by the council that might prohibit allottees from Sinhalese districts from settling in newly developed colonization schemes in Tamil districts. The executive committee of a council has no power to override the wishes of the district minister in case of disagreements because the DDCs Act (No. 35 Part XII) specifies that the president can dissolve the executive committee if the committee does not go along with the district minister's wishes. Moreover, the president can also dissolve a district council by accusing them of being incompetent. Even when a district minister goes along with a council on a controversial project with the prior approval of the line ministries involved, there is always the possibility that the decision will be overridden by the parliament, the president, or both.

The District Development Council chairman and officials encountered serious problems in implementing the DDCs. Bruce Matthews, who interviewed the DDC chairman and the government agent of Jaffna District in 1983, indicates that certain powers that were to be devolved from the ministries of finance, health, and education to the DDC, as proposed in the DDCs Act, were not transferred. The government agent stated that he did not receive the cooperation of government ministries to administer the district or even to implement projects vital to the community, such as expanding the Jaffna General Hospital.[25] Government ministries and departments have even blocked the implementation of development projects that were passed by the chairman and members of the DDCs in Tamil districts. Thus it is apparent that, while on paper the DDCs were supposed to devolve governmental powers to districts in order to satisfy Tamil demands, the chairmen and members of the DDCs were not always able to implement projects they considered essential to local communities. Instead of cooperating with the members of DDCs, the ministers were intent on controlling and restricting the powers of the elected representatives of districts.

The most serious factor limiting the effectiveness of the DDCs was the lack of financial resources. Funds to administer the DDCs were limited because, just as the DDCs were being established, the International Monetary Fund discovered that the Sri Lankan government treasury had been spending generously on items quite beyond agreed-upon limits. In fact, no measures were adopted by the treasury to set aside funds for the new DDC budget. Because there was little support within the bureaucracy to allocate funds to DDCs, those funds were cut back sharply. The revenue from local taxes was insufficient to support local projects, especially when the DDCs were reluctant to raise local taxes, given the state of the local economy in many districts. The funds allocated for old works and new projects for districts have been small and, "considering the wide range of projects that the DDCs may wish to engage in, the budget so far has been completely limited in scope."[26] The government's 1982 allocation for new works under the district budget for the Jaffna District was approximately $1 million, and this was too small to bring about substantial progress toward improving the depressed economy. The Tamils had hoped that large sums of money would be funneled into the Tamil districts via the DDCs to develop major irrigation, agricultural, industrial, and road transportation projects. However, very little public investment has gone into the Tamil areas. Indeed, the government continued its policy, under the guise of having granted substantial concessions to Tamils by establishing the DDCs, to reduce the "once prosperous northern Tamil districts to near destitution and have convinced more than a few Ceylon Tamils that its real aim is tantamount to genocide."[27]

The establishment of District Development Councils did not help to resolve the ethnic problem and the militant separatists continued to push for a violent solution. Likewise, the army continued to use violence against innocent civilians in retaliation for attacks on police stations, army units, government establishments, and government informants by militants. This cycle of violence led ultimately to the trauma of the anti-Tamil 1983 riots, which compelled the government to convene an all-party conference on January 10, 1984, to work out a peaceful settlement to the ethnic conflict. The Indian government persuaded members of the TULF to participate in the conference by convincing them that an acceptable alternative to their demand for a separate state had been negotiated between Indian and Sri Lankan officials, as recorded in the document referred to as Annexure C (see Appendix IV).

Annexure C and the President's Proposals

The TULF found the Annexure C proposals acceptable because they provided for some regional autonomy for Tamil provinces. As noted earlier, the proposals also empowered regional councils to have jurisdiction over large areas; to enact laws on specific subjects; to maintain internal law and order; to administer justice; to undertake social and economic development; to have control over cultural matters and land policy; and to collect funds to initiate development projects.

Because of pressure from Sinhala extremists and opposition parties, the president did not present the proposals at the all-party conference as expected, substituting instead a modified version of the 1980 District Development Councils concept, which the TULF rejected. Negotiations went forward despite the TULF rejection, however, and after nearly eighteen months of talks and continued violence by both separatists and security forces, a ceasefire was arranged. The Thimphu peace talks collapsed because the government failed to present any new proposals that deviated markedly from the original draft proposals on District Development Councils. In rejecting the government's proposals, the TULF reiterated that the Tamil people would not accept any proposals which do not: (1) recognize a Tamil linguistic region, constituting the Northern and Eastern provinces; (2) grant regional autonomy to Northern and Eastern provinces; (3) empower regional bodies in Tamil provinces to enact laws on certain specified subjects relating to social and economic development and maintenance of law and order; and (4) recognize Tamils as a distinct ethnic group in Sri Lanka. It is apparent that the TULF and the separatist groups will agree to a political settlement to the ethnic problem only if an "acceptable and viable alternative" to a separate state is offered by the Sri Lankan government.

By January 1986, various Tamil leaders were united in their demand for the establishment of a federal form of government for Sri Lanka, in which the Northern and Eastern provinces would be recognized as a Tamil linguistic state within the federal union. It is as though the Tamils are beginning to take up again their original demand for the establishment of a federal form of government as envisaged by S. J. V. Chelvanayakam's Federal Party in the 1950s.

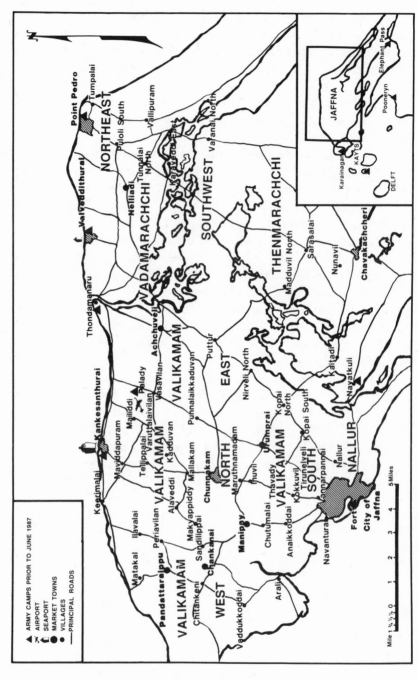

Figure 9. Jaffna Peninsula

Epilogue

SINCE this study was completed in December 1985, dramatic changes have developed in the military strengths and tactics adopted by the Sri Lankan troops and Tamil militants in the intensifying war, in the domination of one militant group over the others in the battle for control of Tamil areas, and in the positions taken by the Sri Lankan government and Tamil leaders on the questions of defining the precise powers to be devolved to provincial or regional councils and identifying the territorial limits of a Tamil linguistic region formed by the linkage or merger of the Northern Province and a major portion of the Eastern Province. Following the collapse of the Thimphu talks and subsequent negotiations, violence was renewed with greater vigor as the negotiators failed to narrow the gap that existed between the expectations of Tamil leaders and the proposals submitted by the government.

Both the government and Tamil militants had used the cease-fire to strengthen their respective military positions and, by the end of 1985, the government was in a much stronger position to launch military operations against militants in the Northern and Eastern provinces. The Sri Lankan government had gradually built up its forces in 1985 by purchasing new helicopter gunships, light aircraft, gunboats, new armored personnel carriers, small arms, and artillery from Pakistan, Israel, and South Africa. Government forces were also trained by SAS British mercenaries, the Israeli Secret Service, and Pakistani military personnel in guerrilla tactics to fight Tamil militants and to fly helicopter gunships and light aircraft. Likewise, Tamil militant groups were well placed to purchase arms in the open market and to operate training camps in South India. They became better equipped and trained in the use of surface-to-air missiles and rocket-propelled grenades, in the placing of land mines to blow up vehicles transporting army personnel, in the use of remote devices to blow up buildings, and in confronting government forces in the open.

At the outset, the government concentrated its military operations in the Eastern Province, where troops mounted a series of attacks on Tamil villages in order to flush out militants. The victims were mostly civilians, many of whom were killed or rendered homeless. Unlike in the Northern Province, the ethnic composition of the population in the Eastern Province has been radically altered by more than forty years of aggressive policy of settling Sinhalese in the predominantly Tamil areas, particularly in the Assistant Government Agent Divisions (AGA Divisions) of Kantalai, Thampalagamam, Morawewa, Gomarankadawala, and Seruwila, as well as in the Urban Council area of Trincomalee in the Trincomalee District. Except for the Kantalai, Seruwila, Gomarankadawala, and Morawewa AGA Divisions, where the Sinhalese are in the majority, Tamil-speaking people predominate in all the other AGA Divisions, including the Thampalagamam AGA Division. The region that lies between Seruwila AGA Division and Kantalai AGA Division and the area that lies within and around the Trincomalee Urban Council limits have become the sites of especially fierce battles waged between government troops and Tamil militants.

Of the 111 army camps distributed in the Northern and Eastern provinces, 36 are located in the Trincomalee District, with 23 serving the area around the town and port of Trincomalee. Tamil militants control the region north and west of the town, where most of the war of terror and counterterror has been fought with government troops and Sinhalese home guards. Thousands of Tamils living in the town of Trincomalee, and in the villages north and west of Trincomalee, such as Nilaveli, Srimapuram, Kuchchaveli, Kanniya, and Thampalagamam, have been killed and their homes and shops burned since August 1985. Because there is a greater ethnic mix in many of these areas, Tamil militants are less entrenched and are vulnerable to attacks by government troops. In an attempt to regain control of these areas, the army conducted a ruthless campaign by burning towns and thereby displacing thousands of Tamil villagers. Tamil militants, for their part, retaliated by attacking Sinhalese peasant colonies and fishing villages in the Eastern Province and thwarted other efforts by the present government to settle refugees from the predominantly Sinhalese community, on sites which were vacated by

Tamils who had fled to the relative safety of refugee camps. Tamil militants considered these attempts by the government to settle Sinhalese refugees to be a deliberate attempt to change the ethnic composition of critical areas in the Eastern Province, so that the merger of the Northern and Eastern provinces into a single Tamil linguistic province, which the militants insist is required for a political settlement of the ethnic conflict, can never be achieved. Violence in the Batticaloa, Mullaitivu, Mannar, and Vavuniya districts continued unabated as government forces and home guards attempted to drive out Tamils from these districts while furnishing protection to Sinhalese villages against militant attacks. More than 100,000 Tamils were rendered homeless in the Northern and Eastern provinces by September 1986 as a result of these military actions. In the Mullaitivu District alone, an estimated 11,000 Tamils were housed in eight refugee camps while twenty-eight refugee camps sheltered as many as 30,000 Tamils in the Eastern Province. In Vavuniya, there were approximately 3,000 Tamils in six camps, but a large number of Sinhalese had begun to leave this district for the Anuradhapura area many months prior to September 1986.

Once the government had accomplished the task of driving out thousands of Tamil inhabitants from vital areas of the Eastern Province through its "search and destroy" operations and was convinced that it would ultimately win its war against militants in this province, it launched an attack against the Tamil stronghold in the Northern Province, particularly the Jaffna Peninsula. The tough stand taken against certain Tamil leaders by the Indian government following the collapse of the Thimphu talks may have given the green light for the Sri Lankan government to declare that Tamil demands for the creation of a single linguistic state were unacceptable and that the government could therefore seek a military solution to the ethnic conflict. In March 1986, the government launched an all-out offensive from the land, air, and sea against militants in the Jaffna region. The aerial bombardments from light aircraft of densely populated Tamil areas, which resulted in the killing of many civilians, prompted international condemnation, as well as censure by some members of human rights and nongovernmental organizations at the 42nd session of the United Nations Human Rights Commission held at Geneva in February and March 1986. India threatened to pull out as a mediator and its External Affairs Minister even accused the Sri Lankan government of perpetrating genocide. The Indian government, however, succeeded in convincing the Sri Lankan government to withdraw its military offensive and set up a time-frame of one month in which to resume serious negotiations. This involved the submission of a counterproposal to the proposals presented by the Tamil United Liberation Movement (TULF) early in 1986. The Sri Lankan government was also aware that, in order to avoid a reduction in foreign aid allocations, a peace settlement had to be negotiated before June of 1986, when a meeting of the country's main aid donors was to take place.

The Sri Lankan government's counterproposals, which were submitted in April of 1986, provided for the establishment of separate provincial councils. These proposals were an improvement over the previous proposals, which placed more emphasis on the devolution of administrative functions to district councils and provincial councils, but the package was not intended to satisfy the militants who had all along insisted that unless provisions were incorporated that would recognize the right of self-determination for Tamils and provide for the establishment of a single Tamil linguistic state that would be administered by a regional council, they would reject them. TULF refused to commence direct talks to thrash out its differences with the government as long as the killing of civilians by government troops continued unabated. In a public statement to the news media, Mr. Amirthalingam of the TULF criticized the proposals on grounds that substantial powers would not be devolved to a Tamil linguistic province, which could be formed by merging the Northern and Eastern provinces. Even before the terms of the proposals were made public, Tamil militants launched a series of systematic bomb attacks at various locations in Colombo, including the explosion aboard the Air Lanka Tristar which killed foreign tourists for the first time. They also exploded a bomb at the Central Telegraph Office. These bomb attacks outside the Jaffna region may have been designed to display their strength and as retaliation for the bombing of the Jaffna Peninsula in March 1986. Nevertheless, the government used these incidents and the TULF's rejection of its counterproposals as excuses to resume its major military offensive against the Tamil stronghold in the Jaffna Peninsula. The government referred to the bombing of the national airline as an act of international terrorism and appealed to Western democracies to assist Sri Lanka in its war against Tamil militants.

The Sri Lankan government launched its major offensive against

Tamil militants in the Jaffna Peninsula immediately after an episode of internecine warfare among the Tamil militants in May 1986. In the power struggle for the control of the Jaffna region, the Tamil Eelam Liberation Organization (TELO) was effectively wiped out by the LTTE, but this did not imply that the Tamil militant resistance was psychologically weakened. The LTTE regrouped quickly and deployed the arms seized from the TELO to defend the peninsula against the three-pronged attack of the army, navy, and air forces. Army advances into the town of Jaffna were halted by militants, who kept up attacks with mortars and rocket-propelled grenades and mined roads as well. The LTTE was able to repulse the attacks from land but was helpless in trying to defend the peninsula against aerial bombardment. In fact, when government troops failed to link up on land, the government resorted to aerial attacks. After week-long fierce fighting in which more than a hundred civilians were killed, government troops were driven back into their barracks. Bombs dropped from planes damaged the General Hospital, teaching institutions, and commercial buildings in the densely populated town of Jaffna, and shelling from gunboats in the east coast of the peninsula destroyed fishing villages and rendered many people homeless. Nevertheless, government plans to link up troops stationed in various camps were foiled and the army continued to be confined to its camps. Roads leading to these camps continue to be mined and the armed militants who are dug in behind sandbags keep constant surveillance over the camps.

The ability of Tamil militants to keep government troops in their camps has brought welcome relief to the people of the peninsula. The army, consisting almost entirely of Sinhalese, had been dispatched periodically to Jaffna since 1958 in order to break up peaceful demonstrations staged by Tamils who wanted to show their disapproval of laws and regulations directed against them. After the militant groups began their violent campaign against the government in 1977 by attacking troops and destroying public buildings, the Jaffna Peninsula and its adjoining islands were placed under military occupation. Sinhalese troops often reacted to attacks with indiscriminate brutality, which often took the form of burning homes, commercial buildings, libraries, and buildings of historical importance, including Hindu temples, and by killing civilians. By 1986, the army camps were under siege, and supplies to these camps had to be delivered by air and sea. Large areas around many of these camps, especially around the Palali Airport and the Jaffna Fort, have been declared security zones and many civilians have been made homeless. Nevertheless, people have resumed normal life in the peninsula although they live in fear of being harassed by army personnel.

The LTTE has taken over the civil administration of the area, maintaining law and order and supplying food and gasoline to the people of the region by purchasing them from the government. The government supplies electricity to the region through the LTTE, which in turn, collects payments for electricity bills. It has also begun to levy taxes at border crossings and on such items as cigarettes and cement to maintain the civil administration. In addition to the Jaffna Peninsula, many populated areas in the Northern Province are under the control of the LTTE, but its domination of the Eastern Province is limited to Tamil areas, where it has blown up army convoys and waged pitched battles with government troops. The Eelam People's Revolutionary Front (EPRLF) was eliminated from the Jaffna Peninsula in December 1986, but the EPRLF, TELO, the Eelam Revolutionary Organization of Students (EROS), and the LTTE continue to operate outside the northern region under the direction of leaders from Tamil Nadu. PLOTE in a recent statement declared that it had suspended its activities in the northern part of Sri Lanka. The competition for control among the militant groups has been shifted to the Eastern Province, and whether the LTTE can overshadow the EPRLF in this province is not certain. It is feasible, however, that the LTTE may coordinate its efforts with EROS and PLOTE, which claim to have substantial support among the Tamils and Muslims of the province, in order to regain some of the areas they lost to government troops in 1985. Nevertheless, the LTTE, whose members have shown very little inclination to compromise on certain issues, is the most dominant force in Tamil areas.

The Sri Lankan government withdrew its offensive after meeting resistance from the militants and after the Indian government condemned the aerial bombings of densely populated areas and threatened to abandon its role of mediator. Moreover, the United States government had asked the Sri Lankan government to cease military action and to seek a political solution. Donor nations, too, became impatient with the escalation of violence, but the killings and reprisals continued into June 1986, as each group tried to drive out the other from vital areas in the Trincomalee District. Tamil militants carried out many bombings, including an explosion in a passenger train, and the bombing of a cement factory in Trincomalee and the soft-drink bottling plant in Colombo, which killed eight people and injured forty. As the violence escalated, public pressure from both within and outside the country compelled the government to revive the peace process. During and just prior to the Jaffna offensive, Indian diplomatic efforts were considered by the Sri Lankan government to be a stumbling block to a settlement of the ethnic problem. By mid-June, however, the government became very sensitive to international condemnation of its military operation, including its concern that the donor countries of the Aid Consortium, which was to meet in Paris on June 19, 1986, might reduce their aid allocation to Sri Lanka if it did not seek a political settlement to the ethnic problem.

On June 18, 1986, only one day before the meeting of the Aid Consortium, the Sri Lankan government published a cabinet-approved peace plan and announced that it would summon a Political Parties Conference (PPC) on June 25, 1986, to discuss its draft proposals for the devolution of greater governmental power to the nine provincial councils in such matters as maintenance of internal law and order, education and culture, land settlements within the province, and agriculture and industry. The TULF boycotted the PPC because of the continuing aerial bombardment of heavily populated Tamil areas in the north and the massacre of Tamils by government troops and home guards in the Eastern Province. It was apparent that the government was determined to demonstrate to the militants that government forces were still in command of the situation, despite the temporary setback in Jaffna. The Sri Lanka Freedom Party (SLFP) boycotted the conference because it claimed that the territorial integrity of Sri Lanka would be sacrificed if the government's proposals were to become law and that too many concessions were being offered to the Tamils. The SLFP, therefore, continued to espouse its policies along pro-Sinhalese communal lines, as has been its tradition since 1956. The Indian government backed the proposals, claiming that they seemed practical enough for resumption of talks and for negotiating alternative provisions that would perhaps allow for possible merger of the Northern and Eastern provinces, which the TULF proposed earlier.

In July 1986, the Indian government persuaded the TULF to enter into direct negotiation with the Sri Lankan government and Tamil militants to agree to a cease-fire. TULF leaders, who strongly believed that any political settlement of the ethnic problem should have the approval of the militants, discussed the main provisions of the proposals with their leaders before meeting with government negotiators in Colombo. The government, however, made it known, from the outset, that it intended to introduce legislation to give effect to its proposals, with or without amendments, even if the various Tamil leaders rejected them. As expected, the provisions dealing with the devolution of powers to provincial councils and the territorial limits of the Tamil linguistic region were found to be unacceptable to the leaders of the TULF and the militant movements. President Jayewardene later declared that he would not introduce the promised legislation unless the militants laid down their arms.

This rejection of the proposals offered by the Sri Lankan government came only one week after the Tamil Nadu police in South India had arrested more than a thousand Tamil militants, including the leaders of EROS, EPRLF, LTTE, PLOTE, and TELO and had confiscated a large number of weapons, ranging from machine guns to surface-to-air missiles, as well as communications equipment. The immediate cause for this crackdown may be attributed to three incidents that were alleged to have been instigated by Tamil militants, one resulting in the shooting of an Indian citizen by a militant and the others involving militant raids on two villages. The timing of this crackdown may have been done as a gesture of goodwill to President Jayewardene, who was to attend the South Asian Association for Regional Cooperation Conference held in Bangalore from November 15 to 17, 1986, and perhaps to put pressure on the militants to accept the government's proposals. The Indian government did not abandon the peace process and is reported to have ordered the Tamil Nadu government to release the communications equipment in order to persuade the militant leaders to have direct talks with Indian negotiators while another group of Indian government negotiators had separate talks with the Sri Lankan government spokesmen. Leaders of the militant groups talked with Indian negotiators, but they rejected the Sri Lankan proposals, since they did not provide for real merger between the two provinces. Indeed, the Sri Lankan government's proposal to carve three provinces out of the Eastern Province, one for each community, was completely contrary to the basic demands of the Tamils that the integrity of their traditional homeland must be preserved at any cost. Despite the failure of the peace talks, however, the fact that the militants, especially the LTTE, were willing to have a dialogue with Indian officials indicates that, for the first time, Tamil leaders were willing to abandon their demand for total independence and seek regional autonomy for a Tamil linguistic state within Sri Lanka.

To the LTTE, the portion of the Jaffna Peninsula where it provides security to the inhabitants, maintains law and order, runs the civil administration, and collects taxes represents part of the Tamil linguistic state. The LTTE even abandoned its supposedly original plan to declare the Jaffna Peninsula an independent region on January 1, 1987. In fact, the LTTE and other militant groups did not entirely reject the government's proposals but merely commented on certain provisions which they felt were inadequate to meet their basic demands. These changes have had a positive impact on the LTTE's relationship with the Sri Lankan government, since the government was willing to have direct talks with the LTTE on ways to solve the ethnic problem.

Three factors might have convinced the government to talk with the LTTE. First, the TULF and the militant groups, especially the most powerful, the LTTE, have shown a willingness to abandon their demand for total independence for Tamil areas and to seek regional autonomy within Sri Lanka. Second, the government had become impatient with India's mediator role since little progress was made in the latter half of 1986 in persuading Tamil leaders to accept government proposals. Third, since the LTTE emerged as the most dominant militant group during the closing days of 1986, the government found it desirable and convenient to negotiate with it directly, since it could speak for other groups and thus holds the key for negotiating a lasting settlement to the ethnic problem. The first direct contact between the government and LTTE resulted in the release of two soldiers, who were held by the latter, in return for two militants. The representatives of the government had a second meeting with the LTTE in December 1986 on the possibility of starting talks to end the conflict. Although the LTTE insisted that, as a prerequisite for commencing talks, Indian participation was essential and that all Tamil political prisoners and detainees should be released, it did not totally reject the idea of commencing peace talks with the government.

With the dawn of 1987, there appeared to be a temporary setback to the peace process, since the Sri Lankan government suspended delivery of gasoline and kerosene to the Jaffna Peninsula in retaliation for the LTTE's moves to issue car license plates, perhaps using

Tamil script, for a fixed fee. Even at this stage, when the prospects of a negotiated settlement look promising, the Sri Lankan government could cut off supplies of essential items, including electricity, and launch an all-out attack on the Jaffna Peninsula in order to crush the militants. Indeed, events of the past three years have shown that there can be peace one day and war the next, and it is difficult to predict whether there will be a prolonged war or a peaceful settlement of the ethnic issue in the immediate future.

The prospects for ending the ethnic conflict in the near future can be evaluated in the light of the dramatic changes that have developed since mid-1985. The Sri Lankan government, which represents the Sinhalese people, is resolved to use its enhanced military capability to uphold the privileged position of Sinhalese-Buddhists on the island and to preserve the territorial integrity of Sri Lanka for the Sinhalese. Leaders of the militant movements, particularly the LTTE, believe that they have the endorsement of the Tamil people to use any form of military tactics to free the Tamils from Sinhalese domination, to preserve their distinct nationality, and to defend the territorial integrity of their traditional homeland in northern and eastern Sri Lanka. Indeed, the Sinhalese and the Tamil people have not, as yet, staged any mass protests to disapprove the policies and tactics that have been adopted by the government and the militants to achieve their respective objectives. It might seem that given the conflicting claims of Sinhalese and Tamils regarding their inalienable rights and privileges in Sri Lanka, there are no solutions to the ethnic problem. However, their conflicting claims can be resolved through the establishment of a Tamil linguistic region within the framework of a federal union of Sri Lanka without endangering the goals of the Sinhalese-Buddhist nation to preserve its identity.

The developments that have occurred since early 1986 regarding the attitudes of both the government and Tamil militants toward their respective demands warrant examination. The government was serious about its original proposals on district councils but later abandoned them and proposed the establishment of provincial councils. Later it proposed, among other options, the possibility of redrawing the provincial borders to create a Tamil majority region in the Eastern Province and link it with the Northern Province by a narrow corridor through a newly created Sinhalese majority region. Although the proposal to carve out a Sinhalese-majority province, a Tamil-majority province, and a Muslim-majority province out of the Eastern Province was rejected by the Tamil leaders as being completely contrary to their basic demands, the fact the government was willing to propose the creation of any Tamil linguistic region is encouraging. This does not imply that the prospects for a compromise are bright. There remain many conflicting issues on the devolution of powers to provincial councils and on the question of merging the Northern Province with a large portion of the Eastern Province. In particular, Tamil leaders questioned the government's rationale for establishing nine provincial councils if they were primarily designed to resolve the ethnic problem. Furthermore, the Tamil leaders would want the Indian government to underwrite and monitor any kind of settlement.

Militant leaders perhaps were compelled by external factors to abandon their original demands for a separate Tamil state and to negotiate for a Tamil linguistic state, preferably within the framework of a federal constitution. This major change may have been a response to the policy of the Indian government, according to which that government opposes the creation of any independent state in India or Sri Lanka. Militants are also increasingly cognizant of the fact that they need to be friendly with India in order to secure the latter's support to monitor and enforce the terms of any proposals that might be negotiated with the government, as well as to ensure the safety of Tamils in Sri Lanka. Nevertheless, most of the militant leaders, especially in the LTTE, are hardliners who would not accept proposals that were not designed to end all aspects of discrimination against minorities and guarantee, among other conditions, the economic development of Tamil-dominated areas, the preservation of the ethnic composition and territorial integrity of their traditional homeland, and the right of the Tamils to live without fear of Sinhalese mobs and the armed forces. By the mid-1980s, moreover, militant groups, especially the LTTE, were in a position to enter peace negotiations from a position of strength.

Had the same package of proposals submitted by the government at the Political Parties Conference in 1986 been implemented unilaterally by this or previous governments in the 1960s or 1970s, the Tamils would have wholeheartedly accepted them. Tamil leaders are reluctant to accept the proposals now for many valid reasons. First, many Tamils are distrustful of the government's intentions and express doubt that it will implement the proposals, especially given pressure from Sinhalese extremists. Second, it will take many years before the majority of Tamils forget the inhumane treatment they were subjected to during the anti-Tamil riots, especially during 1983, and the atrocities perpetrated against civilians by the army of occupation. From 1977 on, government troops have taken advantage of the Prevention of Terrorist Act and Emergency Regulations to arrest hundreds of innocent Tamils, in addition to unleashing violence on the civilian population. Past reports of Amnesty International, including its September 1986 publication, provide testimony to the fact that hundreds of Tamils have disappeared after mass arrests and were killed and tortured during detention. The inflamed passions that have been aroused among the Sinhalese and Tamils by the brutal killings of their loved ones, friends, and neighbors, as well as the burning of homes, which has forced thousands into refugee camps, will take many years to subside. To think that people who were directly and indirectly affected by the violence will return to the devastated areas of Trincomalee, Batticaloa, and Vavuniya and live peacefully as members of an ethnically mixed community is unrealistic. Under these circumstances, the government has had to come to grips with the uncompromising demand for a Tamil linguistic region, comprising the Northern Province and a large portion of the Eastern Province, where Tamil-speaking people can live peacefully.

Questions have been posed by the government on the difficulties of merging the Northern and Eastern provinces because of the presence of a large number of Sinhalese villages in the Trincomalee District, especially around the town and port of Trincomalee and in the Seruwila, Thampalagamam, Kantalai, and Gomarankadawala AGA Divisions. It is feasible to merge Kantalai, Morawewa, and Gomarankadawala with the North-Central Province, while Thampalagamam and the region north of Trincomalee, which have become desolate because of the violence, can form a link between the Northern and Eastern provinces. To avoid further violence and to end the practice of stationing government troops in Tamil-dominated areas, every attempt should be made by the government to designate separate regions or divisions for the Tamil and Sinhalese communities. This would necessitate the movement of the Sinhalese population from the Seruwila and its surroundings to Sinhalese-dominated areas. Indeed, the Allai peasant colonization scheme was initiated by a previous government to settle Sinhalese peasants in Seruwila and in surrounding AGA Divisions. The town of Trincomalee and its surroundings, which have become a ghost region except for the presence of a large number of Tamil refugee camps, should be part of the Tamil linguistic region, while the port of Trincomalee can be administered from Colombo. In the south, the Amparai Electoral District can be merged with the Sinhalese-dominated Uva Province, while the Batticaloa District and a large portion of the Amparai District could form part of the Tamil linguistic region. Constitutional arrangements, however, would have to be made to permit the Muslims, who form the dominant community in the southern portion of the Eastern Province, to administer it as a district within the Tamil-speaking linguistic region.

The desire of the Tamils to establish a Tamil linguistic province by merging portions of the Northern and Eastern provinces can be attributed to many factors. One, the Tamils have always insisted that the Eastern Province is an integral part of the Tamil traditional homeland and that its ethnic composition was deliberately altered by the government's policy of settling Sinhalese in this province. Nevertheless, it is irrelevant whether Tamils constitute the dominant community, but it is important to recognize that Tamils and Muslims, who have lived for centuries as members of the Tamil-speaking community, constitute the vast majority of people in the Eastern Province. Sinhalese settlements were intentionally established in strategic locations in the Eastern Province to alter the contiguity that has traditionally existed between the densely populated Tamil areas of the Northern and Eastern provinces. Most of the fierce fighting between government troops and militants in Trincomalee District was to secure control of vital areas where the Northern and Eastern provinces merge. Tamil leaders of various groups insist that the merger of the Northern and Eastern provinces is a prerequisite for commencing any serious negotiations with the government.

Second, the Northern Province is not as agriculturally and industrially developed, given the large size of its population, compared to other provinces in the Dry Zone. Lack of water resources has limited the capacity of the province to expand the area under cultivation and to raise the yield of various crops. Moreover, since the mid-1950s, its economic development has been neglected by Sinhala-dominated governments. The Northern Province, therefore, relies on other provinces and urban centers to feed its people, to purchase fertilizer, and to market its onions, tobacco, chillies, potatoes, and grapes. The Eastern Province can supply a large quantity of the food that is needed to feed thousands of people who live permanently in the

Northern Province, as well as those who moved into the province as a result of the 1983 anti-Tamil riots. More than a half-million Tamils, many of whom now live as refugees in Tamil districts and those who will return from India and elsewhere once a peace settlement is reached, have to be fed also. Therefore, if the Tamil linguistic region is to be economically viable, the Eastern Province should remain an integral part of it.

Third, the Northern Province lacks productive farmlands to resettle refugees and to rehabilitate large numbers of militants, who have to be compensated for surrendering their arms. The Eastern Province can meet some of the immediate needs of the refugees and militants. It will take decades before the war-torn Tamil areas can be revitalized. Fourth, to avoid the recurrence of communal violence, adequate measures should be taken to ensure that Tamil-speaking people and Sinhalese live in separate regions. It is because of the ethnic mix that Trincomalee District ranks as the leader among districts in the numbers of army camps, in the number of incidents of killings and reprisals, in the number of people rendered homeless, and in the number of refugee camps. Indeed, Tamil militants would be reluctant to relinquish their arms, accept an offer of amnesty by the government, and settle in unsafe areas with ethnically mixed populations where there would always be the possibility of renewed violence and the reappearance of army camps. Under these circumstances, the militants would refuse to surrender their arms. On the other hand, Tamil militants would be required to disarm in order to assure the Sinhalese people that the Tamil linguistic state would pose no danger, actual or potential, to the Sinhalese. Finally, a merger of the Northern and Eastern provinces would facilitate the development of major projects by making it feasible to pool the resources of a large region.

Although many of the provisions in the government's PPC proposals were drawn from the Indian Constitution, as presented in the Chithamparam Papers, prepared by the minister in the central government representing Tamil Nadu, some of the critical provisions were modified to ensure that the Sri Lankan parliament and the president would have overwhelming authority over the provincial councils. In particular, executive power was to be vested with the governor, an appointee of the president, rather than with the elected provincial councils; governors of Indian states hold ceremonial positions, except during times of emergency. Moreover, the draft legislation empowered the parliament to override the legislative authority of the provincial councils and allowed the president to assume emergency powers over the provinces, even when there was no officially proclaimed emergency, in order to deploy the national police and the security forces in the provinces. Even the powers devolved to the provincial councils on matters relating to higher education, land development and land settlement, interprovincial irrigation, and the maintenance of law and order were found to be inadequate. Moreover, no provisions were made in the draft legislation to ensure that provincial councils, especially of the Tamil areas, would be provided with adequate financial resources, from either local or foreign sources, to initiate major development projects and to rebuild the war-torn Tamil areas. Finally, the proposed legislation did not guarantee the territorial integrity and sovereignty of Tamil provinces since the parliament in Colombo had the power to alter any provisions in the constitution, including altering the boundaries of provinces, by a two-thirds majority.

The December 19, 1986, proposals, which were submitted by the Sri Lankan government, were intended to address some of these problems. The Sri Lankan government and Indian mediators had agreed on a plan that called for the merger of a portion of the Amparai District, where the Sinhalese are in a majority, with the Moneragala District and for the recognition of the remaining portions of the Eastern Province as a Tamil linguistic province. If this plan were to be implemented, Tamils would constitute nearly 50 percent and Muslims 35 percent of the population of Eastern Province, respectively. According to this proposal, the Eastern Province would function as separate unit, although the Northern and Eastern provinces would have a single government, the same judicial system, and one university system. This plan, however, did not satisfy Tamil demands for the merger of the Northern and Eastern provinces, especially since the Sinhalese-dominated AGA Divisions in the Trincomalee District would still be an integral part of the Tamil linguistic province. In addition, the constitutional provisions relating to the executive power of the governor and the ease with which provisions can be altered by a two-thirds majority in parliament did not guarantee adequate constitutional safeguards against discrimination by the Sinhalese majority. Whether the Tamil militants would have accepted this plan with further modification is not certain, but the possibility was not pursued by the Sri Lankan government, for no apparent reason. Nevertheless, there was some hope that a breakthrough in the crisis was imminent in December 1986, even though Tamil militants were reluctant to negotiate with the Sri Lankan government and assumed the responsibility of running the civil administration of the Jaffna Peninsula, which had become virtually an independent region.

The government imposed an embargo on fuel, food, and medical supplies on the Jaffna Peninsula, and its security forces embarked on a military offensive in the region in January 1987 in retaliation for the militant takeover of the civil administration. Although attempts made by the security forces to move out of their camps were foiled by Tamil militants, air raids and shellings from the Jaffna fort caused extensive damage to the nearby buildings, such as the main hospital, schools, shops, and temples in the city. In addition to the civilian killings in the city of Jaffna, shelling from gunboats resulted in the death of civilians in the coastal towns of Myliddy and Valveddithurai. The Indian government tried, without success, to compel the Sri Lankan government to end its embargo and to stop the killing of civilians. The LTTE demanded that the 2,000 Tamil detainees, who were held in the Boosa camp, be released and the fuel embargo lifted before they would commence peace talks with the government.

The violence continued unabated for more than three months, and in April 1987, the Sri Lankan government declared a unilateral ceasefire to coincide with the Sinhalese and Tamil new year. The government also declared that it was prepared to lift the embargo and resume peace talks if the militants observed the cease-fire. The ceasefire ended abruptly when more than 125 Sinhalese civilians were machine-gunned to death in a remote jungle near Trincomalee and more than 100 people, most of them Sinhalese, were killed when a bomb exploded in a crowded bus station in Colombo. The government claimed that the LTTE and the EROS perpetrated these violent incidents for the sole purpose of stifling the peace talks and launched a major offensive against Tamil militants. The LTTE and the EROS denied responsibility. This offensive was also triggered by criticisms leveled by SLFP against the UNP for the latter's inability to protect the Sinhalese population and for the lawlessness, as well as the economic problems, that the country faces.

By the end of May 1987, government forces succeeded in occupying a large portion of the Vadamarachchi AGA division, which includes the coastal towns of Valveddithurai, the birthplace of LTTE leader V. Prabakaran, and Point Pedro. The military occupation of this region was accomplished by destroying coastal towns, temples, and homes and by killing civilians in the interior villages. This military offensive compelled large numbers of people in the Vadamarachchi area and a large area around the Palali Airport to evacuate their villages and take shelter in the densely populated AGA divisions, such as Valigamam North, where there is already a scarcity of food, fuel, and medicine due to the embargo. Yet the government refused to permit the International Red Cross and reporters to enter the Jaffna Peninsula in order to relieve the suffering of the people. This prompted some Indian leaders to accuse the Sri Lankan government of conducting genocide against the Tamils and for Tamil leaders to claim that the government was using its tightly controlled media to publicize atrocities that were perpetrated against Sinhalese civilians while refusing to divulge pertinent information on the devastating effects of its military offensive on the civilian population in the Jaffna Peninsula.

In early June, India announced that it intended to furnish much-needed fuel, food, medicine, and clothing to the war-torn area of the Jaffna Peninsula through the Indian Red Cross, transporting relief supplies in a flotilla of fishing boats. On June 3, the day before the boats sailed from South India, more then thirty Sinhalese civilians, most of whom were Buddhist monks, were savagely killed near Amparai by fifty armed men. The government blamed the LTTE for this and other violent acts against Sinhalese civilians. Given the spate of incidents involving raids on paramilitary camps in Sinhalese areas by a left-wing extremist Sinhalese group (identified by the Sri Lankan government as the People's Liberation Front (JVP) it is possible that these acts may have been carried out by groups other than the LTTE and the EROS in order to sabotage the peace talks and create anarchy in the country. On June 4, the Indian fishing boats carrying relief supplies and ninety reporters were forced by the Sri Lankan Navy to return to the South Indian port of Rameswaram, but the supplies were later dropped from Indian transport planes to the people of the Jaffna Peninsula over the objections of the Sri Lankan government, which accused India of violating Sri Lanka's independence and its territorial integrity.

India's insistence on furnishing relief supplies to the Jaffna Peninsula has major implications. First, people from all parts of the subcontinent supported the Indian government in carrying out this relief mission as "a token of India's deep and abiding concern for the suffering of the people of the Jaffna Peninsula." India's position was that the mission was a humanitarian gesture on the part of the people of India, especially when other relief agencies, including the Red Cross, were barred from furnishing relief supplies. Second, although India has not provided military protection to the people of the Jaffna Peninsula, it was prepared to meet the challenge of the Sri Lankan Air Force in the event that its planes were forcefully prevented from dropping supplies. This bold move was intended to reiterate India's policy that any move by either the Sri Lankan government or Tamil militants to resolve the ethnic conflict militarily will be resisted by India. Indeed, India is strongly committed to a peaceful resolution of the ethnic problem and is vehemently opposed to the creation of a separate Tamil state or to any attempt of the Sri Lankan government to subjugate the Sri Lankan Tamils and to dictate the terms under which the latter would be governed. Third, India has gained the respect of Sri Lankan Tamils, including the militants, for carrying out the daring mission. Therefore, the militants might be willing to accept a political settlement, provided that India is prepared to underwrite that settlement. Thus, India is in a stronger position to persuade Tamil militants and the Sri Lankan government to compromise on certain issues related to the government's December 19 proposals, which have stood in the way of negotiating a settlement.

The Sri Lankan government did not halt its military offensive after India dropped relief supplies to the people of the Jaffna Peninsula. Government forces continued to take control of other coastal towns, including Kankesanthurai, the main port of the Jaffna Peninsula, and contemplated advancing toward the city of Jaffna. On June 10, 1987, however, the government announced that it had completed its mission of securing control of the northern coastal towns in the peninsula. It also declared that it had no intention of moving toward the city of Jaffna and called for the resumption of peace talks. Control of the northern coastal towns had been secured in order to stop the flow of military supplies from South India; the city of Jaffna, a militant stronghold, was avoided. Moreover, a southern advance through the heart of Valigamam North AGA division, which is one of the most densely populated rural areas in South Asia, would have resulted in the slaughter of thousands of civilians.

Although the militants are not capable of defending against aerial bombardment, the closely knit settlements, with their tall fences and market gardens, furnish adequate protection for the militants to carry out successful assaults against government troops. Nevertheless, even if the militants are totally defeated and the peninsula comes under the direct control of the government, the ethnic conflict will not be resolved. Indeed, Tamil militants will continue to carry out their operations elsewhere and regain their foothold on the Jaffna Peninsula. Moreover, the odds of the Sri Lankan government or any other government defeating a guerrilla army, which has the support of the local populace, is virtually impossible. Therefore, if there is to be national reconciliation and lasting peace in Sri Lanka, the government must make every effort to negotiate a peace settlement with Tamil leaders, especially the Tamil militants.

A political settlement that will promote national reconciliation can only materialize if Tamil-speaking people, both Tamils and Muslims, are permitted to conduct their own affairs, through a democratically constituted provincial assembly or council vested with substantial legislative and executive powers in matters that effect their economic and social well-being. There is little doubt that there would be national reconciliation and peace in Sri Lanka if the proposed provincial council of the Tamil linguistic region, formed by the linkage of the Northern and Eastern provinces, were vested with substantial powers, similar to those possessed by states in a full-fledged federal system of government. Now that India has the leverage to convince both the militants and the Sri Lankan government to modify their respective demands for total independence or preservation of the unitary character of the constitution, the best hope for a peaceful settlement exists.

10 JUNE 1987

The Bandaranaike-Chelvanayakam Pact
July 26, 1957

Statement on the General Principles of the Agreement:

"Representatives of the Federal Party had a series of discussions with the Prime Minister in an effort to resolve the differences of opinion that had been growing and creating tension.

"At the early stages of these conversations it became evident that it was not possible for the Prime Minister to accede to some of the demands of the Federal Party.

"The Prime Minister stated that from the point of view of the government he was not in a position to discuss the setting up of a federal constitution or regional autonomy or any step which would abrogate the Official Language Act. The question then arose whether it was possible to explore the possibility of an adjustment without the Federal Party abandoning or surrendering any of its fundamental principles and objectives.

"At this stage the Prime Minister suggested an examination of the government's draft Regional Councils Bill to see whether provisions can be made under it to meet reasonably some of matters in this regard which the Federal Party had in view.

"The agreements so reached are embodied in a separate document.

"Regarding the language the Federal Party reiterated its stand for parity, but in view of the position of the Prime Minister in this matter they came to an agreement by way of an adjustment. They pointed out that it was important for them that there should be a recognition of Tamil as a national language and that the administrative work in the Northern and Eastern Provinces should be done in Tamil.

"The Prime Minister stated that as mentioned by him earlier that it was not possible for him to take any step that would abrogate the Official Language Act.

USE OF TAMIL. "After discussions it was agreed that the proposed legislation should contain recognition of Tamil as the language of a national minority in Ceylon, and that the four points mentioned by the Prime Minister should include provision that, without infringing on the position of the Official Language Act, the language of administration in the Northern and Eastern Provinces should be Tamil and any necessary provision be made for non-Tamil speaking minorities in the Northern and Eastern Provinces.

"Regarding the question of Ceylon citizenship for people of Indian descent and revision of the Citizenship Act, the representatives of the Federal Party forwarded their views to the Prime Minister and pressed for an early settlement.

"The Prime Minister indicated that this problem would receive early consideration.

"In view of these conclusions the Federal Party stated that they were withdrawing their proposed satyagraha."

JOINT STATEMENT BY THE PRIME MINISTER AND REPRESENTATIVES OF THE FEDERAL PARTY ON REGIONAL COUNCILS:

"(A) Regional areas to be defined in the Bill itself by embodying them in the schedule thereto.

"(B) That the Northern Province is to form one Regional area whilst the Eastern Province is to be divided into one or more Regional areas.

"(C) Provision is to be made in the Bill to enable two or more regions to amalgamate even beyond provincial limits; and for one Region to divide itself subject to ratification by Parliament. Further provision is to be made in the Bill for two or more regions to collaborate for specific purposes of common interest.

DIRECT ELECTIONS. "(D) Provision is to be made for direct election of regional councillors. Provision is to be made for a delimitation Commission or Commissions for carving out electorates. The question of M.P.'s representing districts falling within regional areas to be eligible to function as chairmen is to be considered. The question of

Government Agents being Regional Commissioners is to be considered. The question of supervisory functions over large towns, strategic towns and municipalities is to be looked into.

SPECIAL POWERS. "(E) Parliament is to delegate powers and specify them in the Act. It was agreed that Regional Councils should have powers over specified subjects including agriculture, cooperatives, land, land development, colonization, education, health, industries and fisheries, housing, and social services, electricity, water schemes and roads. Requisite definition of powers will be made in the Bill.

COLONIZATION SCHEMES. "(F) It was agreed that in the matters of colonization schemes the powers of the Regional Councils shall include the powers to select allottees to whom land within their area of authority shall be alienated and also power to select personnel to be employed for work on such schemes. The position regarding the area at present administered by the Gal Oya Board in this matter requires consideration.

TAXATION AND BORROWING. "(G) The powers in regard to the Regional Councils vested in the Minister of Local Government in the draft Bill to be revised with a view to vesting control in Parliament wherever necessary.
"(H) The Central Government will provide block grants to Regional Councils. The principles on which the grants will be computed will be gone into. The Regional Councils shall have powers of taxation and borrowing."

Source: Government of Ceylon (Sri Lanka), House of Representatives, *Parliamentary Debates (Hansard)*, vol. 30, cols. 1309–1311.

The Senanayake-Chelvanayakam Pact, March 24, 1965

1. Action to be taken early under the Tamil Language Special Provisions Act (No. 28 of 1958), to make provision for the Tamil language to be the language of administration and of record in the Northern and Eastern Provinces. Mr. Senanayake also explained that it was the policy of the Party that a Tamil-speaking person should be entitled to transact business in Tamil throughout the island.

2. Mr. Senanayake stated that it was the policy of his party to amend the Language of the Courts Act to provide for legal proceedings in the Northern and Eastern Provinces to be conducted and recorded in Tamil.

3. Action will be taken to establish District Councils of Ceylon vested with powers over subjects to be mutually agreed between the two leaders. It was agreed, however, that the Government should have power under the law to give directions to such Councils in the national interest.

4. The Land Development Ordinance will be amended to provide that Citizens of Ceylon be entitled to allotment of land under the Ordinance. Mr. Senanayake further agreed that in granting land under Colonization Schemes the following priorities to be observed in the Northern and Eastern Provinces:

(a) Land in the Northern and Eastern Provinces should in the first instance be granted to landless peasants in the District;

(b) Secondly, to Tamil-speaking persons resident in the Northern and Eastern Provinces; and

(c) Thirdly, to other citizens of Ceylon, preference being given to Tamil residents in the rest of the island.

Source: S. Ponnampalam, *Sri Lanka: The National Question and the Tamil Liberation Struggle*, pp. 259–260.

APPENDIX III

Tamil Language (Special Provisions) Regulations, 1966

1. These regulations may be cited as the Tamil Language (Special Provisions) Regulations, 1966.

2. Without prejudice to the operation of the Official Language Act No. 33 of 1956, which declared the Sinhala language to be the official language of Ceylon the Tamil Language will be used:

(a) In the Northern and Eastern Provinces for the transaction of all the Government and public business and the maintenance of public records whether such business is conducted in or by a department or institution of Government, a public corporation or a statutory institution; and

(b) for all correspondence between persons other than officials in their official capacity, educated through the medium of Tamil language and any official in his official capacity, or between any local authority in the Northern and Eastern Provinces which conducts its business in the Tamil Language and any official in his official capacity.

3. For the purpose of giving full force and effect to the principles and provisions of the Tamil Language (Special Provisions) Act No. 28 of 1958, and these regulations all Ordinances and Acts, and all Orders, Proclamations, rules, by-laws, regulations and notifications made or issued under any written law, the Government Gazette and all other official publications, circulars and forms issued used by the Government, public corporations or statutory institutions, shall be translated and published in the Tamil language also.

Source: Government of Ceylon, *Sri Lanka* (Colombo: Department of Public Information), February 1, 1966, p. 4.

Annexure C

In terms of paragraph six of President's statement of December 1st, 1983, the following proposals which have emerged as a result of discussions in Colombo and New Delhi are appended for consideration by the All-Party Conference. These proposals are in the context of unity and integrity of Sri Lanka and will form the basis for formulating the Agenda of the All-Party Conference.

(1) The District Development Councils in a Province be permitted to combine into one or more Regional Councils if they agree by decisions of the Councils and approved by Referendum in that district.

(2) In the case of District Councils of Northern and Eastern Provinces, respectively, as they are not functioning due to the resignation of the majority of members, their union within each province to be accepted.

(3) Each Region will have a Regional Council if so desired. The convention will be established that the leader of the party which commands a majority in the Regional Council would be formally appointed by the President as the chief minister of the Region. The Chief Minister will constitute a Committee of ministers of the Region.

(4) The President and the Parliament will continue to have overall responsibility for all subjects not transferred to the Region and generally for all other matters relating to maintenance of sovereignty, integrity, unity, and security and progress and development of the Republic as a whole.

(5) The legislative power of the region would be vested in the Regional Councils which would be empowered to enact laws and

exercise executive powers in relation thereto on certain specified listed subjects including the maintenance of Internal Law and Order in the Region, the administration of justice, social and economic development, cultural matters and land policy. The list of subjects to be allocated to the Regions will be worked out in detail.

(6) The Regional Councils will have powers to levy taxes, cess of fees and to mobilize resources through loans, the proceeds of which will be credited to a Consolidated Fund set up for that particular Region to which also will be credited grants, allocations or subventions made by the Republic. Financial resources will be apportioned to the Region on the recommendations of the representative Finance Commission appointed from time to time.

(7) Provisions will be made to constitute High Courts in each region. The Supreme Court of Sri Lanka will exercise appellate and constitutional jurisdiction.

(8) Each Region will have a Regional Service constituting (a) officers and public servants of the Region and (b) such other officers and public servants who may be seconded to the Region. Each Region will have a Regional Public Service Commission for recruitment and for exercising disciplinary powers relating to the members of the Regional Service.

(9) The armed forces of Sri Lanka will reflect the national ethnic composition. In the Northern and Eastern Provinces the police force for internal security will also reflect the ethnic composition of these Regions.

(10) A Port Authority under the Central Government will be set up for administering the Trincomalee Port and Harbour. The area that will come under the Port Authority as well as the powers to be assigned to it will be further discussed.

(11) A national policy on land settlement and the basis on which the government will undertake land colonization will have to be worked out. All settlement schemes will be based on ethnic proportion so as not to alter the demographic balance subject to agreements being reached on major projects.

(12) The Constitution and other laws dealing with the official language Sinhala and the national language Tamil be accepted and implemented as well as similar laws dealing with the National Flag and Anthem.

(13) The Conference should appoint a committee to work out constitutional and legal changes that may be necessary to implement

these decisions. The Government will provide its secretariat and necessary legal offices.

(14) The consensus of opinion of the All-Party Conference will itself be considered by the United National Party Executive Committee and presumably by the executive body of the other parties as well before being placed before Parliament for legislative action.

Source: *Tamil Times*, October 1984, p. 5.

President's Proposals to All-Party Conference

The President's Proposals

The following are the proposals presented by the Sri Lankan President Mr. J. R. Jayewardene, to the All-Party Conference:

"System of Government: The basic unit of government to be the pradesheeya mandalaya covering an assistant government's area. The actual composition of its members will have to be decided.

"The next units to be urban councils and municipal councils as at present constituted.

"The third unit should be district councils and their composition and methods of elections and powers and functions will have to be redefined. The area of operation to be the present districts.

"The district councils will be directly elected by the people of the districts. The chairman and the vice-chairman would be the first and second names in the list of the party receiving the highest vote, if elections were to be held on the basis of proportional representation.

"Inter-district co-ordination and collaboration: Inter-district co-ordination to be permitted in defined spheres of activity. District councils must vote for this co-ordination. If they wish to have a referendum in the district a referendum should be held.

"If units are constituted for this purpose they should include the chairman and the vice-chairman of each district council and a limited number of additional representatives elected by each district council. The relationship between such institutions and the district councils from which they are constituted has to be worked out.

"Second Chamber: There are several precedents where the instrument of a second chamber has been successfully employed to ensure a more equitable exercise of political power by all members or sectors of a multi-ethnic society.

"To that extent, if any proposal to establish inter-district collaboration or cooperation is required well-defined spheres of activities may well be examined, since this proposal offers the possibility of various combinations of two or more districts for different purposes as well as establishing co-ordinating bodies for inter-district functional operations. The chairman and the vice-chairman of each district council would be ex-officio members of the Second Chamber. Since these members of the Second Chamber are those who enjoy the confidence of the majority of the members of the district council or the units of co-ordination between districts, the Second Chamber would be a reservoir for the purpose of appointing Ministers to function for inter-district co-ordinating units.

"Ministers who enjoy the support of the majority in either the inter-district co-ordination units or in a district council could be appointed by the President and removed also by him. Their functions, duties and obligations have to be discussed. The question of these Ministers being answerable to the co-ordinating units in the exercise of their executive functions will have to be studied and a procedure for implementing any decisions taken will have to be worked out.

"Composition of the Second Chamber: With regard to the composition, the powers and functions of the Second Chamber, consideration should be paid to President's memorandum presented to the All-Party Conference on the second chamber proposal on July 23rd 1984.

"The Second Chamber may be constituted with adequate representation for all major and minor ethnic communities.

"Provisions may be made for the representation of minority communities from districts where there are substantial or significant concentrations of such minority communities. The district councils in respective districts could also elect or nominate such members. Thus the four ethnic groups on the island, the Sinhala, Sri Lankan Tamils and Tamils of recent Indian origin and Muslims should be represented in such a way as to ensure representation which will create a source of fair participation.

"The two members from each district to be elected at the same time and as at a general election. The second chamber's term of office, therefore, coincides with that of the first chamber. When there is a dissolution of parliament, it would mean the dissolution of both chambers. The district will be the constituency.

"Some powers of Second Chamber: There must be a sharing of powers between the two chambers in regard to the exercise of legislative power in respect of all proposed legislation affecting fundamental rights and language rights guaranteed under the Constitution. In this regard, no proposed legislation should become law unless approved by the president.

"The Second Chamber may be vested with the implementation of provisions of Chapter IV, Section 22 of the Constitution dealing with the national language, Tamil.

"The Second Chamber could also constitute select committees to inquire into and report on all aspects of ethnic disputes such as those relating to university admissions, educational facilities, employment of communities. Land settlement, exercise of language and cultural rights and development of backward regions would also be considered. The recommendations of committee 'B' will be considered in this context.

"The stateless: There was support too for the proposal referred earlier in this report that the stateless (some 90,000 of them) be given citizenship—vide paragraph 9 (3) of the report.

"Ethnic violence and terrorism: There was acceptance too that the causes of ethnic violence and all forms of terrorism in all parts of the country must be eradicated—vide paragraph (4) of the report."

Source: *Tamil Times*, October 1984, p. 15.

Why TULF Rejected President's Proposals

"We are constrained to state that the two Bills before this conference do not embody the scheme of autonomy which could be accepted by the Tamil people or their accredited representatives, the TULF," said Mr. A. Amirthalingam, the leader of the Tamil United Liberation Front, in a statement made on behalf of his party after the All-Party Conference (APC) was formally wound up on 21.12.84.

The following is the full text of the TULF statement:

"In response to an invitation from President Jayewardene dated December 28, 1983, the TULF agreed to attend the All-Party Conference summoned for January 10, 1984, on the basis of certain proposals" to enable them to arrive at an acceptable solution to the present problems facing the Tamil community in Sri Lanka.

When those proposals were abandoned, the TULF would normally have withdrawn from the conference. But we continued to participate and pursue the search for an acceptable viable alternative to our demand for an independent State of Tamil Eelam.

Mrs. Indira Gandhi, the late Prime Minister of India, who "offered her good offices to enable a final solution to be reached" and her Special Envoy Mr. G. Parthasarathy, played a very big part in persuading the TULF to continue the negotiation process.

In view of certain aspersions cast by some people on India's role in this matter, it behooves me to place this fact on record. India has been the biggest factor working for a peaceful political solution.

In the very first statement we made at the conference, we indicated that though we were elected on a mandate to work for a separate

State, if an acceptable and viable alternative is offered, we were willing to recommend it to our people.

Even in the face of total absence of positive response on the part of leading Government Members—even when the majority Sinhala Opposition party avoided the responsibility by walking out—we continued to participate because of our party's commitment to non-violence an integral part of which is the path of negotiation.

We indicated that a solution based on a Tamil linguistic region, consisting of the Northern and Eastern Provinces, granting regional autonomy to the Tamil nation as continued in the proposals placed before this conference by the Ceylon Workers Congress, may be one we could recommend to the Tamil people.

We also said that the regional body should be "empowered to enact laws and exercise thereto on certain specified listed subjects, including the maintenance of internal law and order in the region, the administration of justice, social and economic development, cultural matters and land policy."

A careful study of the provisions of the draft bills placed before the Conference will convince anyone that they fall far short of the regional autonomy indicated above.

When we accepted the scheme of District Development Councils in 1980, it was clearly understood that it was not meant to be an alternative to our demand for a separate State.

It was hoped that it may help to solve some of the pressing problems, like colonization, and ease tensions thereby creating the climate for a solution to the larger political questions.

The total failure of the Government to work that scheme in the proper spirit has largely contributed to the present situation. The repetition of the provisions of the same law in the present draft is totally unacceptable to the Tamil people.

The bills do not embody a proper scheme of devotion or autonomy. Devolution to the larger unit should be done by the constitution and that unit may delegate any functions to the smaller unit.

I am surprised that even these meagre and inadequate provisions are being opposed by some responsible persons.

We have endeavoured both in the All-Party Conference and in informal discussions outside to work out a peaceful solution.

Time is running out. The Tamil areas are under virtual siege. Normal life has come to a standstill. Death, arson, rape, and looting, stalk our areas. Starvation is staring the poor people in the face.

This is the grim reality of the situation in the Northern and Eastern Provinces.

We are constrained to state that the two Bills before this conference do not embody any scheme of autonomy which could be accepted by the Tamil people, or their accredited representatives, the Tamil United Liberation Front."

Source: *Tamil Times*, January 1985.

Notes

Chapter 1

1. Bruce Matthews, "The Situation in Jaffna—And How It Came About," *The Round Table*, p. 193. The Sri Lankan Tamils, who are mainly Saivite Hindus, have never expressed any anxiety about the desire of the Sinhalese people to revive Buddhism, since they perceive Buddhism as an integral part of Hinduism and which expounds the same theme on the view of life. Moreover their most revered god Murugan, the son of Siva, is an important figure in the pantheon of Sinhalese Buddhism. Both communities participate in the pilgrimage to Kataragama in the Moneragala District, which according to traditions is the site at which Murugan fell in love with and married the beautiful woman named Valli of Sinhalese-Veddha descent. Although some scholars are skeptical about the role this pilgrimage and Murugan play in promoting ethnic harmony between the two communities, their hatred for each other could have been worse if the Tamils were as apprehensive as the Sinhalese-Buddhists are about the future of their religion. See Bryan Pfaffenberger, "The Kataragama Pilgrimage: Hindu-Buddhist Interaction and its Significance in Sri Lanka's Polyethnic Social System."

2. See W. Geiger, trans., *The Mahavamsa or the Great Chronicle of Ceylon,* London: Oxford University Press, 1912, pp. 51–61. For an examination of the historical value of the *Pali Chronicles,* see G. C. Mendis, *Problems of Ceylon History.* Commenting on the reliability of the *Mahavamsa,* Mendis states, "though it is on the whole reliable from the first century B.C. it contains far too few details from the writing of history to satisfy modern requirements" (pp. 75–76). Also see G. C. Mendis, *Ceylon Today and Yesterday,* in which the author indicates that the *Mahavamsa* and the *Culavamsa* were compiled by the Buddhist clergy in order to teach the people religious and moral values and to rouse "serene joy and religious emotions among the pious" (p. 87). The *Dipavamsa* is the earliest of all the chronicles and was compiled by an unknown author about the fourth century A.D.

3. To understand the complex beliefs and sentiments held by Sinhalese Buddhists regarding their unique mission to establish a Sinhala-Buddhist society in Sri Lanka and how these beliefs conflict with the demands of the Tamils on language rights and regional autonomy, see Donald E. Smith, "Religion, Politics, the Myth of Reconquest," in T. Fernando and R. N. Kearney, eds., *Modern Sri Lanka: A Society in*

Transition. Also see D. E. Smith, "The Sinhalese Buddhist Revolution," in Donald Smith, ed., *South Asia Politics and Religion,* p. 456.

4. K. M. de Silva, *History of Sri Lanka,* pp. 3–4.

5. Gananath Obeyesekere, "The Vicissitudes of Sinhala-Buddhist Identity Through Time and Change," in Michael Roberts, ed., *Collective Identities, Nationalisms and Protest in Modern Sri Lanka,* p. 282.

6. See C. W. Nicholas and S. Paranavitana, *A Concise History of Ceylon,* p. 58. The authors suggest that dynasties named Pandyans, Cheras, and Cholas ruled South India before the arrival of the Dravidians. The Tamil kingdoms, they suggest, merely adopted the names of these pre-Dravidian dynasties at a later date. This contention is contrary to recent findings that the Dravidians were in the Indus Valley at the time of the Aryan arrival and that they were were driven to the South by new settlers.

7. For a concise study on the current state of knowledge on the origin of Dravidian-speaking people, see Andree F. Sjoberg, ed., *Symposium on Dravidian Civilization,* pp. 3–4 on Aryan contacts with South India.

8. For an impartial analysis of the origin of different racial groups in Sri Lanka, see N. D. Wijesekera, *The People of Ceylon.* He suggests that the Veddhas are not the aboriginal people of Sri Lanka, but they migrated from South India in prehistoric times. He states, "compare the modern Veddhas with the jungle tribes of the Southern part of India, viz., Malavedans, Irulas and Sholagas. A remarkable similarity still prevails. What can be the answer? Migrations of such tribes from India must be most likely answer" (pp. 57–58).

9. K. M. de Silva, *History of Sri Lanka,* pp. 7–8.

10. Although Wijesekera, *People of Ceylon,* does not dispute the link between Vijaya and the origin of the Sinhalese, he emphasizes that in the course of time the purity of the race could not be preserved. He states, "that the Veddhas have contributed to the making of the Sinhalese population is a fact that may be appreciated even today. Strangely enough the up-country Sinhalese preserve these traits in a marked degree. There are not many Sinhalese who show true Nordic characters according to the European standards of judgment. But a large proportion of the population consists of a round-headed element which may be the survival of the Aryan race. They also resemble the Alpine type. To the long-headed Mediterranean type belong the Wanni fold [Dravidian Tamils]. . . . The substratum of the Sinhalese population may be a Negrito type on which were superimposed an Australoid and later Mediterranean type" (p. 49).

11. For an in-depth analysis of the ancient Nagas and the origin of Tamil settlements in Sri Lanka, see C. Rasanayagam, *Ancient Jaffna.* Also see S. Ponnampalam, *Sri Lanka: The National Question and the Tamil Liberation Struggle,* p. 17. Ponnampalam states that the *Mahavamsa* misrepresents the Tamil Nagas and Yaksha as nonhuman people and refers to the accounts in the *Mahabharata* and *Ramayana* in which the Naga kingdoms were conquered by Ravanan, the Tamil Yaksha king of Lanka. He also refers to Ptolemy's description of the Yaksha Tamil people to indicate that the ancestors of present-day Tamils were already on the island when the Sinhalese arrived (pp. 16–20).

12. Wijesekera, *People of Ceylon,* p. 60.

13. See G. P. Malalasekere, *The Pali Literature of Ceylon,* pp. 16–19. Malalasekere indicates that prominent historians and travellers have described Lankapura as

the Yaksha people's capital city of immense wealth; its site can still be pointed out in the district of Matale, in the Central Province. It is also suggested that the Yakshas were Hindus, since Yaksha temples were respected, animals were offered for sacrifice, and special residences were constructed for Brahmins.

14. See K. M. de Silva, ed., *Sri Lanka: A Survey,* pp. 38–85. De Silva indicates that the Tamils were constantly present on the island and the beginnings of Sinhalese-Tamil conflict could be traced to 237 B.C., when two Tamil adventurers ruled the country for twenty-two years. He also states that "Sri Lanka has been from early in its recorded history a multi-racial society in which there was a distinct Dravidian element which could not alter the basic Aryan or North Indian character of the population" (pp. 37–38).

15. For a well-documented, authoritative account of the origins of Sinhalese, Tamil and Muslim (Moor) settlements in Sri Lanka, see S. Arasaratnam, *Ceylon.* Also see K. M. de Silva's well-documented and excellent work on the continuous story of the islands from the early beginnings to the present day, *History of Sri Lanka,* pp. 12–13. De Silva, commenting on the Dravidian presence on the island in protohistorical times, states, "there is no firm evidence as to when the Dravidians first came to the island, but come they did from very early times, either as invaders or as peaceful immigrants" (p. 12).

16. Gail Omvedt, "The Tamil National Question," p. 23.

17. People who were associated with the Megalithic cultures knew the art of using iron implements, of producing a highly polished black and red pottery, and of farming with the aid of tank irrigation. They also placed the remains of their dead in urns before burying them at a single location some distance from their habitat. See Sjoberg, ed., *Symposium on Dravidian Civilization,* p. 8. A number of scholars believe that the Megalithic culture was widespread enough to include peninsular India and Ceylon. Carbon-14 analysis suggests that the knowledge of using iron was known in North India as early as 1100 B.C. and that the Megalithic people were the dominant element in South India at least during the latter part of the first millennium B.C. Also see de Silva, *History of Sri Lanka,* pp. 12–13.

18. J. Emerson Tennent, *Ceylon,* vol. 1, p. 327.

19. Sjoberg, ed., *Symposium on Dravidian Civilization,* p. 17.

20. Nicholas and Paranavitana, *Concise History of Ceylon,* p. 5.

21. E. F. C. Ludowyk, *The Story of Ceylon,* p. 58.

22. K. M. de Silva, ed., *Sri Lanka,* p. 38.

23. For an analysis of Buddhism and politics, see Shelton U. Kodikara, "Communalism and Political Modernization in Ceylon." He states, "a close link had always existed between the state and religion in the traditional Sinhalese political system. The Sinhalese king became the defender of the Buddhist faith and it came to be looked upon as the king's special duty to uphold the religion and its institutions. It was not merely that, in consequence, the Buddhist Sangha came to have a deep influence on royal policy, but the continuance of the Buddha Sasana was identified with the well-being of the Sinhalese royal family" (p. 100). Elsewhere he states that the "recurrent Tamil invasions from South India had posed a serious problem for the Buddha Sasana as well as for the Sinhala nation. It is not surprising, therefore, that the Sangha should be deeply concerned with the present integrity of the Sinhala nation, and that it should play its old role of the protector of Sinhala heritage and

culture" (p. 103). Also see W. Howard Wriggins, *Ceylon: Dilemmas of a New Nation*, pp. 180–184.

24. K. M. de Silva, *History of Sri Lanka*, p. 4.

25. Matthews, "The Situation in Jaffna," p. 192.

26. Obeyesekere, "Vicissitudes of Sinhala-Buddhist Identity," p. 283.

27. K. M. de Silva, *History of Sri Lanka*, pp. 37–38.

28. Ibid., p. 13.

29. Thero Walpola Rahula, *History of Buddhism in Ceylon: The Anuradhapura Period, 3rd century B.C.–10th century A.D.*, p. 79.

30. Obeyesekere, "Vicissitudes of Sinhala-Buddhist Identity," p. 286.

31. K. M. de Silva, *History of Sri Lanka*, p. 38.

32. Ibid., pp. 42–43.

33. The *Rajavaliya* deliberately exaggerated the events following the thirteenth-century invasion of Sri Lanka by Magha of Kalinga. The Tamils are projected as a cruel people who employed barbaric methods to destroy the foundations of Sinhalese-Buddhist society from the thirteenth century. For a detailed analysis of the complex factors that may have contributed to the abandonment of the Rajarata kingdom, see Rhodes Murphy, "The Ruins of Ancient Ceylon." Also see D. C. Vijayavardhana, *The Revolt in the Temple*.

34. For a Tamilian historical perspective of the origin of the Jaffna kingdom, see S. Pathmanathan, *The Kingdom of Jaffna. Part 1 (circa A.D. 1250–1450)*; Arasaratnam, *Ceylon*, p. 104; K. Indrapala, *Dravidian Settlements in Ceylon and the Beginnings of the Kingdom of Jaffna*; and Rasanayagam, *Ancient Jaffna*, pp. 273–390. The Jaffna kingdom came under Sinhalese occupation in 1450 during the reign of Parakramabahu VI, but independence was established within seventeen years. Sinhalese historians C. W. Nicholas and S. Paranavitana, *Concise History of Sri Lanka*, have indicated that "large and gradual increasing Tamil element which formed part of the permanent population of the island from seventh century became predominant in the Northern Province, and secured control of the area in the 13th century; by dint of toil and thrift they have maintained their position to this day and extended it into the Eastern Province" (p. 5). Also see K. M. de Silva, *History of Sri Lanka*, p. 85, in which the author agrees with the Tamil historians that the Jaffna kingdom had control over major portions of the Vanni, including the coastal areas of Puttalam, even though its control over the Vanni was exercised through the Vanni chieftains, who migrated to this region from South India from ancient times; Gananath Obeyesekere, "Political Violence and the Future of Democracy in Sri Lanka," p. 41; and M. D. Raghavan, *India in Ceylonese History, Society and Culture*.

35. Obeyesekere, "Political Violence and the Future of Democracy in Sri Lanka," p. 41.

36. Arasaratnam, *Ceylon*, pp. 98–116.

37. S. Arasaratnam, "Nationalism in Sri Lanka and the Tamils," in Michael Roberts, ed., *Collective Identities, Nationalisms and Protest in Modern Sri Lanka*, p. 509.

38. Ponnampalam, *Sri Lanka*, p. 31. Also see Pfaffenberger, "The Kataragama Pilgrimage," pp. 253–254. Pfaffenberger, commenting on the possibility of Sri Lankan Tamils joining forces with the South Indian Tamils to subjugate the Sinhalese

minority, indicates that the former "maintain few ties with their South Indian neighbors, or with the descendants of Indian tea plantation workers in the central highlands. A thousand years of residence in Sri Lanka and of adoption to the unique ecosystems of the northern and eastern littorals have produced among these indigenous Tamil Hindus, who are called Ceylon Tamils, an identity separate from that of the South Indians" (pp. 253–254).

39. Sir Ivor Jennings, "Nationalism and Political Development in Ceylon (1): The Background of Self-Government," p. 66.

40. S. Arasaratnam, "Nationalism, Communalism, and National Unity in Ceylon," in Philip Mason, ed., *India and Ceylon: Unity and Diversity*, p. 275.

41. The threat of religious and cultural assimilation from English Christians was less of a problem for the Tamil Hindus; the majority of the Western-educated Tamils continued to follow their traditional customs and the Hindu religion. Nevertheless, pressure from the Christian missionaries was strong enough to persuade the religious reformer Arumuga Navalar to meet the challenge by single-handedly reviving Hinduism and improving Tamil literature in the nineteenth century.

42. K. M. de Silva, *History of Sri Lanka*, p. 355.

43. Arasaratnam, "Nationalism in Sri Lanka and the Tamils," p. 502.

44. K. M. de Silva, *History of Sri Lanka*, p. 367. Buddhists consider the full-moon day to be the most auspicious day of every month, since Gautama Buddha's birth, enlightenment, and attainment of Nirvana took place on full-moon days. The Wesak is a festival of lights celebrated every full-moon day to commemorate these auspicious events. While the colonial government permitted the use of alcohol and derived revenue from its sale, the Buddhist "temperance movement" was totally opposed to any alcoholic drink. Therefore the campaign to introduce the Buddhist Temporalities Bill was designed to oppose the social as well as fiscal policies of a Christian government.

45. For a discussion on the Goyigama and Karava caste rivalry and politics see A. Jeyaratnam Wilson, "Race, Religion, Language, and Caste in the Subnationalism in Sri Lanka," in Michael Roberts, ed., *Collective Identities, Nationalism and Protest in Modern Sri Lanka*, p. 466.

46. Jennings, "Nationalism and Political Development in Ceylon," p. 75.

47. Michael Roberts, "Problems of Collective Identity in a Multi-Ethnic Society: Sectional Nationalism Vs. Ceylonese Nationalism 1900–1940," in Michael Roberts, ed., *Collective Identities, Nationalism and Protest in Modern Sri Lanka*, p. 353.

48. Kumari Jayawardena, "Class Formation and Communalism," p. 59.

49. Obeyesekere, "Vicissitudes of Sinhala-Buddhist Identity," p. 303.

50. Michael Roberts, "Problems of Collective Identity in a Multi-Ethnic Society," p. 350.

51. K. M. de Silva, *History of Sri Lanka*, p. 397.

52. Ibid.

53. Wilson, "Race, Religion, Language, and Caste," p. 467.

54. Arasaratnam, "Nationalism in Sri Lanka and the Tamils," p. 503.

55. Wilson, "Race, Religion, Language, and Caste," p. 464.

56. Arasaratnam, "Nationalism in Sri Lanka and the Tamils," p. 502.

57. Michael Roberts, ed., *Collective Identities, Nationalism and Protest in Modern Sri Lanka*, p. 67.

58. Michael Roberts, "Nationalism in Economic and Social Thought 1915–1945," in Michael Roberts, ed., *Collective Identities, Nationalism and Protest in Modern Sri Lanka*. These two ordinances prohibited the government from granting land to Tamils of Indian origin for the purpose of cultivation and settlement.

59. Ibid.

60. Wilson, "Race, Religion, Language, and Caste," p. 465.

61. Roberts, *Collective Identities,* p. 73.

62. Arasaratnam, "Nationalism in Sri Lanka and the Tamils," p. 505.

63. Matthews, "The Situation in Jaffna," p. 194. Also see Wriggins, *Ceylon: Dilemmas of a New Nation.* This outstanding work analyzes in an in-depth and impartial manner how ethnic factors have guided political trends in Sri Lanka since independence. In particular, the deep-seated differences between the Sinhalese and the Tamils that threaten the survival of Sri Lanka as a united nation are explained with references to intergroup prejudices (pp. 231–233).

64. A. Jeyaratnam Wilson, "The Governor General and the Dissolutions of Parliament, December 5, 1959 and April 23, 1960," p. 95; A. Jeyaratnam Wilson, "Minority Safeguards in the Ceylon Constitution," pp. 73–79. A. Jeyaratnam Wilson has written extensively on minority safeguards in the Ceylon Constitution and is an authority on various schemes that have been proposed by Sinhalese and Tamil leaders for the devolution of governmental powers to Tamil areas under a federal form of government, regional councils, provincial councils, and district development councils. Also see Sydney Bailey, *Parliamentary Government in Southern Asia,* p. 37.

65. S. Namasivayagam, *Parliamentary Government in Ceylon, 1948–1958,* p. 97.

66. A. Jeyaratnam Wilson, "Politics and Political Development since 1948," in K. M. de Silva, ed., *Sri Lanka: A Survey,* p. 287.

67. For a critical evaluation of the ethnic, economic, and political factors that contributed to the denial of citizenship and voting rights to Indian Tamils, see Wriggins, *Ceylon: Dilemmas of a New Nation,* pp. 212–228. Also see I. D. S. Weerawardana, "Minority Problems in Ceylon," pp. 278–287.

68. Arasaratnam, "Nationalism in Sri Lanka and the Tamils," p. 506. See also Walter Schwarz, *The Tamils of Sri Lanka,* pp. 11–12, and Rachel Kurian et al., "Plantation Politics," p. 85. Under the Citizenship Act of 1948, Indian Tamils could no longer become citizens of Sri Lanka by virtue of their birth on the island and had to prove three or more generations of paternal ancestry to become citizens by descent. It was impossible for most of the Indian Tamils to furnish such proof and they were made stateless. Moreover, most of the Indian Tamils, who had participated in the country's general elections from 1931, were also disenfranchised under the Indian and Pakistani Residents (Citizenship) Act of 1949 and the Ceylon Parliamentary Elections Amendment Act of 1949. Only 134,316 Tamils of Indian origin received citizenship under the Indian and Pakistani (Citizenship) Act and more than 975,000 were rendered stateless. A major step toward solving the Indian statelessness problem occurred in 1964 when, under the terms of the Srimavo-Shastri Pact, 300,000 of the approximately 975,000 stateless Indians were to be granted Sri Lankan citizenship while India promised to grant citizenship to 525,000. No decision was made on the remaining 150,000 until 1974 when Mrs. Bandaranaike and Mrs. Indira Gandhi agreed to speed up the process of registration and to split the remain-

ing 150,000 Indians between the two countries, with each granting citizenship rights to 75,000. Therefore, India was to grant citizenship rights to 600,000 Tamils of Indian origin while Sri Lanka was supposed to absorb the remaining 375,000. Despite the fact that 600,000 Tamils of Indian origin were entitled to Indian citizenship, only 505,000 opted to apply for such citizenship. Moreover, only 400,000 of the 505,000 applicants were repatriated to India by the time the pact ended in October 31, 1981. Therefore, the Indian government has yet to grant citizenship rights to approximately 95,000 Tamils of Indian origin. In January 1986, the Indian government agreed to grant citizenship to approximately 85,000 Tamils of Indian origin who applied for Indian citizenship before the Srimavo-Shastri pact expired in 1981. On the other hand, the government of Sri Lanka granted citizenship to 94,000 Tamils of Indian origin who did not apply for Indian citizenship and remained stateless. Thus, it is estimated that more than 470,000 Tamils of Indian origin were granted Sri Lankan citizenship if these 94,000 Tamils were added to 375,000 Tamils who were entitled for Sri Lankan citizenship rights under the Srimavo-Shastri pact of 1964. This number does not include the natural increase in the population that has occurred since 1964.

Chapter 2

1. K. M. de Silva, *History of Sri Lanka*, p. 496.

2. Robert Kearney, "Nationalism, Modernization, and Political Mobilization in a Plural Society," in Michael Roberts, ed., *Collective Identities, Nationalism and Protest in Modern Sri Lanka*, p. 449.

3. Michael Roberts, ed., *Collective Identities, Nationalism and Protest in Modern Sri Lanka*, p. 73.

4. K. M. de Silva, *History of Sri Lanka*, p. 498.

5. Kearney, "Nationalism, Modernization, and Political Mobilization," p. 450.

6. E. R. Sarachandra, "Some Problems Connected with Cultural Revival in Ceylon," *Culture*, pp. 1-11.

7. Robert N. Kearney, *Communalism and Language in the Politics of Ceylon*, p. 137.

8. Shelton U. Kodikara, "Communalism and Political Modernization in Ceylon," pp. 100-105. Kodikara indicates that the monks of Eksath Bhikkhu Peramuna "not only published political literature but addressed meetings and campaigned from door to door with the slogan that a vote for the UNP was a vote for Catholics, and vote for the MEP a vote for Buddhists" (p. 102).

9. K. M. de Silva, *History of Sri Lanka*, p. 497.

10. A. Jeyaratnam Wilson, "Politics and Political Development since 1948," in K. M. de Silva, ed., *Sri Lanka: A Survey*, p. 301.

11. Kearney, *Communalism and Language in the Politics of Ceylon*, p. 83.

12. See Xavier S. Thaninayagam, "Tamil Culture—Its Past, Its Present and Its Future with Special Reference to Ceylon."

13. Robert N. Kearney, "Language and the Rise of Tamil Separatism in Sri Lanka," p. 528.

14. L. H. Mettananda threatened to fast to death if the Official Language bill included provisions for the "reasonable use of Tamil."

15. Donald E. Smith, "Religion, Politics, and the Myth of Reconquest," in T. S. Fernando and R. S. Kearney, eds., *Modern Sri Lanka: A Society in Transition*, p. 90.

16. Ibid., p. 85.

17. K. M. de Silva, "Politics and Constitutional Change in Sri Lanka," p. 53.

18. B. Thillainathan, "Ceylon: The Federal Principles," p. 11.

19. Kearney, *Communalism and Language in the Politics of Ceylon*, pp. 144–146.

20. Wilson, "Politics and Political Development since 1948," p. 303.

21. Tarzie Vittachi, *Emergency '58: The Story of the Ceylon Race Riots*.

22. Roberts, ed., *Collective Identities, Nationalism and Protest*, p. 71.

23. Kearney, *Communalism and Language in the Politics of Ceylon*, p. 147.

24. Suntharalingam regarded Eelam as the Tamil people's deity that should be revered. To him the Tamil people's salvation depended on the establishment of the separate Tamil state of Eelam. Indeed, Eelam has become such an obsession to some Tamil militants that they are prepared to sacrifice their lives to secure it.

25. Kearney, *Communalism and Language in the Politics of Ceylon*, p. 108.

26. Kodikara, "Communalism and Political Modernization in Ceylon," p. 104. Also see Government of Ceylon, *Proposals for the Establishment of District Councils under the Direction and Control of the Central Government*.

27. S. Arasaratnam, "Nationalism in Sri Lanka and the Tamils," p. 510.

28. Government of Ceylon (Sri Lanka), *The Constitution of Sri Lanka*, p. 4.

29. Kearney, "Language and the Rise of Tamil Separatism," p. 530.

30. Robert N. Kearney, "Democracy and the Stress of Modernization in Sri Lanka," p. 72.

31. C. R. de Silva, "The Impact of Nationalism on Education: The Schools Take-Over (1961) and the University Admissions Crisis, 1970–1975," in Michael Roberts, ed., *Collective Identities, Nationalism and Protest in Modern Sri Lanka*, p. 475. See also Kearney, "Language and the Rise of Tamil Separatism," p. 530.

32. C. R. de Silva, "The Impact of Nationalism on Education," p. 490.

33. Robert N. Kearney, "Ethnic Conflict and the Tamil Separatist Movement in Sri Lanka," p. 905.

34. Bruce Matthews, "The Situation in Jaffna—And How It Came About," p. 194.

35. A. Sivanandan, "Sri Lanka: Racism and Politics of Underdevelopment," p. 22.

36. Bruce Matthews, "District Development Councils in Sri Lanka," p. 1115.

37. Kearney, "Ethnic Conflict and the Tamil Separatist Movement," p. 907.

38. W. Howard Wriggins, "The Present Situation and Outlook For Sri Lanka," in *Proceedings Before the Subcommittee on Asian and Pacific Affairs and the Subcommittee on Human Rights and International Organizations*, Committee on Foreign Affairs, U.S. House of Representatives, August 2, 1984. Wriggins is professor of political science at Columbia University and former U.S. Ambassador to Sri Lanka.

39. W. I. Siriweera, "Recent Developments in Sinhala-Tamil Relations," p. 905.

40. Kearney, "Ethnic Conflict and the Tamil Separatist Movement," p. 905.

41. The abuse of human rights was brought to light by Amnesty International, *Report of a Mission to Sri Lanka 1975*. A report published by Amnesty International in 1982 indicates that the government used torture and political killings against the Tamils even though it has the responsibility under the International Covenant on

Civil and Political Rights not to do so even in a national emergency. In addition, the report goes on to state that the government introduced the Prevention of Terrorist Act in order to increase the power of the security forces and removed basic protection for human rights of detainees under the Act. The report also claims that the lack of discipline among the security forces had predictable results in the torture and ill-treatment of detainees. Subsequent reports released by Amnesty International confirm the widespread use of torture against political detainees. A report released in New York by the American Association for International Commission of Jurists, headed by Professor Virginia A. Leary, of the State University of New York at Buffalo Law School, criticizes the Sri Lankan government for not pursuing a vigorous policy of investigation and prosecution of police and army personnel who were responsible for setting fire to homes, public buildings, and businesses in May–June 1981. The Commission also reported that police officers convicted of acting illegally have been promoted by decisions made at the cabinet level by ministers.

42. W. Howard Wriggins, "Sri Lanka in 1981: Year of Austerity, Development Councils, and Communal Disorders," p. 175.

43. Matthews, "District Development Councils in Sri Lanka," p. 1124. The author provides a detailed and critical analysis of the District Development Councils.

44. Kearney, "Ethnic Conflict and the Tamil Separatist Movement," p. 907.

45. Sivanandan, "Sri Lanka," p. 33.

46. Ibid., p. 33.

47. Matthews, "District Development Councils in Sri Lanka," p. 1127.

48. S. W. R. de. A. Samarasinghe, "Sri Lanka in 1983: Ethnic Conflicts and the Search for Solutions," p. 2512.

49. Ibid.

50. Kearney, "Ethnic Conflict and the Tamil Separatist Movement," p. 906. The militants are referred to as "tigers," insurgents, rebels, guerrillas, terrorists, extremists, separatists, freedom fighters, "the boys," and Marxists by different groups of people and the government. Also see Bryan Pfaffenberger, "Fourth World Colonialism, Indigenous Minorities, and Tamil Separatism in Sri Lanka," *The Bulletin of Concerned Asian Scholars*, pp. 15–27. Pfaffenberger describes the traditional role played by the Vellala caste, an aristocratic caste, in the political, economic, and social affairs of the Jaffna region and how the human rights of the minority groups are often ignored. He even states that the Vellalas are more interested in preserving their own interests and Jaffna traditions in Tamil Eelam than the rights and aspirations of the Tamils and Muslims of eastern Sri Lanka. Contrary to Pfaffenberger's assertions there are strong indications that the Tamil-speaking people have begun to set aside their caste and regional differences in order to secure their rights, although clashes over caste differences continue to keep the leadership of some militant groups apart. There is no evidence, given the socialist aspirations of some of the leaders of the groups, that the militant movements are dominated by the Vellala caste and that members of the other castes or Tamils of the Eastern Province are excluded. Moreover, contrary to the government's claims, Tamil militants are not conspiring with Sinhalese militants of the South to establish a Marxist state by overthrowing the government. Indeed, the only aim of all Tamil militants is to establish Eelam through violent struggle.

51. For an in-depth analysis of the provisions of the 1979 Prevention of Terrorism

Act, the riots of 1977 and 1983, and the police and army rampages in Jaffna, see S. Ponnampalam, *Sri Lanka: The National Question and the Tamil Liberation Struggle*, pp. 189–227. See also S. J. Thambiah, *Sri Lanka: Ethnic Fratricide and the Dismantling of Democracy*, p. 6. He indicates that the Emergency Regulation 15a is the "most draconian measure ever perpetrated in Sri Lanka."

52. The incident of the killing of the fifty-one Tamil prisoners in the Welikade prison in Colombo was presented by Amy Young to the *Subcommittee on Asian and Pacific Affairs and the Subcommittee on Human Rights and International Organizations*, Committee on Foreign Affairs, U.S. House of Representatives, August 2, 1984. Amy Young is the executive director of the International Human Rights Law Group, a nongovernmental organization, with headquarters in Washington, D.C.

53. Thambiah, *Sri Lanka: Ethnic Fratricide and the Dismantling of Democracy*, p. 17, indicates that the thirteen soldiers may have been killed in retaliation to Tamil charges "the army of occupation in Jaffna with going on punitive expedition killing innocent civilians and torturing several hundreds without cause." Also see paper by Brian Senewiratne, "The July 1983 Massacre: Unanswered Questions," p. 6, in which he states "The July holocaust was only the culmination of a continuing series of acts of violence by the militant youth on the Security Forces, and reprisals by the Security Forces on the innocent civilian population in Jaffna. In particular, there was increasing anti-Tamil racial violence in Trincomalee in June and July 1983 which the government did nothing to discourage and by their silence, encouraged."

54. *India Abroad*, August 5, 1985, p. 3.

55. Gananath Obeyesekere, "Political Violence and the Future of Democracy in Sri Lanka," pp. 44–50, analyzes in great detail under the heading "The Institutionalization of Political Violence," the circumstances leading to the rise of the Jatika Sevaka Sangamaya as a militant organization which has been put to political use by members of parliament.

56. Allen K. Jones, *Time for Decision: Sri Lankan Tamils in the West*. Jones is consultant to the U.S. Committee for Refugees.

57. Kearney, "Ethnic Conflict and the Tamil Separatist Movement," p. 906.

58. Gail Omvedt, "The Tamil National Question," p. 23.

59. See D. B. S. Jeyaraj, "How Strong are the 'Boys'?," for a detailed account of the militant organizations.

60. A. Jeyaratnam Wilson, "Sri Lanka and Its Future: Sinhalese Versus Tamils," in A. Jeyaratnam Wilson and Dennis Dalton, eds., *The States of South Asia: Problems of National Integration*, p. 295.

61. Young, *Subcommittee on Asian and Pacific Affairs*.

Chapter 3

1. Archaeological finds have indicated the existence of a formerly widespread Megalithic culture in peninsular India and Sri Lanka and it is believed that some of the Dravidian-speaking people may have participated in this culture in prehistoric times. See Andree F. Sjoberg, ed., *Symposium on Dravidian Civilization*.

2. N. P. Perera, "Early Agricultural Settlements in Sri Lanka in Relation to Natural Resources."

3. K. M. de Silva, *History of Sri Lanka*, p. 7.

4. C. R. de Silva, "The Sinhalese-Tamil Rift in Sri Lanka," in A. Jeyaratnam

Wilson and Dennis Dalton, eds., *The States of South Asia*, p. 156. For a history of Tamil settlements in northern Sri Lanka, see K. Indrapala, "Dravidian Settlements in Ceylon and the beginnings of the Kingdom of Jaffna"; S. Pathmanathan, *The Kingdom of Jaffna, Part I (circa A.D. 1250-1450);* and S. Arasaratnam, *Ceylon.*

5. Arasaratnam, *Ceylon*, p. 101.

6. Perera, "Early Agricultural Settlements in Sri Lanka," pp. 69–70.

7. It is not certain what the size of the population of ancient Sri Lanka was, although one ancient manuscript claims that it was as high as seventy million while the more reasonable estimate is approximately four million. For information on the population estimates of ancient Sri Lanka, see E. B. Denham, *Ceylon at the Census of 1911;* Bertram H. Farmer, *Pioneer Peasant Colonization in Ceylon*, pp. 15–16; and Rhodes Murphy, "The Ruins of Ancient Ceylon," p. 186.

8. Government of Ceylon, Department of Census and Statistics, *Ceylon Year Book* (1954), p. 61.

9. See J. E. Tennent, *Ceylon;* D. C. Vijayavardhana, *The Revolt in the Temple,* p. 66; Murphy, "Ruins of Ancient Ceylon," pp. 181–200; Farmer, *Pioneer Peasant Colonization*, pp. 16–22; and K. M. de Silva, *Sri Lanka: A Survey,* p. 42–43.

10. Murphy, "Ruins of Ancient Ceylon," pp. 189–190.

11. See ibid., p. 188. Murphy, commenting on the destructive nature of rains and floods in the Dry Zone, states that "the rains are potent destroyers. The record is 31 inches in 24 hours, at a station north of Trincomalee, but nearly all dry-zone stations experience 6 inches in 24 hours several times each year, and often the fall is heavier; an inch in five minutes is not uncommon. Floods resulting from rains like these, or from the cumulative rains of even a normal, let alone the recurrent excessive monsoon, bring certain havoc to any untended irrigation system." Also see B. H. Farmer, *Ceylon: A Divided Nation,* p. 14, on the disastrous effects of the floods of 1956–1957 on irrigation systems in the Dry Zone.

12. Farmer, *Pioneer Peasant Colonization,* p. 12.

13. Murphy, "Ruins of Ancient Ceylon," p. 197. The destruction caused to major irrigation systems in the Dry Zone by floods is so frequent that Parakramabahu I had to organize a massive labor force "to restore several of the irrigation works he had himself built in the early part of his reign."

14. Garrett C. Mendis, *Ceylon Today and Yesterday,* p. 213.

15. Farmer, *Pioneer Peasant Colonization,* pp. 12–13. Farmer indicates that the immediate hinterland of Trincomalee as well as the area around the Kantalai tank were "almost completely empty" during the early period of British rule.

16. S. Arasaratnam, "Nationalism in Sri Lanka and the Tamils," in Michael Roberts, ed., *Collective Identities, Nationalism, and Protest in Modern Sri Lanka,* p. 511.

17. Arasaratnam, *Ceylon,* p. 124.

18. Ibid., p. 108.

19. W. Howard Wriggins, *Ceylon: Dilemmas of a New Nation,* p. 270.

20. Farmer, *Pioneer Peasant Colonization,* p. 76. Farmer's book is one of the best sources on how man has responded to the limitations imposed by the Dry Zone environment on human settlements and agricultural activities. It is also a valuable source of information on the nature and distribution of population, agrarian problems, and peasant colonization of the Dry Zone prior to 1954.

21. P. C. Bansil, *Ceylon Agriculture: A Perspective,* p. 67.

22. Farmer, *Pioneer Peasant Colonization*, p. 209.

23. Government of Ceylon, Department of Census and Statistics, *Ceylon Year Book* (1963), p. 47.

24. Farmer, *Pioneer Peasant Colonization*, p. 229.

25. Ibid., p. 203.

26. K. M. de Silva, "Discrimination in Sri Lanka," in V. Venhoven, ed., *Case Studies on Human Rights and Fundamental Freedoms: A World Survey*, pp. 73–119.

27. Peter Richards and W. Gooneratne, *Basic Needs, Poverty and Government Policies in Sri Lanka*, p. 124; Department of Census and Statistics, *Ceylon Year Book* (1963), p. 53.

28. Government of Ceylon, Department of Census and Statistics, *Statistical Pocket Book of the Democratic Socialist Republic of Sri Lanka*, p. 168.

29. Government of Ceylon, Department of Census and Statistics, *Ceylon Year Book* (1982), p. 58.

30. Ibid., pp. 167–168.

31. Central Bank of Ceylon, *Review of the Economy*, Table 22.

32. Farmer, *Pioneer Peasant Colonization*, pp. 12–13.

33. Ibid., pp. 164–165.

34. For a detailed study of the geology, landforms, water resources, and soils of the Dry Zone, see K. Kularatnam, "The Face of Ceylon," *The Proceedings of the Ninth Annual Session, Ceylon Association for the Advancement of Science*, Part II; E. K. Cook, *Ceylon, Its Geography, Resources, and People*. Also see F. D. Adams, "The Geology of Ceylon," pp. 425–511; W. Luther Jeyasingham, "The Urban Geography of Jaffna"; F. R. Moorman and C. R. Panabokke, "Soils of Ceylon"; and C. H. L. Srimane, "Geology for Water Supply," *Proceedings of the Eight Annual Session, Ceylon Association for the Advancement of Science*, pp. 5–6.

35. For a comprehensive account on the climatic potential for cultivating various crops on a regional basis in Sri Lanka, see Manfred Domros, *The Agroclimate of Ceylon*, pp. 100–103. Climatic limitations on agriculture and water resources development in the Tamil areas are well-documented in this work. Also see G. Thambyapillai, "Dry Zone of Ceylon."

36. Domros, *Agroclimate of Ceylon*, pp. 22–31.

37. Ibid., p. 29. Also see C. W. Thornthwaite Associates, "Average Climatic Water Balance Data of the Continents, Part II. Asia," *Publication in Climatology*, pp. 56–58. This author uses Thornthwaite's system to estimate the water balance parameters because it is the best available system to classify regions based on records dealing with standardized mean monthly temperature and monthly rainfall data, which have considerable longevity for most areas in the world.

38. The Mahaweli Ganga Diversion Project was designed primarily to develop agriculture in the predominantly Sinhalese areas, although the people of the Tamil districts face more serious problems with overcrowding, farming, unemployment, and food scarcity than the residents of other districts in the Dry Zone. In fact, water resource development in the Dry Zone continues to be largely restricted to Sinhalese districts or to those areas of the Tamil districts where colonization schemes are already established or in the process of being established. Other plans involving the transfer of surplus water from the Mahaweli Ganga into the rivers of the Northern Province and of converting the Jaffna lagoon into a fresh water lake have received the lowest

priority. See R. L. Brohier, "Jaffna Peninsula Lagoon Scheme," *Transactions for 1952 of the Engineering Association of Ceylon*, pp. 207–209.

39. Bansil, *Ceylon Agriculture*, p. 67.

40. Ibid., p. 17.

41. Peter Richards and E. Stoutjeesdeijk, *Agriculture in Ceylon 1975*, p. 98.

42. The procedures presented by Barbara Harriss, "Paddy and Rice Situation in Sri Lanka," in B. H. Farmer, ed., *Green Revolution*, pp. 20–30, were adopted to compute the annual production of paddy per capita. Accordingly, the net extent harvested is estimated at 82.5 percent of the gross extent sown (to discount portions of the land in bunds, ridges, and threshing places). It is also estimated that only 85 percent of the population has to be included for computing the total consumptive need for a region, since 30 percent of the population is below the age of ten years and consumes only 50 percent of the adult requirements.

43. Arasaratnam, *Ceylon*, p. 518.

Chapter 4

1. For a comprehensive analysis of the agrarian problems and population densities in the Jaffna region, see S. Selvanayagam, "Agrarian Problems and Prospects of Developing the Jaffna Region of Ceylon," *Young Socialist*, May 1967, pp. 55–60; S. Selvanayagam, "Population Densities and Land Use in the Jaffna Region of Ceylon," pp. 33–42. Also B. L. C. Johnson and M. LeM. Schrivenor, *Sri Lanka*, p. 47. It is estimated that approximately 46 percent of the paddy holdings were less than 1.2 hectares and 32 percent of the agricultural families were landless in the early 1950s. In the 1960s, approximately 81 percent of the paddy holdings were less than 0.8 hectares, and it is estimated that the holdings are much smaller in the 1980s.

2. The population of the Jaffna region is approximately 95 to 98 percent of the Jaffna District. It is estimated that the population of the region increased from 241,454 in 1871 to 760,000 in 1981, an increase of 214 percent. The density of population increased from 1,429 to 4,544 persons per square kilometer during the same period, an increase of 218 percent. See Selvanayagam, "Population Densities and Land Use," pp. 35–36.

3. W. Robert Holmes, *Jaffna 1980 (Sri Lanka)*, pp. 176–187.

4. K. M. de Silva, *History of Sri Lanka*, pp. 350–355.

5. A. Sivanandan, "Sri Lanka: Racism and the Politics of Underdevelopment," pp. 3–4.

6. W. Howard Wriggins, *Ceylon: Dilemmas of a New Nation*, p. 234. For explanations as to why Jaffna Tamils sought employment in the public service and why they succeeded in their endeavor, see pp. 234–235.

7. Government of Ceylon, "Report of the General and Economic Conditions of the Ceylonese in Malaysia," *Sessional Paper*, p. 1.

8. C. R. de Silva, "The Impact of Nationalism on Education: The Schools Take-Over (1961) and the University Admissions Crisis 1970–1975," in Michael Roberts, ed., *Collective Identities, Nationalism and Protests in Modern Sri Lanka*, p. 487.

9. Government of Ceylon, Department of Census and Statistics, *Sri Lanka Year Book* (1982), p. 173.

10. Editorial Notes, "Notes and Documents: Human Rights Violations in Sri

Lanka," pp. 142–148. These notes were prepared from the "Memorandum on Human Rights Violations and Ethnic Violence in Sri Lanka" researched by the Gemeenchappelijk Overleg Medefinancierings Organisaties (Netherlands, 1983). Jenny Bourne has included additional notes. The tables and statistics are based on data released by private agencies and government departments in Sri Lanka. The sources include *Census of Population and Housing* (1981); *Census of Public and Corporation Sector Employment* (1980) released by the Department of Census and Statistics and Ministry of Planning Implementation; *Report on Consumer Finance and Socio-Economic Survey, 1978/1979;* and university admission figures released by Division of Planning and Research, University Grant Commission, 1983.

11. The General Certificate of Education Ordinary Level replaced the Senior School Certificate (SSC) and is issued to students who pass a prescribed number of subjects in a public examination conducted by the Department of Education at the end of the tenth year of schooling. The certificate provides the minimum qualification for securing clerical employment in public service. The General Certificate of Education Advanced Level replaced the High School Certificate (SSE) and is issued after a student passes a prescribed number of subjects in a public examination conducted by the Department of Education at the end of the twelfth year of schooling. A person has to obtain a high point average in a combination of subjects to secure admission to university.

12. Editorial Notes, "Notes and Documents," pp. 149–150.

13. Walter Schwarz, *The Tamils of Sri Lanka,* p. 12.

14. C. R. de Silva, "Weightage in University Admissions: Standardisation and District Quotas."

15. C. R. de Silva, "Weightage in University Admissions."

16. Ibid.

17. C. R. de Silva, "Impact of Nationalism on Education," p. 490.

18. C. R. de Silva, "Impact of Nationalism on Education," p. 495. Also see Editorial Notes, "Notes and Documents," p. 146.

19. C. R. de Silva, "The Sinhalese-Tamil Rift in Sri Lanka," in A. Jeyaratnam Wilson and Dennis Dalton, eds., *The States of South Asia: Problems of National Integration,* p. 170.

20. C. R. de Silva, "Impact of Nationalism on Education," p. 497.

21. Michael Roberts, ed., *Collective Identities, Nationalism, and Protest in Modern Sri Lanka,* p. 71.

22. Robert N. Kearney, "Language and the Rise of Tamil Separatism in Sri Lanka," p. 531.

23. Editorial Notes, "Notes and Documents," p. 149.

24. Schwarz, *Tamils of Sri Lanka,* p. 13.

25. Ibid.

26. S. Ponnampalam, *Sri Lanka: The National Question and the Tamil Liberation Struggle,* p. 174.

27. Angelito Peries, "Historical Background to the Genocide of Thamils in Sri Lanka," p. 19.

28. Editorial Notes, "Notes and Documents," pp. 141–142.

29. Ibid.

30. Ponnampalam, *Sri Lanka,* p. 175.

31. Central Bank of Ceylon, *Review of the Economy,* p. 90.

32. Editorial Notes, "Notes and Documents," p. 153.

33. For detailed analysis of the market-oriented farming system in the Jaffna region, see S. Selvanayagam, "Market Gardening in the Jaffna Region"; S. Selvanayagam, "Intensive Farming and Agricultural Trends in the Jaffna Region of Ceylon"; C. Manogaran, "Traditional Versus Modern Agriculture: A Study of Peasant Farming in Ceylon (Sri Lanka)"; W. Robert Holmes, *Jaffna 1980;* and B. L. C. Johnson and M. LeM. Schrivenor, *Sri Lanka,* pp. 44–47. For historical trends in the production of onions and chillies, see Department of Census and Statistics, *The Ceylon Year Book;* Government of Sri Lanka, *Administrative Report of the Government Agent of Jaffna District* (1968, p. A15; 1970, pp. A29–A38; and 1973, pp. A21–A22); and Central Bank of Ceylon, *Review of the Economy.*

34. Holmes, *Jaffna 1980,* pp. 367–375.

35. Ponnampalam, *Sri Lanka,* p. 168.

36. See Department of Census and Statistics, *Statistical Pocket Book of the Democratic Socialist Republic of Sri Lanka* (1983), p. 18.

37. Schwarz, *The Tamils of Sri Lanka,* pp. 13–14.

38. C. R. de Silva, "The Sinhalese-Tamil Rift in Sri Lanka," p. 161.

Chapter 5

1. See Government of Ceylon, *Proposals for the Establishment of District Councils under the Direction and Control of the Central Government.* Also see Bruce Matthews, "District Development Councils in Sri Lanka," *Asian Survey,* p. 1119. This article traces the history of unsuccessful attempts made by special commissions and governments to decentralize administrative functions to local governments at the district and provincial levels. Matthews provides a critical evaluation of the structure, composition, and functions of District Development Councils as they relate to Tamil demands for decentralization of legislative, executive, and financial powers to governmental units at the regional level.

2. Matthews, "District Development Councils," p. 1119.

3. Editorial Notes, "Notes and Documents: Human Rights Violations in Sri Lanka," p. 157.

4. B. Thillainathan, "Ceylon: The Federal Principle," p. 11.

5. Robert N. Kearney, *Communalism and Language in the Politics of Ceylon,* pp. 144–146.

6. Ibid., pp. 147–149.

7. W. I. Siriweera, "Recent Developments in Sinhala-Tamil Relations," p. 903.

8. S. Ponnampalam, *Sri Lanka: The National Question and the Tamil Liberation Struggle,* p. 192; S. Ponnampalam, *A Draft Constitution of the People's Republic of Tamil Eelam.*

9. Central Bank of Ceylon, *Review of the Economy,* 1982, p. 102.

10. N. T. Uphoff and M. J. Esman, "Local Organization for Rural Development in Asia," *Development Digest,* Volume XIII, Number 3, July 1975, pp. 31–46. See World Bank (Staff), "World Bank Policy on Rural Development," which recom-

mends that for rural development schemes to be successful, some functions of regional and local planning should be delegated to planners and specialists who are knowledgeable of the local needs and conditions of different regions in any country.

11. Government of Ceylon, Department of Census and Statistics, *Sri Lanka Year Book* (1982), p. 67.

12. Albert Waterson, "A Viable Model for Rural Development," pp. 3–11.

13. World Bank, "World Bank Policy on Rural Development."

14. Government of Ceylon, Department of Census and Statistics, *Sri Lanka Year Book* (1982), pp. 67–71; Central Bank of Ceylon, *Review of Economy,* 1982, pp. 102–104.

15. Government of Ceylon, Department of Census and Statistics, *Sri Lanka Year Book* (1982).

16. Editorial Notes, "Notes and Documents," p. 152.

17. W. Howard Wriggins, "Sri Lanka in 1981: Year of Austerity, Development Councils, and Communal Disorders," pp. 175–177; Matthews, "District Development Councils," pp. 1117–1134.

18. See Matthews, "District Development Councils." Detailed information on structure, composition, and functions are provided in the notes.

19. Ibid., p. 1121.

20. N. T. Uphoff and M. J. Esman, "Local Organization for Rural Development in Asia."

21. Wriggins, "Sri Lanka in 1981," p. 176.

22. Matthews, "District Development Councils," p. 1130.

23. Wriggins, "Sri Lanka in 1981," p. 176.

24. S. W. R. de. A. Samarasinghe, "Sri Lanka in 1983: Ethnic Conflicts and the Search for Solutions," p. 251.

25. Bruce Matthews, "The Situation in Jaffna—And How It Came About," p. 195. Matthews cites an example of how the Ministry of Health turned down the Jaffna District Development Council's decision to extend a "much needed wing for the Jaffna General Hospital" to emphasize the fact that DDCs have very little power to implement development plans that are crucial to the well-being of the Tamil people.

26. See Editorial Notes, "Notes and Documents," p. 157; also see Matthews, "The Situation in Jaffna," p. 195. Matthews states that a "critical factor limiting the integrity and efficacy of the DDCs was unreliable financial support from Colombo. He indicates that funds allocated to DDCs by parliament were not funnelled toward the development of large district-level projects. Instead, the funds allocated to each DDC are divided among MPs to develop their own pet projects in their own constituencies. Apparently, some MPs consider DDCs to be glorified local government bodies or municipalities which require very little financial support from the Colombo government" (p. 195). Matthews also indicates that some MPs "are not interested in the DDCs as a second tier of government, and give the system only nominal cooperation" (p. 202).

27. Bryan Pfaffenberger, "Fourth World Colonialism, Indigenous Minorities, and Tamil Separatism in Sri Lanka," p. 16.

Bibliography

Government Publications

Central Bank of Ceylon. *Review of the Economy.* Colombo, 1977–1983.

Government of Ceylon (Sri Lanka). *Administrative Report of the Government Agent of Jaffna District for 1966–1970.* Colombo: Government Press, 1968–1973.

———. *The Constitution of Sri Lanka.* Colombo: Government Press, 1972.

———. *Census of Population and Housing,* Colombo: Government Press, 1981.

———. Department of Census and Statistics. *Ceylon/Sri Lanka Year Book, 1948–1983.* Colombo: Government Press, 1949–1984.

———. House of Representatives. *Parliamentary Debates (Hansard),* vol. 30, cols. 1309–1311.

———. *Proposals for the Establishment of District Councils under the Direction and Control of the Central Government,* Colombo: Government Printing Press, June 1968.

———. *Government Gazette 14653 of 2. 3. 1966.* Colombo: Government Press, 1966.

———. *Report of the Tobacco Commission.* Sessional Paper XIV. Colombo: Government Press, 1955.

———. Department of Census and Statistics, Ministry of Planning Implementations, *Socio-Economic Indicators of Sri Lanka.* Colombo: Government Press, 1983.

———. *Sri Lanka.* Colombo: Department of Public Information, February 1, 1966.

———. Department of Census and Statistics. *Statistical Pocket Book of the Democratic Socialist Republic of Sri Lanka, 1980–1983.* Colombo: Government Press, 1981–1984.

———. "Report of the General and Economic Conditions of the Ceylonese in Malaysia." *Sessional Papers,* vol. 9. Colombo. 1946.

Books, Monographs, and Pamphlets

Amnesty International. *Report of an Amnesty International Mission to Sri Lanka 1975.* London: Amnesty International Publication, 1976.

———. *Report of an Amnesty International Mission to Sri Lanka, 31 January–9 February 1982.* London: Amnesty International Publication, 1983.

Arasaratnam, Sinappah. *Ceylon*. Englewood Cliffs, New Jersey: Prentice-Hall, 1964.
———. "Nationalism, Communalism, and National Unity in Ceylon." In Philip Mason, ed., *India and Ceylon: Unity and Diversity,* pp. 260–278. New York: Oxford University Press, 1967.
———. "Nationalism in Sri Lanka and the Tamils." In Michael Roberts, ed., *Collective Identities, Nationalisms and Protest in Modern Sri Lanka,* pp. 500–519. Colombo: Marga Institute, 1979.
Arumugam, S. *Water Resources of Ceylon*. Water Resources Board, 1969.
Bailey, Sydney. *Parliamentary Government in Southern Asia*. New York: International Secretariat Institute of Pacific Relations, 1953.
Banks, Michael. "Caste in Jaffna." In E. R. Leach, ed., *Aspects of Caste in South India, Ceylon and Northwest Pakistan,* pp. 61–77. Cambridge: Cambridge University Press, 1960.
Bansil, P. C. *Ceylon Agriculture: A Perspective*. Delhi: Dhanapat Rai and Sons, 1971.
Cook, E. K. *Ceylon, Its Geography, Resources, and People*. Madras: Macmillan, 1931. Revised by K. Kularatnam as *Ceylon: Its Geography, Its Resources, and Its People*. Madras: Macmillan, 1951.
De Silva, Chandra R. "The Impact of Nationalism on Education: The Schools Take-Over (1961) and the University Admissions Crisis 1970–1975." In Michael Robert, ed., *Collective Identities, Nationalism and Protest in Modern Sri Lanka,* pp. 474–499. Colombo: Marga Institute, 1979.
———. "The Sinhalese-Tamil Rift in Sri Lanka." In A. J. Wilson and Dennis Dalton, eds., *The States of South Asia,* pp. 155–174. Honolulu: The University of Hawaii, 1982.
De Silva, Kingsley M. "Discrimination in Sri Lanka." In V. Venhoven, ed., *Case Studies on Human Rights and Fundamental Freedoms: A World Survey,* vol. 3, pp. 73–119. The Hague: Martinus Nijhoff, 1976.
———. *History of Sri Lanka*. Berkeley: University of California, 1981.
De Silva, K. M., ed. *Sri Lanka: A Survey,* London: C. Hurst and Company, 1977.
Denham, E. B. *Ceylon at the Census of 1911,* Colombo, 1912.
Domros, Manfred. *The Agroclimate of Ceylon*. Wisbaden: Franz Steiner Verlag Gmbh, 1974.
Farmer, Bertram H. *Pioneer Peasant Colonization in Ceylon*. New York: Oxford University Press, 1957.
———. *Ceylon: A Divided Nation*. London: London University Press, 1963.
———, ed., *Green Revolution*. Boulder, Colorado: Westview Press, 1977.
Geiger, Wilhem, trans. *The Mahavamsa or the Great Chronicle of Ceylon*. London: Oxford University Press, 1912.
Holmes, W. Robert. *Jaffna 1980*. Jaffna, Sri Lanka: The Christian Institute for the Study of Religion and Society of Jaffna College, 1980.
Indrapala, Karthigesu. "Dravidian Settlements in Ceylon and the Beginnings of the Kingdom of Jaffna." Ph.D. thesis, University of London, 1966.
Jeyasingham, W. Luther. "The Urban Geography of Jaffna." Ph.D. Dissertation, Clark University, Massachusetts, 1958.
Johnson, B. L. C. and M. LeM. Scrivenor. *Sri Lanka*. Exeter, New Hampshire: Heinemann, 1980.

Jones, Allen K. *Time for Decision: Sri Lankan Tamils in the West.* Washington, D.C.: American Council For Nationalities Service, 1985.

Kearney, Robert N. *Communalism and Language in the Politics of Ceylon.* Durham, North Carolina: Duke University Press, 1967.

———. *The Politics of Ceylon (Sri Lanka).* Ithaca: Cornell University Press, 1973.

———. "Nationalism, Modernization, and Political Mobilization in a Plural Society." In Michael Roberts, ed. *Collective Identities, Nationalism and Protest in Modern Sri Lanka,* pp. 440–461. Colombo: Marga Institute, 1979.

Kularatnam, K. "The Face of Ceylon," *The Proceedings of the Ninth Annual Session, Ceylon Association for the Advancement of Science,* Part II. Colombo, 1954.

Ludowyk, E. F. C. *The Story of Ceylon.* London: Faber and Faber, 1962.

Malalasekere, G. P. *The Pali Literature of Ceylon,* vol. 10. Colombo: RAS Publication, 1928.

Mendis, Garrett C. *Ceylon Today and Yesterday.* Colombo: Newspapers of Ceylon, Ltd., 1963.

———. *Problems of Ceylon History.* Colombo: The Colombo Apothecaries, Co. Ltd., 1966.

Namasivayagam, S. *Parliamentary Government in Ceylon, 1948-1958.* Colombo: K. V. G. de Silva, 1959.

Nicholas, Cyril W., and Paranavitana, Senerat. *A Concise History of Ceylon.* Colombo: Ceylon University Press, 1961.

Nyrop, R. R. et al., *Area Handbook for Ceylon.* Washington, D.C.: U.S. Government Press, 1971.

Obeyesekere, Gananath. "The Vicissitudes of Sinhala-Buddhist Identity Through Time and Change." In Michael Roberts, ed., *Collective Identities, Nationalism, and Protest in Modern Sri Lanka,* pp. 279–312. Colombo: Marga Institute, 1979.

Pathmanathan, S. *The Kingdom of Jaffna, Part I (circa A.D. 1250-1450).* Colombo: Arul M. Rajendram, 1978.

Peries, Angelito. "Historical Background to the Genocide of Thamils in Sri Lanka." Unpublished manuscript, November 1983.

Perinbanayagam, R. S. *The Karmic Theater: Self, Society, and Astrology in Jaffna.* Amherst: University of Massachusetts Press, 1982.

Ponnampalam, S. *Sri Lanka: The National Question and the Tamil Liberation Struggle.* London: Zed Books Ltd., 1983.

Raghavan, M. D. *India in Ceylonese History, Society and Culture.* Bombay: Asia House, 1964.

Rahula, Thero Walpola M. *History of Buddhism in Ceylon: The Anuradhapura Period, 3rd century B.C.-10th century A.D.* Colombo: M. D. Gunasena, 1956.

Rasanayagam, C. *Ancient Jaffna.* Madras: Everymans Publisher, 1926.

Richards, Peter, and E. Stoutjeesdeijk. *Agriculture in Ceylon 1975.* Paris: Development Center of the Organization For Cooperation and Development, 1970.

Richards, Peter, and W. Gooneratne. *Basic Needs, Poverty and Government Policies in Sri Lanka.* Geneva: ILO, 1980.

Roberts, Michael, ed. *Collective Identities, Nationalism, and Protest in Modern Sri Lanka,* Colombo: Marga Institute, 1979.

———. "Problems of Collective Identity in a Multi-Ethnic Society: Sectional Nationalism Vs. Ceylonese Nationalism 1900-1940." In Michael Roberts, ed.,

Collective Identities, Nationalism and Protest in Modern Sri Lanka, pp. 337–360. Colombo: Marga Institute, 1979.

————. "Nationalism in Economic and Social Thought 1915–1945." In Michael Roberts, ed., *Collective Identities, Nationalism and Protest in Modern Sri Lanka*, pp. 386–419. Colombo: Marga Institute, 1979.

Sjoberg, Andree F., ed. *Symposium on Dravidian Civilization*. Asian Series of the Center for Asian Studies of the University of Texas, at Austin. New York: Jenkins Publishing Co., 1971.

Smith, Donald E. "The Sinhalese Buddhist Revolution." In Donald Smith, ed., *South Asia Politics and Religion*. Princeton: Princeton University Press, 1966.

————. "Religion, Politics, the Myth of Reconquest." In T. Fernando and R. N. Kearney, eds., *Modern Sri Lanka: A Society in Transition*, pp. 83–99. Foreign and Comparative Studies/South Asia Series, No. 4. Syracuse: Maxwell School of Citizenship and Public Affairs, 1979.

Snodgrass, Donald R. *Ceylon: An Export Economy in Transition*. Illinois: Richard D. Irwin, Inc., 1966.

Schwarz, Walter. *The Tamils of Sri Lanka*. London: The Minority Rights Group Ltd., Report No. 25, 1983.

Tennent, J. Emerson. *Ceylon*, vols. I and II. London: Longmans Press, 1859.

Thambiah, S. J. *Sri Lanka: Ethnic Fratricide and the Dismantling of Democracy*. Chicago: University of Chicago Press, 1985.

Vijayavardhana, D. C. The Revolt in the Temple. Colombo: Sinha Publications, 1953.

Vittachi, Tarzie. *Emergency '58: The Story of the Ceylon Race Riots*. London: A. Deutsch, 1958.

Wijesekera, N. D. *The People of Ceylon*, Colombo: M. D. Gunasena and Co., 1965.

Wilson, A. Jeyaratnam. "Politics and Political Development since 1948." In K. M. de Silva, ed., *Sri Lanka: A Survey*, pp. 281–311. London: C. Hurst and Co., 1977.

————. "Race, Religion, Language, and Caste in the Subnationalism in Sri Lanka." In Michael Roberts, ed., *Collective Identities, Nationalism and Protest in Modern Sri Lanka*, pp. 462–473. Colombo: Marga Institute, 1979.

————. "Sri Lanka and Its Future: Sinhalese Versus Tamils." In A. Jeyaratnam Wilson and Dennis Dalton, eds., *The States of South Asia: Problems of National Integration*, pp. 295–312. Honolulu: The University Press of Hawaii, 1982.

Wilson, A. Jeyaratnam, and Dennis Dalton, eds. *The States of South Asia: Problems of National Integration*. Honolulu: The University Press of Hawaii, 1982.

Wriggins, W. Howard. *Ceylon: Dilemmas of a New Nation*. Princeton: Princeton University Press, 1960.

————. "The Present Situation and Outlook For Sri Lanka." Oral Presentation before the Subcommittee on Asian and Pacific Affairs and the Subcommittee on Human Rights and International Organizations. Committee on Foreign Affairs, U.S. House of Representatives, August 2, 1984.

Young, Amy. "Situation and Outlook in Sri Lanka." Oral Presentation before the Subcommittee on Asian and Pacific Affairs and the Subcommittee on Human Rights and International Organizations. Committee on Foreign Affairs, U.S. House of Representatives, August 2, 1984.

Articles and Periodicals

Adams, F. D. "The Geology of Ceylon." *Canadian Journal of Research* 1 (1929): 425–511.

Amnesty International. "File on Torture: Sri Lanka," *News Letter* 15, 10 (October 1985).

Brohier, R. L. "Underground Water Supply of Northern Ceylon." *Bulletin of Ceylon Geographic Society* 4, 1–2 (September 1949): 39–42.

———. "The Jaffna Peninsula Lagoon Scheme." *Transactions for 1952 Engineering Society of Ceylon,* Part I: 207–209.

De Silva, C. R. "Weightage in University Admissions: Standardization and District Quotas." *Modern Ceylon Studies* 5, 2 (1972).

———. "Weightage in University Admissions." Paper presented to the Ceylon Studies Seminar, series no. 2, 1975.

De Silva, Kingsley M. "Politics and Constitutional Change in Sri Lanka." *Round Table* 276 (January 1979): 49–57.

Editorial Notes, "Notes and Documents: Human Rights Violations in Sri Lanka." *Race and Class* 26, no. 1 (1984): 111–157.

Dunmoye, R. Ayo. "Ethnic Ideology, Bourgeois Democracy, and Nigerian Politics." *The Journal of Ethnic Studies* 12, 1 (Spring 1984): 123–137.

India Abroad, August 5, 1985, p. 3.

Jayawardena, Kumari. "Class Formation and Communalism." *Race and Class* 6, 1 (1984): 51–61.

Jennings, Sir Ivor. "Race, Religion and Economic Opportunity in the University of Ceylon." *University of Ceylon Review* 2, 1–2 (October 1944): 1–13.

———. "Nationalism and Political Development in Ceylon (1): The Background of Self-Government." *Secretariat Paper,* no. 10, pp. 62–84. New York: Institute of Pacific Relations, 1950.

Jeyeraj, D. B. S. "How Strong are the 'Boys'?" *Frontline,* March 23–April 5, 1985.

Jeyaseelan, K. N. "A Soil Catena Associated with the Jaffna Limestone." Proceedings of the Annual Session of the Ceylon Association for the Advancement of Science (unpublished), 1958.

Joachim, A. W. R. "The Soils of Ceylon." *Bulletin of the Ceylon Geographical Society* 8, nos. 3 and 4 (July–December 1954): 67–71.

Kearney, Robert N. "Democracy and the Stress of Modernization in Sri Lanka." *Journal of Asian and Middle Eastern Studies* 1, 3 (Spring 1978): 87–98.

———. "Language and the Rise of Tamil Separatism in Sri Lanka." *Asian Survey* 18, 6 (June 1978): 521–534.

———. "Ethnic Conflict and the Tamil Separatist Movement in Sri Lanka." *Asian Survey* 25, 9 (September 1985): 898–917.

Kodikara, Shelton U. "Communalism and Political Modernization in Ceylon." *Modern Ceylon Studies* 4, 3 (January 1970): 94–114.

Kurian, Rachel et al. "Plantation Politics," *Race and Class* 26, 1 (1984): 83–95.

Manogaran, C. "Traditional Versus Modern Agriculture: A Study of Peasant Farming in Ceylon (Sri Lanka)." *Geographiska Annaler* 56, Series B, 2 (1974): 68–77.

Matthews, Bruce. "District Development Councils in Sri Lanka." *Asian Survey* 22, 1 (November 1982): 1117–1134.

————. "The Situation in Jaffna—And How It Came About." *The Round Table* 290 (April 1984): 188–204.

Moorman, F. R., and C. R. Panabokke. "Soils of Ceylon." *Tropical Agriculture* 117, 1 (January–March 1961): 22–23.

Murphy, Rhodes. "The Ruins of Ancient Ceylon." *Journal of Asian Studies* 16, 2 (1956): 181–200.

Obeyesekere, Gananath. "Political Violence and the Future of Democracy in Sri Lanka." *Internationales Asienforum* 15, no. 1/2 (May 1984): 39–60.

Omvedt, Gail. "The Tamil National Question." *The Bulletin of Concerned Asian Scholars* 16, 1 (January–March 1984): 23–26.

Ponnampalam, S. "A Draft Constitution of the People's Republic of Tamil Eelam." Paper presented at the Second World Thamil Eelam Convention, Nanuet, New York, June 1984.

Perera, N. P. "Early Agricultural Settlements in Sri Lanka in Relation to Natural Resources." *Ceylon Historical Journal* 25, 1–4 (October 1978): 59–73.

Pfaffenberger, Bryan. "The Kataragama Pilgrimage: Hindu-Buddhist Interaction and Its Significance in Sri Lanka's Polyethnic Social System." *Journal of Asian Studies* 38 (February 1979): 253–270.

————. "Fourth World Colonialism, Indigenous Minorities, and Tamil Separatism in Sri Lanka." *The Bulletin of Concerned Asian Scholars* 16, 1 (January–March 1984): 15–22.

Sarachandra, E. R. "Some Problems Connected with Cultural Revival in Ceylon." *Bulletin of the Institute of Traditional Culture* (Madras), Part I (1962): 1–11.

Samarasinghe, S. W. R. de A. "Sri Lanka in 1983: Ethnic Conflicts and the Search for Solutions." *Asian Survey* 24, 2 (February 1984): 250–256.

Selvanayagam, S. "Population Densities and Land Use in the Jaffna Region," *Ceylon Geographer* (Colombo) (1965): 33–42.

————. "Market Gardening in the Jaffna Region." *Ceylon Journal of Historical and Social Studies* 9, 2 (July–December 1966): 172–176.

————. "Intensive Farming and Agricultural Trends in the Jaffna Region of Ceylon." *National Agricultural Society of Ceylon* 3, 1 (July–December 1966): 21–35.

————. "Agrarian Problems and Prospects of Developing the Jaffna Region of Ceylon." *Young Socialist* 4, 2 (May 1967): 55–60.

Siriweera, W. I. "Recent Developments in Sinhala-Tamil Relations." *Asian Survey* 20, 9 (September 1980): 903–913.

Sivanandan, A. "Sri Lanka: Racism and Politics of Underdevelopment." *Race and Class* 26, 1 (1984): 22–38.

Sivanandan, A., ed. "Human Rights Violations in Sri Lanka" (Notes and Documents). *Race and Class* 26, 1 (1984): 111–157.

Social Studies Circle of the Sri Lankan Worker-Peasant Institute. "Anti-Tamil Riots and the Political Crisis in Sri Lanka." *The Bulletin of Concerned Asian Scholars* 16, 1 (January–March 1984): 27–29.

Srimane, C. H. L. "Geology for Water Supply." *Proceedings of the Eighth Annual Session,* p. 5–6. Ceylon Association for the Advancement of Science, 1952.

Thambiah, S. J. "Ethnic Representation in Ceylon's Higher Administrative Service, 1870–1946." *University of Ceylon Review* 23, 2–3 (April–July 1955): 113–134.

Thambyapillai, G. "Dry Zone of Ceylon." *Journal of Agricultural Society of Ceylon* 2, 1 (1965).

Thaninayagam, Xavier S. "Tamil Culture—Its Past, Its Present and Its Future with Special Reference to Ceylon." *Tamil Culture* 4, 14 (October 1955): 341–364.

Thillainathan, B. "Ceylon: The Federal Principles." *Eastern World* 16 (November 1962): 11–12.

Thirlaway, H. I. S. "Ruhuna and Soil Conservation." *Loris Journal* 3 (1945): 1–5.

Thornthwaite, C. W. and Associates. "Average Climatic Water Balance Data of the Continents, Part II. Asia." *Publication in Climatology,* vol. 16, 1 (1963): 56–58. Centerton, New Jersey: Laboratory of Climatology.

Uphoff, Norman T., and M. J. Esman. "Local Organization for Rural Development in Asia." *Development Digest* 8, 3 (July 1975): 31–46.

Waterson, Albert. "A Viable Model for Rural Development." *Development Digest* 8, 3 (July 1975): 3–11.

Weerawardana, I. D. S. "The General Elections in Ceylon, 1952." *Ceylon Historical Journal* 2, 1–2 (July–October 1952): 111–178.

———. "Minority Problems in Ceylon." *Pacific Affairs* 25, 3 (September 1952): 278–287.

Wilson, A. Jeyaratnam. "Minority Safeguards in the Ceylon Constitution." *Journal of Historical and Social Studies* 1, 1 (January 1958): 73–95.

———. "Culture and Language Rights in the Multi-National Society." *Tamil Culture* 7 (January 1958): 22–32.

———. "The Governor General and the Dissolutions of Parliament, December 5, 1959 and April 23, 1960." *The Ceylon Journal of Historical and Social Studies* 3, 2 (1960): 194–207.

———. "Racial Strife in Sri Lanka: the Role of an Intermediary." *Conflict Quarterly* (Canada) (Spring-Summer 1982): 53–64.

World Bank (Staff). "World Bank Policy on Rural Development." *Development Digest* 13, 3 (July 1975): 12–30.

Wriggins, W. Howard. "Sri Lanka in 1981: Year of Austerity, Development Councils, and Communal Disorders." *Asian Survey* 22, 2 (February 1982): 171–179.

Index

About the Author

Chelvadurai Manogaran received his early education in Sri Lanka, including a B.A. degree from the University of Ceylon (Sri Lanka), during a critical period in the modernization of that country. He received his M.A. from Clark University (Massachusetts) and his Ph.D. from Southern Illinois University. As a geographer and climatologist, he has an abiding interest in agricultural and water resource development in Sri Lanka. He has published articles in *Geographisca Annaler, Water Resources Research, Forest Science,* and *Physical Geography.* He is currently associate professor of geography and international studies at the University of Wisconsin-Parkside.

Production Notes

This book was designed by Roger Eggers.
Composition and paging were done on the
Quadex Composing System and typesetting on
the Compugraphic 8400 by the design and production staff of University of Hawaii Press.

The text and display typeface is Garamond
No. 49.

Offset presswork and binding were done by
Vail-Ballou Press, Inc. Text paper is Writers RR
Offset, basis 50.